Essentials of Organization Theory & Design

SECOND EDITION

Richard L. Daft

Vanderbilt University

SOUTH-WESTERN

THOMSON LEARNING

Australia · Canada · Mexico · Singapore · Spain · United Kingdom · United States

Essentials of Organization Theory and Design, 2e by Richard L. Daft
Vice President/Publisher: Jack W. Calhoun
Executive Editor: John Szilagyi
Developmental Editor: Denise Simon
Marketing Manager: Rob Bloom
Production Editor: Kelly Keeler
Manufacturing Coordinator: Sandee Milewski
Internal Design: A Small Design Studio/Ann Small
Cover Design: Paul Neff Design
Cover Image: © Josef Beck/FPG
Production House: DPS Associates, Inc.
Printer: Phoenix Color

Printed in the United States of America
1 2 3 4 5 03 02 01 00

For more information contact South-Western College Publishing, 5101 Madison Road, Cincinnati, Ohio, 45227 or find us on the Internet at http://www.swcollege. com

For permission to use material from this text or product, contact us by
• **telephone: 1–800–730–2214**
• **fax: 1–800–730–2215**
• **web: http://www.thomsonrights.com**

Library of Congress Cataloging-in-Publication Data

Daft, Richard L.

    Essentials of organization theory and design / Richard L. Daft.—2nd ed.
      p. cm.
    Based on: Daft, Richard L. Organization theory and design. 7th ed. 2000.
    ISBN 0-324-02097-X
    1. Organization. 2. Organizational effectiveness. I. Title.

    HD31 .D132 2000
    658.1—dc21

                                 00-036995

This book is printed on acid-free paper.

Contents

$\mathcal{P}$ reface

The purpose of this *Essentials* textbook is to describe traditional ideas and concepts that form a concise and accurate foundation about organization theory and design. The world of organizations is changing rapidly, which prompts many instructors to take a personal approach to teaching organization theory and design. *Essentials of Organization Theory and Design* contains all the fundamental concepts on organization structure, environment, effectiveness, innovation and change, size, life cycle, technology, culture, decision making, and power and politics. *Essentials* was written to enable students to acquire the fundamental concepts within a course in which the instructor provides outside cases, readings, exercises, and other teaching materials that reflect the instructor's own unique approach to the subject. This is a valuable alternative to a full-service textbook because it allows instructors to tailor their courses to meet a variety of teaching objectives.

Instructors can use this text as a foundation upon which to design their own courses, in which they supplement the text's basic picture of organization theory and design with their own up-to-the minute cases, readings, and videos. In addition, because this text focuses on the basics, instructors are free to choose whether and how to incorporate more recent organization design ideas and approaches to suit their own course objectives. The book offers instructors maximum flexibility to build their own organization theory and design courses upon a solid foundation of time-tested, fundamental concepts and models. If an instructor wants to use a textbook for the most recent trends, concepts, teaching cases, corporate examples, and student exercises, I recommend the comprehensive textbook, *Organization Theory and Design,* 7th ed. (South-Western, 2001).

I want to thank John Szilagyi for providing the motivation for this *Essentials* text. In addition, Kelly Keeler, production editor, and Denise Simon, development editor, did a great job of pulling together all the things needed to produce this book. Karen Bowerman did her usual excellent job of providing teaching notes.

As always, I want to give special thanks to my editorial associate, Pat Lane. Pat provided enormous help in identifying and pulling together the true essentials of organization theory and design needed for this text. Pat also skillfully drafted materials on a variety of topics and did an outstanding job with the copyedited manuscripts and page proofs.

Richard L. Daft
Nashville, Tennessee

PART 1

Introduction to Organizations

Chapter 1
Organizations and Organization Theory

CHAPTER 1

Organizations and Organization Theory

*T*wenty years ago, owning stock in IBM was like owning a gold mine. The overwhelming success of the IBM PC sent the company's already high profits soaring, and IBM was ranked as the world's largest company in terms of stock market value. Big Blue, as the company was known, was creating jobs around the world, its workforce ultimately swelling to 407,000.

A decade later, those who had invested their lives—or their money—in a company they thought could never fail watched long-cherished dreams go down the drain. The company went from earning a $6 billion profit to reporting a whopping $5 billion loss two years later. IBM stock lost more than $75 billion in value, an amount equal to the gross domestic product of Sweden. Everyone associated with the once-great company suffered.

Yet today, IBM has shifted into growth mode again, with hot-selling new products, cutting-edge information services, and growing profits. The shifting fortunes of IBM represent a classic story of organizational decline and renewal.

The introduction of the System/360 line of mainframe computers in the mid-1960s sealed IBM's leadership in the computer industry. Yet many believe this marked the beginning of IBM's decline as well. Retired IBM executive Malcolm Robinson, who rose to a senior post in IBM Europe, said, "The scale of the [System/360 project] created a complexity in the business that almost couldn't be handled. It was chaos for a while. So an organization had to be created to bring things under control and make sure that kind of breakdown never happened again. And that really may have been what made the bureaucracy take off."[1] Statistics indicate that Robinson was right. IBM's personnel count went up almost 130 percent between 1963 and 1966, while sales rose about 97 percent.

Too many people and too many meetings caused IBM executives to make mistakes. Decisions that should have been made quickly in response to changes in the computer market were delayed or ignored because of the cumbersome management system that demanded everything be done "the IBM way." When IBM's new chairman took over after the resignation of John Akers in the early 1990s, he said of the troubled company, "It was bureaucracy run amok."

IBM lost the vision and flexibility needed to adapt to changes in the industry. The company was late getting into the personal computer market, choosing to steer what company executives thought was a safe course—preserving the company's mainframe profits. By the time IBM decided to enter the personal computer game in earnest, the death knell was already starting to toll on the profits from mainframes. And, although the IBM PC was an instant success, the PC war was already lost. IBM failed to take advantage of new technologies and opportunities for collaboration with fledgling companies such as Microsoft. In addition, executives didn't recognize that the values and policies of the past—the caution, the obsessive training of employees, a focus on following rather than anticipating customer needs, and a guarantee of lifetime employment—were no longer effective in the fast-paced, rapidly changing environment.

In 1993, Louis V. Gerstner stepped in as IBM's new chairman and CEO, determined to shine up the company's image by creating a culture in which employees seize opportunities, minimize bureaucracy, and put the good of the company ahead of their separate departments and divisions. In his first year on the job, he revamped IBM's finances, brought in outsiders to head up several critical divisions, and dramatically altered financial incentives for top executives, basing about 75 percent of their variable pay on the overall performance of the company. Today, sweaters, chinos, and loafers have replaced starched white shirts and blue suits in many IBM offices, an outward symbol that the company's stiff, bureaucratic culture has given way to a more relaxed, adaptable one. Gerstner, known for his sometimes lightning-quick decisions, dismantled a top-management committee that often stifled action and began talking to employees and customers directly through e-mail.

Today, IBM is pursuing the fastest growing segment of the information technology marketplace—the demand for electronic business services—by selling services, hardware, software and know-how that can address virtually any IT dilemma. When Gerstner announced recently that IBM earns more money from Internet business than the top 25 Internet companies combined, Big Blue's stock prices soared.

Gerstner came to IBM with a vision of a future in which major corporations will buy computing power and applications software the way they buy electric service, never even knowing or caring where the computer that does the work is located. As that vision becomes a reality, IBM is poised at the forefront to reap the benefits. Gerstner's strategies have combined the IBM name, a hip advertising campaign, and the widest range of products, services, and experts in the information services industry to bring about one of the most remarkable turnarounds in corporate America.[2]

Welcome to the real world of organization theory. IBM managers were deeply involved in organization theory each day of their working lives—but they never realized it. Company managers didn't fully understand how the organization related to the environment or how it should function internally. Familiarity with organization theory helps managers such as Lou Gerstner analyze and diagnose what is happening and the changes needed to keep the company competitive. Organization theory gives us the tools to explain the decline and turnaround of IBM. It helps us understand and explain what happened in the past, as well as what may happen in the future, so that we can manage our organizations more effectively.

ORGANIZATION THEORY IN ACTION

TOPICS

Each of the topics to be covered in this book is illustrated in the IBM case. Consider, for example, IBM's failure to respond to or control such elements as customers, suppliers, and competitors in the fast-paced external environment; its inability to coordinate departments and design control systems that promoted efficiency; slow decision making, such as delaying action on exploiting the potential of new technology; handling the problem of large size; the absence of a forceful top management team that allowed IBM to drift further and further into chaos; and an outmoded corporate culture that stifled innovation and change. These are the subjects with which organization theory is concerned. Organization theory can also explain how Lou Gerstner and his top managers found the right structure and strategies that helped revitalize the giant company.

Of course, organization theory is not limited to IBM. Every organization, every manager in every organization, is involved in organization theory. Johnsonville Foods, a Sheboygan, Wisconsin, sausage maker, turned a floundering family business into a dynamic fast-growing company by reorganizing into self-directed teams. Hewlett-Packard Company—which was suffering from some of the same problems as IBM in the 1980s—went through a major, highly successful reorganization, using concepts based in organization theory. Today, H-P is one of the fastest-growing companies in the computer industry. Xerox Corporation has gone through a similar transformation. The turnaround plan for Xerox included slashing costs, selling off the company's financial services divisions, streamlining the supply chain, and reducing product development time. And Xerox continues to restructure to meet changing competitive conditions. The company recently announced that it will cut 10 percent of the workforce, close factories, and hire outside companies to handle storage and distribution. Xerox plans to use the savings to build up high-margin businesses such as servicing equipment and creating computer networks, as well as increase marketing efforts to compete with Hewlett-Packard in lower-cost office machines.[3]

Organization theory draws lessons from these organizations and makes those lessons available to students and managers. The story of IBM's decline is important because it demonstrates that even large, successful organizations are vulnerable, that lessons are not learned automatically, and that organizations are only as strong as their decision makers. The stories of Johnsonville Foods, Hewlett-Packard, Xerox, and IBM also illustrate that organizations are not static; they continuously adapt to shifts in the external environment. Today, many companies are facing the need to transform themselves into dramatically different organizations because of new challenges in the environment.

PURPOSE OF THIS CHAPTER

The purpose of this chapter is to explore the nature of organizations and organization theory today. Organization theory has developed from the systematic study of organizations by scholars. Concepts are obtained from living, ongoing organizations. Organization theory can be practical, as illustrated in the IBM case. It helps people understand, diagnose, and respond to emerging organizational needs and problems.

The next section begins with a formal definition of organization and then explores introductory concepts for describing and analyzing organizations. Next, the scope and nature of organization theory are discussed more fully. Succeeding sections examine the history of organization theory and design and how organization theory can help people manage complex organizations in today's rapidly changing world.

WHAT IS AN ORGANIZATION?

Organizations are hard to see. We see outcroppings, such as a tall building or a computer workstation or a friendly employee; but the whole organization is vague and abstract and may be scattered among several locations. We know organizations are there because they touch us every day. Indeed, they are so common that we take them for granted. We hardly notice that we are born in a hospital, have our birth records registered in a government agency, are educated in schools and universities, are raised on food produced on corporate farms, are treated by doctors engaged in a joint practice, buy a house built by a construction company and sold by a real estate agency, borrow money from a bank, turn to police and fire departments when trouble erupts, use moving companies to change residences, receive an array of benefits from government agencies, spend forty hours a week working in an organization, and are even laid to rest by an undertaker.[4]

DEFINITION

Organizations as diverse as a church, a hospital, and IBM have characteristics in common. The definition used in this book to describe organizations is as follows: **organizations** are (1) social entities that (2) are goal directed, (3) are designed as deliberately structured and coordinated activity systems, and (4) are linked to the external environment.

The key element of an organization is not a building or a set of policies and procedures; organizations are made up of people and their relationships with one another. An organization exists when people interact with one another to perform essential functions that help attain goals. Recent trends in management recognize the importance of human resources, with most new approaches designed to empower employees with greater opportunities to learn and contribute as they work together toward common goals. Managers deliberately structure and coordinate organizational resources to achieve the organization's purpose. However, even though work may be structured into separate departments or sets of activities, most organizations today are striving for greater horizontal coordination of work activities, often using teams of employees from different functional areas to work together on projects. Boundaries between departments as well as those between organizations are becoming more flexible and diffuse as companies face the need to respond to changes in the external environment more rapidly. An organization cannot exist without interacting with customers, suppliers, competitors, and other elements of the external environment. Today, some companies are even cooperating with their competitors, sharing information and technology to their mutual advantage.

IMPORTANCE OF ORGANIZATIONS

It may seem hard to believe today, but "organizations" as we know them are relatively recent in the history of humankind. Even in the late 19th century there were few organizations of any size or importance—no labor unions, no trade associations, few large businesses, non-profit organizations or governmental departments. What a change has occurred since then! The Industrial Revolution and the development of large organizations transformed all of society. Gradually, organizations became central to people's lives and today they exert a tremendous influence in our society.[5]

Organizations are all around us and shape our lives in many ways. But what contributions do organizations make? Why are they important? Exhibit 1.1 lists seven reasons organizations are important to you and to society. First, organizations bring together resources to accomplish specific goals. Consider MaMaMedia Inc. (*www.mamamedia.com*), founded by Irit Harel. To accomplish the goal of providing an entertaining children's Web site based on the educational research of the legendary MIT Media Lab, Harel had to raise more than $11 million; negotiate alliances with partners such as Scholastic, Inc., Netscape Communications, America Online, and General Mills; recruit quality employees who believed in the theory that interactive play promotes learning; develop activities that promote constructive creativity; and line up advertisers and sponsors for the site.[6]

Organizations also produce goods and services that customers want at competitive prices. Companies look for innovative ways to produce and distribute goods and services more efficiently. One way is through e-commerce and advanced information technology, and through the use of computer-based manufacturing technologies. Redesigning organizational structures and management practices can also contribute to increased efficiency. Organizations create a drive for innovation rather than a reliance on standard products and outmoded ways of doing things.

Organizations adapt to and influence a rapidly changing environment. Some large companies have entire departments charged with monitoring the external environment and finding ways to adapt to or influence that environment. One of the most significant changes in the external environment today is globalization. Organizations such as Coca-Cola, AES Corporation, Heineken Breweries, and Xerox are involved in strategic alliances and partnerships with companies around the world in an effort to influence the environment and compete on a global scale.

Through all of these activities, organizations create value for their owners, customers, and employees. Managers need to understand which parts of the operation create value and which parts do not; a company can be profitable only when the value it creates is greater than the cost of resources. McDonald's made a thorough study of how to use its core competencies to create better value for customers. The study resulted in the introduction of Extra Value Meals and the decision to open restaurants in different locations, such as inside Wal-Mart and Sears stores.[7] Finally, organizations have to cope with and accommodate today's challenges of workforce diversity and growing concerns over ethics and social responsibility, as well as find effective ways to motivate employees to work together to accomplish organizational goals.

EXHIBIT 1.1   *Importance of Organizations*

1. Bring together resources to achieve desired goals and outcomes
2. Produce goods and services efficiently
3. Facilitate innovation
4. Use modern manufacturing and computer-based technology
5. Adapt to and influence a changing environment
6. Create value for owners, customers, and employees
7. Accommodate ongoing challenges of diversity, ethics, and the motivation and coordination of employees

Organizations shape our lives, and well-informed managers can shape organizations. An understanding of organization theory enables managers to design organizations to function more effectively.

ORGANIZATIONS AS SYSTEMS

OPEN SYSTEMS

One significant development in the study of organizations was the distinction between closed and open systems.[8] A **closed system** would not depend on its environment; it would be autonomous, enclosed, and sealed off from the outside world. Although a true closed system cannot exist, early organization studies focused on internal systems. Early management concepts, including scientific management, leadership style, and industrial engineering, were closed-system approaches because they took the environment for granted and assumed the organization could be made more effective through internal design. The management of a closed system would be quite easy. The environment would be stable and predictable and would not intervene to cause problems. The primary management issue would be to run things efficiently.

An **open system** must interact with the environment to survive; it both consumes resources and exports resources to the environment. It cannot seal itself off. It must continuously change and adapt to the environment. Open systems can be enormously complex. Internal efficiency is just one issue—and sometimes a minor one. The organization has to find and obtain needed resources, interpret and act on environmental changes, dispose of outputs, and control and coordinate internal activities in the face of environmental disturbances and uncertainty. Every system that must interact with the environment to survive is an open system. The human being is an open system. So is the planet earth, the city of New York, and IBM. Indeed, one problem at IBM was that top managers seemed to forget they were part of an open system. They isolated themselves within the IBM culture and failed to pay close attention to what was going on with their customers, suppliers, and competitors. The rapid changes over the past few decades, including globalization and increased competition, the explosion of the Internet and e-business, and the growing diversity of the population and workforce, have forced many managers to reorient toward an open-systems mindset and recognize their business as part of a complex, interconnected whole.

To understand the whole organization, it should be viewed as a system. A **system** is a set of interacting elements that acquires inputs from the environment, transforms them, and discharges outputs to the external environment. The need for inputs and outputs reflects dependency on the environment. Interacting elements mean that people and departments depend on one another and must work together.

Exhibit 1.2 illustrates an open system. Inputs to an organization system include employees, raw materials and other physical resources, information, and financial resources. The transformation process changes these inputs into something of value that can be exported back to the environment. Outputs include specific products and services for customers and clients. Outputs may also include employee satisfaction, pollution, and other by-products of the transformation process.

A system is made up of several **subsystems**, as illustrated at the bottom of Exhibit 1.2. These subsystems perform the specific functions required for organizational survival, such as production, boundary spanning, maintenance, adaptation, and management. The production subsystem produces the product and service outputs of the organization. Boundary subsystems are responsible for exchanges with the external environment. They include activities such as purchasing supplies or marketing products. The maintenance subsystem maintains the smooth operation and upkeep of the organization's physical and human elements. The adaptive subsystems are responsible for organizational change and adaptation. Management is a distinct subsystem, responsible for coordinating and directing the other subsystems of the organization.

EXHIBIT 1.2   *An Open System and Its Subsystems*

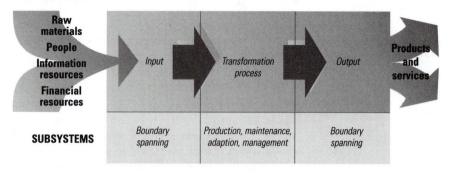

ORGANIZATIONAL CONFIGURATION

Various parts of the organization are designed to perform the key subsystem functions illustrated in Exhibit 1.2. One framework proposed by Henry Mintzberg suggests that every organization has five parts.[9] These parts, illustrated in Exhibit 1.3, include the technical core, top management, middle management, technical support, and administrative support. The five parts of the organization may vary in size and importance depending on the organization's environment, technology, and other factors.

Technical Core. The technical core includes people who do the basic work of the organization. It performs the production subsystem function and actually produces the product and service outputs of the organization. This is where the primary transformation from inputs to outputs takes place. The technical core is the production department in a manufacturing firm, the teachers and classes in a university, and the medical activities in a hospital. At IBM, the technical core produces hardware, software, and e-business services for clients.

Technical Support. The technical support function helps the organization adapt to the environment. Technical support employees such as engineers and researchers scan the environment for problems, opportunities, and technological developments. Technical support is responsible for creating innovations in the technical core, helping the organization to change and adapt. Technical support at IBM is provided by departments such as technology, research and development, and marketing research.

Administrative Support. The administrative support function is responsible for the smooth operation and upkeep of the organization, including its physical and human elements. This includes human resource activities such as recruiting and hiring, establishing compensation and benefits, and employee training and development, as well as maintenance activities such as cleaning of buildings and service and repair of machines. Administrative support functions in a corporation such as IBM might include the human resources department, organizational development, the employee cafeteria, and the maintenance staff.

Management. Management is a distinct subsystem, responsible for directing and coordinating other parts of the organization. Top management provides direction, strategy, goals, and policies for the entire organization or major divisions. Middle management is responsible for implementation and coordination at the departmental level. In traditional organizations, middle managers are responsible for mediating between top management and the technical core, such as implementing rules and passing information up and down the hierarchy.

In real-life organizations, the five parts are interrelated and often serve more than one subsystem function. For example, managers coordinate and direct other parts of the system, but they may also be involved in administrative and technical support. In addition,

EXHIBIT 1.3   *Five Basic Parts of an Organization*

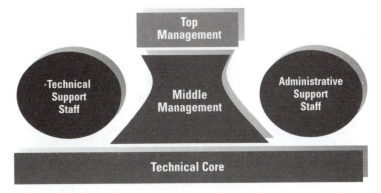

Source: Based on Henry Mintzberg, *The Structuring of Organizations* (Englewood Cliffs, N.J.: Prentice-Hall, 1979), 215–297; and Henry Mintzberg, "Organization Design: Fashion or Fit?" *Harvard Business Review* 59 (January-February 1981): 103-116.

several of the parts serve the *boundary spanning* function mentioned in the previous section. For example, in the administrative support realm, human resources departments are responsible for working with the external environment to find quality employees. Purchasing departments acquire needed materials and supplies. In the technical support area, research and development departments work directly with the external environment to learn about new technological developments. Managers perform boundary spanning as well, such as when Lou Gerstner of IBM works directly with major customers. The important boundary spanning subsystem is embraced by several areas, rather than being confined to one part of the organization.

DIMENSIONS OF ORGANIZATION DESIGN

The systems view pertains to dynamic, ongoing activities within organizations. The next step for understanding organizations is to look at dimensions that describe specific organizational design traits. These dimensions describe organizations much the same way that personality and physical traits describe people.

Organizational dimensions fall into two types: structural and contextual. **Structural dimensions** provide labels to describe the internal characteristics of an organization. They create a basis for measuring and comparing organizations. **Contextual dimensions** characterize the whole organization, including its size, technology, environment, and goals. They describe the organizational setting that influences and shapes the structural dimensions. Contextual dimensions can be confusing because they represent both the organization and the environment. Contextual dimensions can be envisioned as a set of overlapping elements that underlie an organization's structure and work processes. To understand and evaluate organizations, one must examine both structural and contextual dimensions.[10] These dimensions of organization design interact with one another and can be adjusted to accomplish the purposes listed earlier in Exhibit 1.1.

STRUCTURAL DIMENSIONS

1. *Formalization* pertains to the amount of written documentation in the organization. Documentation includes procedures, job descriptions, regulations, and policy manuals. These written documents describe behavior and activities. Formalization is often measured by simply counting the number of pages of documentation within the organization. Large state universities, for example, tend to be high on formalization because they have several volumes of written rules for such things as registration,

dropping and adding classes, student associations, dormitory governance, and financial assistance. A small, family-owned business, in contrast, may have almost no written rules and would be considered informal.

2. *Specialization* is the degree to which organizational tasks are subdivided into separate jobs. If specialization is extensive, each employee performs only a narrow range of tasks. If specialization is low, employees perform a wide range of tasks in their jobs. Specialization is sometimes referred to as the *division of labor*.

3. *Hierarchy of authority* describes who reports to whom and the span of control for each manager. The hierarchy is depicted by the vertical lines on an organization chart, as illustrated in Exhibit 1.4. The hierarchy is related to *span of control* (the number of employees reporting to a supervisor). When spans of control are narrow, the hierarchy tends to be tall. When spans of control are wide, the hierarchy of authority will be shorter.

4. *Centralization* refers to the hierarchical level that has authority to make a decision. When decision making is kept at the top level, the organization is centralized. When decisions are delegated to lower organizational levels, it is decentralized. Organizational decisions that might be centralized or decentralized include purchasing equipment, establishing goals, choosing suppliers, setting prices, hiring employees, and deciding marketing territories.

5. *Professionalism* is the level of formal education and training of employees. Professionalism is considered high when employees require long periods of training to hold jobs in the organization. Professionalism is generally measured as the average number of years of education of employees, which could be as high as twenty in a medical practice and less than ten in a construction company.

6. *Personnel ratios* refer to the deployment of people to various functions and departments. Personnel ratios include the administrative ratio, the clerical ratio, the professional staff ratio, and the ratio of indirect to direct labor employees. A personnel ratio is measured by dividing the number of employees in a classification by the total number of organizational employees.

CONTEXTUAL DIMENSIONS

1. *Size* is the organization's magnitude as reflected in the number of people in the organization. It can be measured for the organization as a whole or for specific components, such as a plant or division. Because organizations are social systems, size is typically measured by the number of employees. Other measures such as total sales or total assets also reflect magnitude, but they do not indicate the size of the human part of the social system.

2. *Organizational technology* refers to the tools, techniques, and actions used to transform inputs into outputs. It concerns how the organization actually produces the products and services it provides for customers and includes such things as computer-aided manufacturing, advanced information systems, and the Internet. An automobile assembly line, a college classroom, and an overnight package delivery system are technologies, although they differ from one another.

3. The *environment* includes all elements outside the boundary of the organization. Key elements include the industry, government, customers, suppliers, and the financial community. Environmental elements that affect an organization the most are often other organizations.

4. The organization's *goals and strategy* define the purpose and competitive techniques that set it apart from other organizations. Goals are often written down as an enduring statement of company intent. A strategy is the plan of action that describes resource allocation and activities for dealing with the environment and for reaching the organization's goals. Goals and strategies define the scope of operations and the relationship with employees, customers, and competitors.

5. An organization's *culture* is the underlying set of key values, beliefs, understandings, and norms shared by employees. These underlying values may pertain to ethical

EXHIBIT 1.4   Organization Chart Illustrating the Hierarchy of Authority for a Community Job Training Program

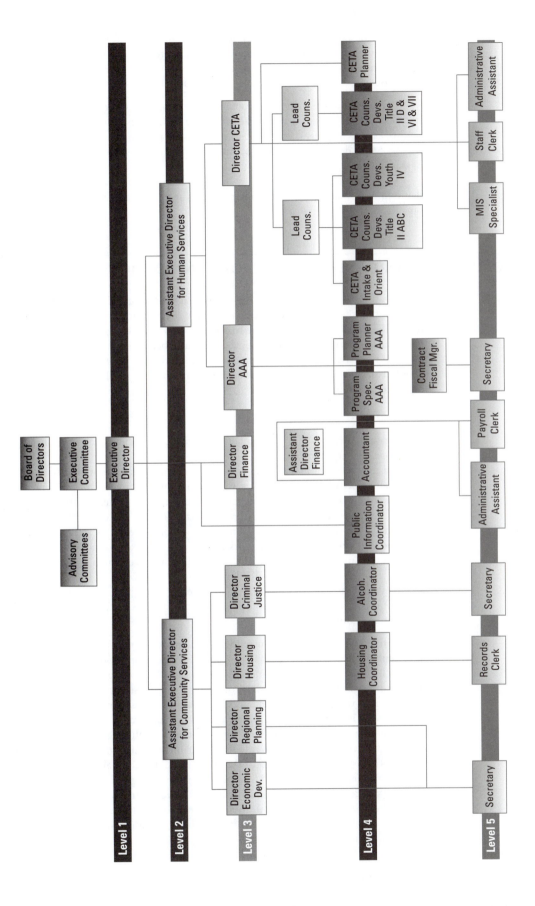

behavior, commitment to employees, efficiency, or customer service, and they provide the glue to hold organization members together. An organization's culture is unwritten but can be observed in its stories, slogans, ceremonies, dress, and office layout.

The eleven contextual and structural dimensions discussed here are interdependent. For example, large organization size, a routine technology, and a stable environment all tend to create an organization that has greater formalization, specialization, and centralization. More detailed relationships among the dimensions are explored in later chapters of this book.

These dimensions provide a basis for the measurement and analysis of characteristics that cannot be seen by the casual observer, and they reveal significant information about an organization.

THE EVOLUTION OF ORGANIZATION THEORY AND DESIGN

Organization theory is not a collection of facts; it is a way of thinking about organizations. Organization theory is a way to see and analyze organizations more accurately and deeply than one otherwise could. The way to see and think about organizations is based on patterns and regularities in organizational design and behavior. Organization scholars search for these regularities, define them, measure them, and make them available to the rest of us. The facts from the research are not as important as the general patterns and insights into organizational functioning.

HISTORY

Organization design and management practices have varied over time in response to changes in the larger society.

You may recall from an earlier management course that the modern era of management theory began with the classical management perspective in the late nineteenth and early twentieth century. The emergence of the factory system during the Industrial Revolution posed problems that earlier organizations had not encountered. As work was performed on a much larger scale by a larger number of workers, people began thinking about how to design and manage work in order to increase productivity and help organizations attain maximum efficiency. The classical perspective, which sought to make organizations run like efficient, well-oiled machines, is associated with the development of hierarchy and bureaucratic organizations and remains the basis of much of modern management theory and practice. Two subfields of the classical perspective are scientific management and administrative principles.

Scientific Management. Pioneered by Frederick Winslow Taylor, **scientific management** postulates that decisions about organizations and job design should be based on precise, scientific study of individual situations.[11] To use this approach, managers develop precise, standard procedures for doing each job, select workers with appropriate abilities, train workers in the standard procedures, carefully plan work, and provide wage incentives to increase output. Taylor's approach is illustrated by the unloading of iron from rail cars and reloading finished steel for the Bethlehem Steel plant in 1898. Taylor calculated that with correct movements, tools, and sequencing, each man was capable of loading 47.5 tons per day instead of the typical 12.5 tons. He also worked out an incentive system that paid each man $1.85 per day for meeting the new standard, an increase from the previous rate of $1.15. Productivity at Bethlehem Steel shot up overnight. These insights helped to establish organizational assumptions that the role of management is to maintain stability and efficiency, with top managers doing the thinking and workers doing what they are told.

Fayol

Administrative Principles. Whereas scientific management focused primarily on the technical core—on work performed on the shop floor—**administrative principles** looked at the design and functioning of the organization as a whole. For example, Henri Fayol proposed fourteen principles of management, such as "each subordinate receives orders from only one superior" (unity of command) and "similar activities in an organization should be grouped together under one manager" (unity of direction). These principles formed the foundation for modern management practice and organization design. Fayol believed these principles could be applied in any organizational setting. The scientific management and administrative principles approaches were very powerful and gave organizations fundamental new ideas for establishing high productivity and increasing prosperity. Administrative principles in particular contributed to the development of **bureaucratic organizations**, which emphasized designing and managing organizations on an impersonal, rational basis through such elements as clearly defined authority and responsibility, formal recordkeeping, and uniform application of standard rules. Although the term *bureaucracy* has taken on negative connotations in today's organizations, bureaucratic characteristics worked extremely well for the needs of the Industrial Age. Following classical management theory, other academic approaches emerged to address issues such as the social context and workers' needs.

The Hawthorne Studies. Early work on industrial psychology and human relations received little attention because of the prominence of scientific management. However, a major breakthrough occurred with a series of experiments at a Chicago electric company, which came to be known as the **Hawthorne Studies**. Interpretations of these studies concluded that positive treatment of employees improved their motivation and productivity. The publication of these findings led to a revolution in worker treatment and laid the groundwork for subsequent work examining treatment of workers, leadership, motivation, and human resource management. These human relations and behavioral approaches added new and important contributions to the study of management and organizations.

However, the hierarchical system and bureaucratic approaches that developed during the Industrial Revolution remained the primary approach to organization design and functioning well into the 1970s and 1980s. In general, this approach has worked well for most organizations until the past few decades. However, during the 1980s, it began to lead to problems. Increased competition, especially on a global scale, changed the playing field. Many North American companies were saddled with bloated administrative ratios and professional staff ratios. International competition from Europe and Japan provided the rude awakening. For example, Xerox discovered it was using 1.3 overhead workers for every direct worker, while its Japanese affiliate needed only 0.6 overhead workers. By the 1980s North American companies had to find a better way. AT&T cut thirty thousand managers during the 1980s. The merger of Chevron and Gulf led to the dismissal of eighteen thousand employees, many of whom were managers. GE laid off fifty thousand salaried employees.[12]

The 1980s produced new corporate cultures that valued lean staff, flexibility, rapid response to the customer, motivated employees, caring for customers, and quality products. The world was changing fast because corporate boundaries were altered by waves of merger activity, much of it international, and increased international competition.

Today, the world—and thus the world of business—is undergoing a change more profound and far-reaching than any experienced since the dawn of the modern age and the scientific revolution. Just as civilization was altered irrevocably in the transition from the agrarian to the industrial age, emerging events are changing the ways in which we interact with one another in our personal and professional lives. Old organization forms and management methods are inadequate to cope with new problems in the emerging postmodern world.[13] One net effect of the evolving business environment and the evolving study of organization theory is the use of contingency theory to describe and convey organizational concepts.

CONTINGENCY THEORY

Organizations are not all alike. Many problems occur when all organizations are treated as similar, which was the case with scientific management and administrative principles approaches that attempted to design all organizations alike. However, the structures and systems that work in the retail division of a conglomerate will not be appropriate for the manufacturing division. The organization charts and financial procedures that are best for a new entrepreneurial Internet firm like MaMaMedia will not work for a large food processing plant.

Contingency means that one thing depends on other things, and for organizations to be effective, there must be a "goodness of fit" between their structure and the conditions in their external environment.[14] What works in one setting may not work in another setting. There is not one best way. Contingency theory means "it depends." For example, some organizations may experience a certain environment, use a routine technology, and desire efficiency. In this situation, a management approach that uses bureaucratic control procedures, a functional structure, and formal communication would be appropriate. Likewise, free-flowing management processes work best in an uncertain environment with a nonroutine technology. The correct management approach is contingent on the organization's situation.

THE ROLE OF ORGANIZATION THEORY AND DESIGN

What topics are relevant to organization theory and design? How does a course in management or organizational behavior differ from a course in organization theory? To answer these questions, let's examine the value a person gains through the study of organization theory and consider the concept of levels of analysis.

THE VALUE OF ORGANIZATION THEORY

How can a study of organization theory help during this time of complexity and transition? For people who are or will be managers, organization theory provides significant insight and understanding to help them be better managers in a rapidly changing world. For example, one of the greatest threats to organizations today is the inability of management to adapt to the speed and chaos of technological change. Although companies have made massive investments in technology, they are only beginning to implement the organizational and management changes needed to make technology and the Internet competitive weapons. Understanding organization theory and design can help managers make those necessary changes by helping them see and understand how technology interacts with other elements of the organization and its environment. As in the case of IBM, many managers learn organization theory by trial and error. At IBM, managers did not initially understand the situation they were in or the contingencies to which they should respond.

In a very real sense, organization theory can make managers more competent and more influential by giving them an understanding of how organizations work. The study of organizations helps people see and understand things other people cannot see and understand. Organization theory provides ideas, concepts, and ways of thinking and interpreting that help managers effectively guide their organizations. When the old approaches are no longer working, organization theory helps managers understand why and develop new approaches to meet changing conditions.

LEVELS OF ANALYSIS

In systems theory, each system is composed of subsystems. Systems are nested within systems, and one **level of analysis** has to be chosen as the primary focus. Four levels of analysis normally characterize organizations, as illustrated in Exhibit 1.5. The individual human being is the basic building block of organizations. The human being is to the

EXHIBIT 1.5   *Levels of Analysis in Organizations*

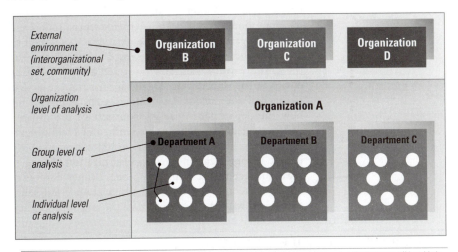

Source: Based on Andrew H. Van De Ven and Diane L. Ferry, *Measuring and Assessing Performance* (New York: Wiley, 1980), 8; and Richard L. Daft and Richard M. Steers, *Organizations: A Micro/Macro Approach* (Glenview, Ill.: Scott, Foresman, 1986), 8.

organization what a cell is to a biological system. The next higher system level is the group or department. These are collections of individuals who work together to perform group tasks. The next level of analysis is the organization itself. An organization is a collection of groups or departments that combine into the total organization. Organizations themselves can be grouped together into the next higher level of analysis, which is the interorganizational set and community. The interorganizational set is the group of organizations with which a single organization interacts. Other organizations in the community also make up an important part of an organization's environment.

Organization theory focuses on the organizational level of analysis but with concern for groups and the environment. To explain the organization, one should look not only at its characteristics but also at the characteristics of the environment and of the departments and groups that make up the organization. The focus of this book is to help you understand organizations by examining their specific characteristics, the nature and relationships among groups and departments that make up the organization, and the collection of organizations that make up the environment.

Are individuals included in organization theory? Organization theory does consider the behavior of individuals, but in the aggregate. People are important, but they are not the primary focus of analysis. Organization theory is distinct from organizational behavior. **Organizational behavior** is the micro approach to organizations because it focuses on the individuals within organizations as the relevant units of analysis. Organizational behavior examines concepts such as motivation, leadership style, and personality and is concerned with cognitive and emotional differences among people within organizations. **Organization theory** is a macro examination of organizations because it analyzes the whole organization as a unit. Organization theory is concerned with people aggregated into departments and organizations and with the differences in structure and behavior at the organization level of analysis. Organization theory is the sociology at organizations, while organizational behavior is the psychology of organizations.

A new approach to organization studies is called meso theory. Most organizational research and many management courses specialize in either organizational behavior or organization theory. **Meso theory** (*meso* means "in between") concerns the integration of both micro and macro levels of analysis. Individuals and groups affect the organization and the organization in return influences individuals and groups. To thrive in organizations, managers and employees need to understand multiple levels simultaneously. For example, research may show that employee diversity enhances innovation. To facilitate innovation, managers need to understand how structure and context (organization theory) are related to interactions among diverse employees (organizational behavior) to foster innovation, because both macro and micro variables account for innovations.[15]

For its part, organization theory is directly relevant to top- and middle-management concerns and partly relevant to lower management. Top managers are responsible for the entire organization and must set goals, develop strategy, interpret the external environment, and decide organization structure and design. Middle management is concerned with major departments, such as marketing or research, and must decide how the department relates to the rest of the organization. Middle managers must design their departments to fit work-unit technology and deal with issues of power and politics, intergroup conflict, and information and control systems, each of which is part of organization theory. Organization theory is only partly concerned with lower management because this level of supervision is concerned with employees who operate machines, type letters, teach classes, and sell goods. Organization theory is concerned with the big picture of the organization and its major departments.

DISCUSSION QUESTIONS

1. What is the definition of *organization*? Briefly explain each part of the definition.
2. What is the difference between an open system and a closed system? Can you give an example of a closed system?
3. Explain how Mintzberg's five basic parts of the organization perform the subsystem functions shown at the bottom of Exhibit 1.2. If an organization had to give up one of these five parts, which one could it survive the longest without? Discuss.
4. What is the difference between formalization and specialization? Do you think an organization high on one dimension would also be high on the other? Discuss.
5. What does *contingency* mean? What are the implications of contingency theories for managers?
6. What levels of analysis are typically studied in organization theory? How would these contrast with the level of analysis studied in a course in psychology? Sociology? Political science?
7. Why might human organizations be considered more complex than machine-type systems? What is the implication of this complexity for managers?

NOTES

1. Carol J. Loomis, "Dinosaurs?" *Fortune*, 3 May 1993, 36–42.

2. The analysis of IBM was based on Paul Carroll, *Big Blues: The Unmaking of IBM* (New York: Crown, 1993); Brent Schlender, "Big Blue Is Betting on Big Iron Again," *Fortune*, 29 April 1996, 102–112; Ira Sager, "The View from IBM," *Business Week*, 30 October 1995, 142–152; David Kirkpatrick, "First: With New PCs and a New Attitude, IBM Is Back," *Fortune*, 11 November 1996, 28–29; Judith H. Dobrzynski, "Rethinking IBM," *Business Week*, 4 October 1993, 86–97; Michael W. Miller and Laurence Hooper, "Akers Quits at IBM Under Heavy Pressure; Dividend Is Slashed," *The Wall Street Journal*, 27 January 1993, A1, A6; John W. Verity, "IBM: A Bull's-Eye and a Long Shot," *Business Week*, 13 December 1993, 88–89; G. Pascal Zachary and Stephen Kreider Yoder, "Computer Industry Divides into Camps of Winners and Losers," *The Wall Street Journal*, 27 January 1993, A1,

A4; and David Kirkpatrick, "IBM: From Big Blue Dinosaur to E-Business Animal," *Fortune*, 26 April 1999, 116+; D. Quinn Mills, "The Decline and Rise of IBM," *Sloan Management Review*, Summer 1996, 78–82; and Sara Nathan, "IBM Stock Surges 9%," *USA Today*, 1B.

3. John A. Byrne, "Management Meccas," *Business Week*, 18 September 1995, 122–134; Catherine Arnst, "Now HP Stands for Hot Products," *Business Week*, 14 June 1993, 36; and Rachel Layne, "Xerox to Cut 9,000 Jobs," 7 April 1998, *http://www.naplesnews.com/today/business/d191799a.htm* accessed May 17, 1999; and "Competing through Constellations: The Case of Fuji Xerox," *Strategy & Business,* First Quarter, 1997, *http://www.strategy-business.com/casestudy/97108/page5.html* accessed on May 17, 1999.

4. Howard Aldrich, *Organizations and Environments* (Englewood Cliffs, N.J.: Prentice-Hall, 1979), 3.

5. Robert N. Stern and Stephen R. Barley, "Organizations and Social Systems: Organization

Theory's Neglected Mandate," *Administrative Science Quarterly* 41 (1996): 146-162.

6. Anne Stuart, "Kid Stuff," *CIO Web Business*, Section 2, 1 April 1999, 20-21.

7. Michael A. Hitt, R. Duane Ireland, and Robert E. Hoskisson, *Strategic Management: Competitiveness and Globalization* (St. Paul, Minn.: West, 1995), 238.

8. James D. Thompson, *Organizations in Action* (New York: McGraw-Hill, 1967), 4–13.

9. Henry Mintzberg, *The Structuring of Organizations* (Englewood Cliffs, N.J.: Prentice-Hall, 1979), 215-297; and Henry Mintzberg, "Organization Design: Fashion or Fit?" *Harvard Business Review* 59 (January-February 1981): 103-116.

10. The following discussion was heavily influenced by Richard H. Hall, *Organizations: Structures, Processes, and Outcomes* (Englewood Cliffs, N.J.: Prentice-Hall, 1991); D. S. Pugh, "The Measurement of Organization Structures: Does Context Determine Form?" *Organizational Dynamics* 1 (Spring 1973): 19–34; and D. S. Pugh, D. J. Hickson, C. R. Hinings, and C. Turner, "Dimensions of Organization Structure," *Administrative Science Quarterly* 13 (1968): 65–91.

11. Robert Kanigel, *The One Best Way: Frederick Winslow Taylor and the Enigma of Efficiency* (New York: Viking, 1997); and Alan Farnham, "The Man Who Changed Work Forever," *Fortune*, July 21, 1997, 114. For a discussion of the impact of scientific management on American industry, government, and nonprofit organizations, also see Mauro F. Guillén, "Scientific Management's Lost Aesthetic: Architecture, Organization, and the Taylorized Beauty of the Mechanical," *Administrative Science Quarterly* 42 (1997) 682-715.

12. Amanda Bennett, *The Death of the Organization Man* (New York: William Morrow, 1990).

13. Ian I. Mitroff, Richard O. Mason, and Christine M. Pearson, "Radical Surgery: What Will Tomorrow's Organizations Look Like?" *Academy of Management Executive* 8, no. 2 (1994): 11–21; Nicholas Imparato and Oren Harari, "When New Worlds Stir," *Management Review* (October 1994): 22–28; William Bergquist, *The Postmodern Organization: Mastering the Art of Irreversible Change* (San Francisco: Jossey-Bass, 1993).

14. Johannes M. Pennings, "Structural Contingency Theory: A Reappraisal," *Research in Organizational Behavior* 14 (1992): 267–309.

15. Robert House, Denise M. Rousseau, and Melissa Thomas-Hunt, "The Meso Paradigm: A Framework for the Integration of Micro and Macro Organizational Behavior," *Research in Organizational Behavior* 17 (1995): 71–114.

PART 2

Organizational Purpose and Structural Design

CHAPTER

Strategy, Organization Design, and Effectiveness

Organizational Purpose
Mission • Operative Goals

Organizational Strategies and Design
Porter's Competitive Strategies • How Strategies Affect Organization Design
• Other Factors Affecting Organization Design

Organizational Effectiveness

Contingency Effectiveness Approaches
Goal Approach • Resource-Based Approach • Internal Process Approach
• Stakeholder Approach

*A*n **organizational goal** is a desired state of affairs that the organization attempts to reach.[1] A goal represents a result or end point toward which organizational efforts are directed. For example, at France's Danone Group, maker of Dannon yogurt, the goals include increasing sales outside of Europe, pushing into emerging markets of Asia and Latin America, refocusing on core products, and boosting profitability.[2] The choice of goals and strategy affects organization design, as we will discuss in this chapter.

PURPOSE OF THIS CHAPTER

Top managers give direction to organizations. They set goals and develop the strategies for their organization to attain those goals. The purpose of this chapter is to help you understand the types of goals organizations pursue and some of the competitive strategies managers develop to reach those goals. We will examine two significant frameworks for determining strategic action and look at how strategies affect organization design. The chapter also describes the most popular approaches to measuring the effectiveness of organizational efforts. To manage organizations well, managers need a clear sense of how to measure effectiveness.

ORGANIZATIONAL PURPOSE

Organizations are created and continued in order to accomplish something. All organizations, including Sears, the American Red Cross, IBM, the Methodist Church, the U.S. Department of Agriculture, and the local video rental store, exist for a purpose. This purpose may be referred to as the overall goal, or mission. Different parts of the organization establish their own goals and objectives to help meet the overall goal, mission, or purpose of the organization.

Many types of goals exist in an organization, and each type performs a different function. One major distinction is between the officially stated goals, or mission, of the organization and the operative goals the organization actually pursues.

MISSION

The overall goal for an organization is often called the **mission**—the organization's reason for existence. The mission describes the organization's vision, its shared values and beliefs, and its reason for being. It can have a powerful impact on an organization.[3] The mission is sometimes called the **official goals**, which are the formally stated definition of business scope and outcomes the organization is trying to achieve. Official goal statements typically define business operations and may focus on values, markets, and customers that distinguish the organization. Whether called a mission statement or official goals, the organization's general statement of its purpose and philosophy is often written down in a policy manual or the annual report. The mission statement for Hallmark is shown in Exhibit 2.1. Note how the overall mission, values, and goals are all defined.

OPERATIVE GOALS

Operative goals designate the ends sought through the actual operating procedures of the organization and explain what the organization is actually trying to do.[4] Operative goals describe specific measurable outcomes and are often concerned with the short run. Operative versus official goals represent actual versus stated goals. Operative goals typically pertain to the primary tasks an organization must perform, similar to the subsystem activities identified in Chapter 1.[5] These goals concern overall performance, boundary spanning, maintenance, adaptation, and production activities. Specific goals for each primary task provide direction for the day-to-day decisions and activities within departments.

Overall Performance. Profitability reflects the overall performance of for-profit organizations. Profitability may be expressed in terms of net income, earnings per share, or

EXHIBIT 2.1   *Hallmark's Mission Statement*

THIS IS HALLMARK

We believe:

That our *products and services* must enrich people's lives
   and enhance their relationships.
That *creativity and quality*—in our concepts, products
   and services—are essential to our success.
That the *people* of Hallmark are our company's
   most valuable resource.
That distinguished *financial performance* is a must,
   not as an end in itself, but as a means
   to accomplish our broader mission.
That our *private ownership* must be preserved.

The values that guide us are:

Excellence in all we do.
Ethical and moral conduct at all times
   and in all our relationships.
Innovation in all areas of our business as a means
   of attaining and sustaining leadership.
Corporate social responsibility to Kansas City
   and to each community in which we operate.

*These beliefs and values guide our business strategies,
our corporate behavior, and our relationships
with suppliers, customers, communities, and each other.*

Source: Hallmark, Cards, Inc. Used with permission.

return on investment. Other overall goals are growth and output volume. Growth pertains to increases in sales or profits over time. Volume pertains to total sales or the amount of products or services delivered. Executives at Procter & Gamble have set a growth goal to double consumer-products sales to $70 billion by 2006.[6]

Not-for-profit organizations such as labor unions do not have goals of profitability, but they do have goals that attempt to specify the delivery of services to members within specified budget expense levels. Growth and volume goals also may be indicators of overall performance in not-for-profit organizations.

Resources. Resource goals pertain to the acquisition of needed material and financial resources from the environment. They may involve obtaining financing for the construction of new plants, finding less expensive sources for raw materials, or hiring top-quality college graduates. Many high-tech companies are having trouble hiring well-educated, computer-literate knowledge workers because of today's tight labor market. Companies such as Sun Microsystems are investing heavily in online recruiting programs to help them meet their resource goals in this area.

Market. Market goals relate to the market share or market standing desired by the organization. Market goals are the responsibility of marketing, sales, and advertising departments.

An example of a market goal is Cisco Systems' desire to be the leading maker of switches and other gear that keep the Internet running. Cisco has captured 80 percent of the market for Internet high-end routers. Cementos Mexicanos (Cemex) has 60 percent of the market for cement in Mexico and is the leading supplier in several emerging markets.[7] Both companies have an operative goal of having the largest market share in a specific industry.

Employee Development. Employee development pertains to the training, promotion, safety, and growth of employees. It includes both managers and workers. At Fetzer Vineyards, a primary goal is to contribute to the continuous growth and development of employees. The goal includes providing a comprehensive employee education program, with classes such as English as a second language, decision making, and communication. According to Barbara Wallace, Fetzer's director of human resources, ". . . our company feels that developing people's capabilities strengthens the organization. It's a way of creating loyalty."[8]

Innovation and Change. Innovation goals pertain to internal flexibility and readiness to adapt to unexpected changes in the environment. Innovation goals are often defined with respect to the development of specific new services, products, or production processes. For example, 3M has a goal of generating enough new products so that 30 percent of sales come from products introduced within the past four years.[9]

Productivity. Productivity goals concern the amount of output achieved from available resources. They typically describe the amount of resource inputs required to reach desired outputs and are thus stated in terms of "cost for a unit of production," "units produced per employee," or "resource cost per employee." For example, Rubbermaid set a productivity goal of increasing the number of units produced per worker per day. Total output increased from three hundred units per worker per day in 1952 to five hundred units in 1980 and 750 in 1988. Another productivity goal was to reduce the number of sales representatives and to increase the work force by only 50 percent while doubling sales. The resulting increases in productivity produced fresh profits for Rubbermaid.[10]

Successful organizations such as Rubbermaid and 3M use a carefully balanced set of operative goals. For example, although profitability is important, some of today's best companies recognize that a single-minded focus on bottom-line profits may not be the best way to achieve high performance. In a rapidly changing environment, innovation and change goals are increasingly important, even though they may initially cause a *decrease* in profits. Employee development goals are critical for helping to maintain a motivated, committed work force in a tight labor market.

ORGANIZATIONAL STRATEGIES AND DESIGN

A **strategy** is a plan for interacting with the competitive environment to achieve organizational goals. Some managers think of goals and strategies as interchangeable, but for our purposes, goals define where the organization wants to go and strategies define how it will get there. For example, a goal may be to achieve 15 percent annual sales growth; strategies to reach that goal might include aggressive advertising to attract new customers, motivating salespeople to increase the average size of customer purchases, and acquiring other businesses that produce similar products. Strategies can include any number of techniques to achieve the goal. The essence of formulating strategies is choosing whether the organization will perform different activities than its competitors or will execute similar activities more efficiently than its competitors do.[11]

One model for formulating strategies is the Porter model of competitive strategies, which provides a framework for competitive action. After describing the model, we will discuss how the choice of strategies affects organization design.

PORTER'S COMPETITIVE STRATEGIES

Michael E. Porter studied a number of businesses and introduced a framework describing three competitive strategies: low-cost leadership, differentiation, and focus.[12] The focus strategy, in which the organization concentrates on a specific market or buyer group, is further divided into *focused low cost* and *focused differentiation*. This yields four basic strategies, as illustrated in Exhibit 2.2. To use this model, managers evaluate two factors, competitive advantage and competitive scope. With respect to advantage, managers determine whether to compete through lower cost or through the ability to offer unique or distinctive products and services that can command a premium price. Managers then determine whether the organization will compete on a broad scope (competing in many customer segments) or a narrow scope (competing in a selected customer segment or group of segments). These choices determine the selection of strategies, as illustrated in Exhibit 2.2.

Differentiation. In a **differentiation** strategy, organizations attempt to distinguish their products or services from others in the industry. An organization may use advertising, distinctive product features, exceptional service, or new technology to achieve a product perceived as unique. This strategy usually targets customers who are not particularly concerned with price, so it can be quite profitable. Maytag appliances, Tommy Hilfiger clothing, and Starbucks Coffee are examples of products from companies using a differentiation strategy.

A differentiation strategy can reduce rivalry with competitors and fight off the threat of substitute products because customers are loyal to the company's brand. However, companies must remember that successful differentiation strategies require a number of costly activities, such as product research and design and extensive advertising. Companies that pursue a differentiation strategy need strong marketing abilities and creative employees who are given the time and resources to seek innovations.

Low-Cost Leadership. The **low-cost leadership** strategy tries to increase market share by emphasizing low cost compared to competitors. With a low-cost leadership strategy, the organization aggressively seeks efficient facilities, pursues cost reductions, and uses tight controls to produce products more efficiently than its competitors.

This strategy is concerned primarily with stability rather than taking risks or seeking new opportunities for innovation and growth. A low-cost position means the company

EXHIBIT 2.2   *Porter's Competitive Strategies*

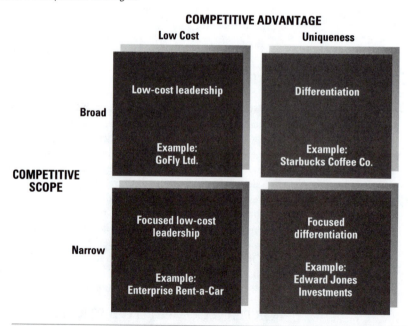

Source: Adapted from Michael E. Porter, *Competitive Advantage: Creating and Sustaining Superior Performance* (New York: The Free Press, 1985), 12. Used with permission.

can undercut competitors' prices and still offer comparable quality and earn a reasonable profit. GoFly Ltd., a startup airline based in London, England, is using a low-cost strategy to compete successfully against major carriers such as British Airways. CEO Barbara Cassani monitors costs closely so GoFly can keep prices low. For example, the company doesn't use travel agents, requiring that customers book flights directly by phone or on the Web. Rather than serving free food and drinks, GoFly offers travelers a choice of quality refreshments at a fair price.[13]

A low-cost strategy can help a company defend against current competitors because customers cannot find lower prices elsewhere. In addition, if substitute products or potential new competitors enter the picture, the low-cost producer is in a better position to prevent loss of market share.

Focus. With Porter's third strategy, the **focus strategy**, the organization concentrates on a specific regional market or buyer group. The company will try to achieve either a low-cost advantage or a differentiation advantage within a narrowly defined market. One example of focus strategy is Enterprise Rent-a-Car, which has made its mark by focusing on a market in which the major companies like Hertz and Avis don't even compete—the low-budget insurance replacement market. Customers whose cars have been wrecked or stolen have one less thing to worry about when Enterprise delivers a rental car right to their driveway. Enterprise has been able to grow rapidly by using a focused low-cost strategy. Edward Jones, a St. Louis-based brokerage house, succeeded by building its business in rural and small-town America and providing investors with conservative, long-term investments. Peter Drucker (the ultimate management guru, who has worked as a consultant to Edward Jones) points out that the firm's safety-first orientation means it delivers a product "that no Wall Street house has ever sold before: peace of mind." The company is expanding rapidly, aiming to become the "Wal-Mart of Wall Street," by using this focused differentiation strategy.[14]

HOW STRATEGIES AFFECT ORGANIZATION DESIGN

Choice of strategy affects internal organization characteristics. Organization design characteristics need to support the firm's competitive approach. For example, a company wanting to grow and invent new products looks and "feels" different from a company that is focused on maintaining market share for long-established products in a stable industry.

With a low-cost leadership strategy, managers take an efficiency approach to organization design, whereas a differentiation strategy calls for a flexible learning approach. A low-cost leadership strategy (efficiency) is associated with strong, centralized authority and tight control, standard operating procedures, and emphasis on efficient procurement and distribution systems. Employees generally perform routine tasks under close supervision and control and are not empowered to make decisions or take action on their own. A differentiation strategy, on the other hand, requires that employees be constantly experimenting and learning. Structure is fluid and flexible, with strong horizontal coordination. Empowered employees work directly with customers and are rewarded for creativity and risk-taking. The organization values research, creativity, and innovativeness over efficiency and standard procedures.

OTHER FACTORS AFFECTING ORGANIZATION DESIGN

Strategy is one important factor that affects organization design. Ultimately, however, organization design is a result of numerous contingencies, which will be discussed throughout this book. The emphasis given to efficiency and control versus learning and flexibility is determined by the contingencies of strategy, environment, size and life cycle, technology, and organizational culture. The organization is designed to "fit" the contingency factors, as illustrated in Exhibit 2.3.

For example, in a stable environment, the organization can have a traditional structure that emphasizes vertical control, efficiency, specialization, standard procedures, and centralized decision making. However, a rapidly changing environment may call for a

EXHIBIT 2.3   *Contingency Factors Affecting Organization Design*

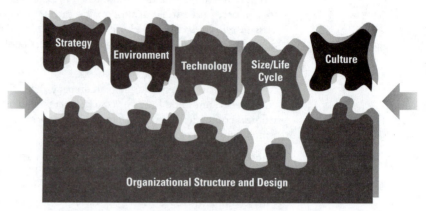

The Right Mix of Design Characteristics Fit the Contingency Factors

more flexible structure, with strong horizontal coordination and collaboration through teams or other mechanisms. Environment will be discussed in detail in Chapter 4. In terms of size and life cycle, young, small organizations are generally informal and have little division of labor, few rules and regulations, and ad hoc budgeting and performance systems. Large organizations such as IBM or Sears, on the other hand, have an extensive division of labor, numerous rules and regulations, and standard procedures and systems for budgeting, control, rewards, and innovation. Size and stages of the life cycle will be discussed in Chapter 6.

Design must also fit the workflow technology of the organization. For example, with mass production technology, such as a traditional automobile assembly line, the organization functions best by emphasizing efficiency, formalization, specialization, centralized decision making, and tight control. An e-business, on the other hand, may need to be very informal and flexible. Technology's impact on design will be discussed in detail in Chapter 5. A final contingency that affects organizational design is corporate culture. An organizational culture that values teamwork, collaboration, creativity, and open communication among all employees and managers, for example, would not function well with a tight, vertical structure and strict rules and regulations. The role of culture is discussed in Chapter 7.

One responsibility of managers is to design organizations that fit the contingency factors of strategy, environment, size and life cycle, technology, and culture. Finding the right "fit" leads to organizational effectiveness, whereas a poor fit can lead to decline or even the demise of the organization.

ORGANIZATIONAL EFFECTIVENESS

Understanding organizational goals and strategies, as well as the concept of fitting design to various contingencies, is a first step toward understanding organizational effectiveness. Organizational goals represent the reason for an organization's existence and the outcomes it seeks to achieve. The next few sections of the chapter explore the topic of effectiveness and how effectiveness is measured in organizations.

Goals were defined earlier as the desired future state of the organization. Organizational **effectiveness** is the degree to which an organization realizes its goals.[15] Effectiveness is a broad concept. It implicitly takes into consideration a range of variables at both the organizational and departmental levels. Effectiveness evaluates the extent to which multiple goals—whether official or operative—are attained.

Efficiency is a more limited concept that pertains to the internal workings of the organization. Organizational efficiency is the amount of resources used to produce a unit of output.[16] It can be measured as the ratio of inputs to outputs. If one organization can achieve a given production level with fewer resources than another organization it would be described as more efficient.[17]

Sometimes efficiency leads to effectiveness. In other organizations, efficiency and effectiveness are not related. An organization may be highly efficient but fail to achieve its goals because it makes a product for which there is no demand. Likewise, an organization may achieve its profit goals but be inefficient.

Overall effectiveness is difficult to measure in organizations. Organizations are large, diverse, and fragmented. They perform many activities simultaneously. They pursue multiple goals. And they generate many outcomes, some intended and some unintended.[18] Managers determine what indicators to measure in order to gauge the effectiveness of their organizations. One study found that many managers have a difficult time with the concept of evaluating effectiveness based on characteristics that are not subject to hard, quantitative measurement.[19] However, top executives at some of today's leading companies are finding new ways to measure effectiveness, using indicators such as "customer delight" and employee satisfaction. A number of approaches to measuring effectiveness look at which measurements managers choose to track. These *contingency effectiveness approaches* are based on looking at which part of the organization managers consider most important to measure.

CONTINGENCY EFFECTIVENESS APPROACHES

Contingency approaches to measuring effectiveness focus on different parts of the organization. Traditional approaches include the goal approach, the resource-based approach, and the internal process approach, as illustrated in Exhibit 2.4. Organizations bring resources in from the environment, and those resources are transformed into outputs delivered back into the environment, as shown in the exhibit. The **goal approach** to organizational effectiveness is concerned with the output side and whether the organization achieves its goals in terms of desired levels of output.[20] The **resource-based approach** assesses effectiveness by observing the beginning of the process and evaluating whether the organization effectively obtains resources necessary for high performance. The **internal process approach** looks at internal activities and assesses effectiveness by indicators of internal health and efficiency.

These traditional approaches all have something to offer, but each one tells only part of the story. A more recent **stakeholder approach** (also called the constituency approach) acknowledges that each organizatioan has many constituencies that have a stake

EXHIBIT 2.4   *Contingency Approaches to the Measurement of Organizational Effectiveness*

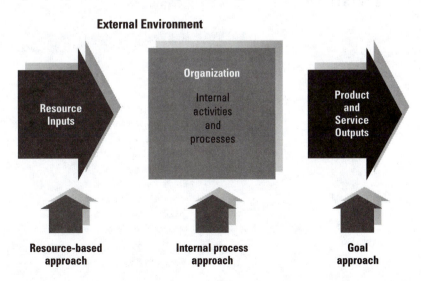

in its outcomes. The stakeholder approach focuses on the satisfaction of stakeholders as an indicator of the organization's performance.[21]

GOAL APPROACH

The goal approach to effectiveness consists of identifying an organization's output goals and assessing how well the organization has attained those goals.[22] This is a logical approach because organizations do try to attain certain levels of output, profit, or client satisfaction. The goal approach measures progress toward attainment of those goals. For example, an important measure for the Women's National Basketball Association is number of tickets sold per game. During the league's first season, President Val Ackerman set a goal of 4,000 to 5,000 tickets per game. The organization actually averaged nearly 9,700 tickets per game, indicating that the WNBA was highly effective in meeting its goal for attendance.[23]

Indicators. The important goals to consider are operative goals. Efforts to measure effectiveness have been more productive using operative goals than using official goals.[24] Official goals tend to be abstract and difficult to measure. Operative goals reflect activities the organization is actually performing.

One example of multiple goals is from a survey of U.S. business corporations.[25] Their reported goals are shown in Exhibit 2.5. Twelve goals were listed as being important to these companies. These twelve goals represent outcomes that cannot be achieved simultaneously. They illustrate the array of outcomes organizations attempt to achieve.

Usefulness. The goal approach is used in business organizations because output goals can be readily measured. Business firms typically evaluate performance in terms of profitability, growth, market share, and return on investment. However, identifying operative goals and measuring performance of an organization are not always easy. Two problems that must be resolved are the issues of multiple goals and subjective indicators of goal attainment.

Since organizations have multiple and conflicting goals, effectiveness often cannot be assessed by a single indicator. High achievement on one goal may mean low achievement on another. Moreover, there are department goals as well as overall performance goals. The full assessment of effectiveness should take into consideration several goals simultaneously.

The other issue to resolve with the goal approach is how to identify operative goals for an organization and how to measure goal attainment. For business organizations, there are often objective indicators for certain goals, such as profit or growth. However, subjective assessment is needed for other goals, such as employee welfare or social responsibility.

EXHIBIT 2.5   *Reported Goals of U.S. Corporations*

Goal	% Corporations
Profitability	89
Growth	82
Market share	66
Social responsibility	65
Employee welfare	62
Product quality and service	60
Research and development	54
Diversification	51
Efficiency	50
Financial stability	49
Resource conservation	39
Management development	35

Source: Adapted from Y. K. Shetty, "New Look at Corporate Goals," *California Management Review* 22, no. 2 (1979), 71–79.

Someone has to go into the organization and learn what the actual goals are by talking with the top management team. Once goals are identified, subjective perceptions of goal attainment have to be used when quantitative indicators are not available. Managers rely on information from customers, competitors, suppliers, and employees, as well as their own intuition, when considering these goals. Jerre Stead, Chairman and CEO of Ingram Micro Inc., the world's largest distributor of computer-technology products and services, communicates directly with hundreds of customers each week to measure the company's goal of achieving "customer delight." "These direct interactions don't provide hard numbers," he says, "but I sure do learn a lot."[26]

Although the goal approach seems to be the most logical way to assess organizational effectiveness, managers and evaluators should keep in mind that the actual measure of effectiveness is a complex process.

RESOURCE-BASED APPROACH

The resource-based approach looks at the input side of the transformation process shown in Exhibit 2.4. It assumes organizations must be successful in obtaining and managing valued resources in order to be effective. From a resource-based perspective, organizational effectiveness is defined as the ability of the organization, in either absolute or relative terms, to obtain scarce and valued resources and successfully integrate and manage them.[27]

Indicators. Obtaining and successfully managing resources is the criterion by which organizational effectiveness is assessed. In a broad sense, indicators of effectiveness according to the resource-based approach encompass the following dimensions:

- Bargaining position—the ability of the organization to obtain from its environment scarce and valued resources, including financial resources, raw materials, human resources, knowledge, and technology.
- The abilities of the organization's decision makers to perceive and correctly interpret the real properties of the external environment.
- The abilities of managers to use tangible (e.g., supplies, people) and intangible (e.g., knowledge, corporate culture) resources in day-to-day organizational activities to achieve superior performance.
- The ability of the organization to respond to changes in the environment.

Usefulness. The resource-based approach is valuable when other indicators of performance are difficult to obtain. In many not-for-profit and social welfare organizations, for example, it is hard to measure output goals or internal efficiency. Some for-profit organizations also use a resource-based approach. For example, Mathsoft, Inc., which provides a broad range of technical-calculation and analytical software for business and academia, evaluates its effectiveness partly by looking at how many top-rate Ph.D.s it can recruit. CEO Charles Digate believes Mathsoft has a higher ratio of Ph.D.s to total employees than any other software company, which directly affects product quality and the company's image.[28]

Although the resource-based approach is valuable when other measures of effectiveness are not available, it does have shortcomings. For one thing, the approach only vaguely considers the organization's link to the needs of customers in the external environment. A superior ability to acquire and use resources is important only if resources and capabilities are used to achieve something that meets a need in the environment. The resource-based approach is most valuable when measures of goal attainment cannot be readily obtained.

INTERNAL PROCESS APPROACH

In the internal process approach, effectiveness is measured as internal organizational health and efficiency. An effective organization has a smooth, well-oiled internal process. Employees are happy and satisfied. Departmental activities mesh with one another to ensure high productivity. This approach does not consider the external environment. The important element in effectiveness is what the organization does with the resources it has, as reflected in internal health and efficiency.

Indicators. One indicator of internal process effectiveness is the organization's economic efficiency. However, the best-known proponents of a process model are from the human relations approach to organizations. Such writers as Chris Argyris, Warren G. Bennis, Rensis Likert, and Richard Beckhard have all worked extensively with human resources in organizations and emphasize the connection between human resources and effectiveness.[29] Writers on corporate culture and organizational excellence have stressed the importance of internal processes. Results from a study of nearly two hundred secondary schools showed that both human resources and employee-oriented processes were important in explaining and promoting effectiveness in those organizations.[30]

These are indicators of an effective organization as seen from an internal process approach:

- Strong corporate culture and positive work climate
- Team spirit, group loyalty, and teamwork
- Confidence, trust, and communication between workers and management
- Decision making near sources of information, regardless of where those sources are on the organizational chart
- Undistorted horizontal and vertical communication; sharing of relevant facts and feelings
- Rewards to managers for performance, growth, and development of subordinates and for creating an effective working group
- Interaction between the organization and its parts, with conflict that occurs over projects resolved in the interest of the organization.[31]

Usefulness. The internal process approach is important because the efficient use of resources and harmonious internal functioning are ways to measure effectiveness. Today, most managers believe that happy, committed, actively involved employees and a positive corporate culture are important measures of effectiveness. Gary White, CEO of The Gymboree Corp., for example, believes that keeping employees happy is the key to long-term success for his company, which runs parent-child play programs and operates more than 500 retail clothing stores.

The internal process approach also has shortcomings. Total output and the organization's relationship with the external environment are not evaluated. Also, evaluations of internal health and functioning are often subjective, because many aspects of inputs and internal processes are not quantifiable. Managers should be aware that this approach alone represents a limited view of organizational effectiveness.

STAKEHOLDER APPROACH

The stakeholder approach integrates diverse organizational activities by focusing on organizational stakeholders. A **stakeholder** is any group within or outside an organization that has a stake in the organization's performance. Creditors, suppliers, employees, and owners are all stakeholders. Each stakeholder will have a different criterion of effectiveness because it has a different interest in the organization. Each stakeholder group has to be surveyed to learn whether the organization performs well from its viewpoint.

Indicators. The initial work on evaluating effectiveness on the basis of stakeholders included ninety-seven small businesses in Texas. Seven stakeholder groups relevant to those businesses were surveyed to determine the perception of effectiveness from each viewpoint.[32] The following table shows each stakeholder and its criterion of effectiveness.

Stakeholder	Effectiveness Criteria
1. Owners	Financial return
2. Employees	Worker satisfaction, pay, supervision
3. Customers	Quality of goods and services
4. Creditors	Creditworthiness
5. Community	Contribution to community affairs
6. Suppliers	Satisfactory transactions
7. Government	Obedience to laws, regulations

The survey of stakeholders showed that a small business found it difficult to simultaneously fulfill the demands of all groups. One business may have high employee satisfaction, but the satisfaction of other groups may be lower. Nevertheless, measuring all seven stakeholders provides a more accurate view of effectiveness than any single measure. Evaluating how organizations perform across each group offers an overall assessment of effectiveness.

Usefulness. The strength of the stakeholder approach is that it takes a broad view of effectiveness and examines factors in the environment as well as within the organization. The stakeholder approach includes the community's notion of social responsibility, which is not formally measured in the goal, resource-based, and internal process approaches. The stakeholder approach also handles several criteria simultaneously—inputs, internal processing, outputs—and acknowledges that there is no single measure of effectiveness. The well-being of employees is just as important as attaining the owner's financial goals.

The stakeholder approach is gaining in popularity, based on the view that effectiveness is a complex, multidimensional concept that has no single measure.[33] Recent research has shown that the assessment of multiple stakeholder groups is an accurate reflection of effectiveness, especially with respect to organizational adaptability.[34] Moreover, research shows that firms really do care about their reputational status and do attempt to shape stakeholders' assessments of their performance.[35] If an organization performs poorly according to several interest groups, it is probably not meeting its effectiveness goals.

DISCUSSION QUESTIONS

1. How might a company's goals for employee development be related to its goals for innovation and change? To goals for productivity? Can you discuss ways these types of goals might conflict in an organization?
2. What is the difference between a goal and a strategy as defined in the text? Identify both a goal and a strategy for a campus or community organization with which you are involved.
3. Discuss the difference between a low-cost leadership and a differentiation strategy described in Porter's model of competitive strategies. Identify a company you are familiar with that illustrates each strategy and explain why.
4. Suppose you have been asked to evaluate the effectiveness of the police department in a medium-sized community. Where would you begin, and how would you proceed? What effectiveness approach would you prefer?
5. What are the advantages and disadvantages of the resource-based approach versus the goal approach for measuring organizational effectiveness?
6. A noted organization theorist once said, "Organizational effectiveness can be whatever top management defines it to be." Discuss.

NOTES

1. Amitai Etzioni, *Modern Organizations* (Englewood Cliffs, N.J.: Prentice-Hall, 1964), 6.
2. Gail Edmondson, "Danone Hits Its Stride," *Business Week*, 1 February 1999, 52–53.
3. David L. Calfee, "Get Your Mission Statement Working!" *Management Review* (January 1993) 54–57: John A. Pearce II and Fred David, "Corporate Mission Statements: The Bottom Line," *Academy of Management Executive* 1 (1987): 109–16; and Christopher K. Bart, "Sex, Lies, and Mission Statements," *Business Horizons*, November-December, 1997, 23–28.
4. Charles Perrow, "The Analysis of Goals in Complex Organizations," *American Sociological Review* 26 (1961): 854–66.
5. Johannes U. Stoelwinder and Martin P. Charns, "The Task Field Model of Organization Analysis and Design," *Human Relations* 34 (1981): 743– 62; Anthony Raia, *Managing by Objectives* (Glenview, Ill.: Scott, Foresman, 1974).
6. Peter Galuszka and Ellen Neuborne with Wendy Zellner, "P&G's Hottest New Product: P&G," *Business Week*, 5 October 1998, 92, 96.
7. Walid Mougayar, Michael Mattis, Kate McKinley, and Nissa Crawford, "Business 2.0 100: And the Winner is . . . Cisco Systems," *Business 2.0* (May 1999): 59–63; and Oren Harari, "The Concrete Intangibles," *Management Review*, May 1999, 30–33.
8. Miriam Schulman, "Winery with a Mission," *Issues in Ethics* (Spring 1996): 14–15.

9. Rahul Jacob, "Corporate Reputations," *Fortune*, 6 March 1995, 54–67.

10. Alex Taylor III, "Why the Bounce at Rubbermaid," *Fortune*, 13 April 1987, 77–78.

11. Michael E. Porter, "What is Strategy?" *Harvard Business Review* (November-December 1996,): 61–78.

12. Michael E. Porter, *Competitive Strategy: Techniques for Analyzing Industries and Competitors* (New York: Free Press, 1980).

13. Lucy McCauley, ed., "Unit of One: Measure What Matters," *Fast Company*, May 1999, 97+.

14. Greg Burns, "It Only Hertz When Enterprise Laughs," *Business Week*, 12 December 1994, 44; Richard Teitelbaum, "The Wal-Mart of Wall Street," *Fortune*, 13 October 1997, 128-130.

15. Etzioni, *Modern Organizations*, 8.

16. Etzioni, *Modern Organizations*, 8; Gary D. Sandefur, "Efficiency in Social Service Organizations," *Administration and Society* 14 (1983): 449–68.

17. Richard M. Steers, *Organizational Effectiveness: A Behavioral View* (Santa Monica, Calif.: Goodyear, 1977), 51.

18. Karl E. Weick and Richard L. Daft, "The Effectiveness of Interpretation Systems," in Kim S. Cameron and David A. Whetten, eds., *Organizational Effectiveness: A Comparison of Multiple Models* (New York: Academic Press, 1982).

19. David L. Blenkhorn and Brian Gaber, "The Use of 'Warm Fuzzies' to Assess Organizational Effectiveness," *Journal of General Management*, 21, no. 2 (Winter 1995): 40–51.

20. Steven Strasser, J. D. Eveland, Gaylord Cummins, O. Lynn Deniston, and John H. Romani, "Conceptualizing the Goal and Systems Models of Organizational Effectiveness—Implications for Comparative Evaluation Research," *Journal of Management Studies* 18 (1981): 321–40.

21. Anne S. Tusi, "A Multiple-Constituency Model of Effectiveness: An Empirical Examination at the Human Resource Subunit Level," *Administrative Science Quarterly* 35 (1990): 458, 483; Charles Fombrun and Mark Shanley, "What's in a Name? Reputation Building and Corporate Strategy," *Academy of Management Journal* 33 (1990): 233–58; Terry Connolly, Edward J. Conlon, and Stuart Jay Deutsch, "Organizational Effectiveness: A Multiple-Constituency Approach," *Academy of Management Review* 5 (1980): 211–17.

22. James L. Price, "The Study of Organizational Effectiveness," *Sociological Quarterly* 13 (1972): 3–15.

23. McCauley, "Measure What Matters."

24. Richard H. Hall and John P. Clark, "An Ineffective Effectiveness Study and Some Suggestions for Future Research," *Sociological Quarterly* 21 (1980): 119–34; Price, "Study of Organizational Effectiveness;" Perrow, "Analysis of Goals."

25. Y. K. Shetty, "New Look at Corporate Goals," *California Management Review* 22, no. 2 (1979), 71–79.

26. McCauley, "Measure What Matters."

27. The discussion of the resource-based approach is based in part on Michael V. Russo and Paul A. Fouts, "A Resource-Based Perspective on Corporate Environmental Performance and Profitability," *Academy of Management Journal* 40, No. 3 (June 1997): 534-559; and Jay B. Barney, J. L. "Larry" Stempert, Loren T. Gustafson, and Yolanda Sarason, "Organizational Identity Within the Strategic Management Conversation: Contributions and Assumptions," in *Identity in Organizations: Building Theory through Conversations,* David A. Whetten and Paul C. Godfrey, eds. (Thousand Oaks, CA: Sage Publications, 1998): 83-98.

28. Lucy McCauley, "Measure What Matters."

29. Chris Argyris, *Integrating the Individual and the Organization* (New York: Wiley, 1964); Warren G. Bennis, *Changing Organizations* (New York: McGraw-Hill, 1966); Rensis Likert, *The Human Organization* (New York: McGraw-Hill, 1967); Richard Beckhard, *Organization Development Strategies and Models* (Reading, Mass.: Addison-Wesley, 1969).

30. Cheri Ostroff and Neal Schmitt, "Configurations of Organizational Effectiveness and Efficiency," *Academy of Management Journal* 36 (1993): 1345–61; Peter J. Frost, Larry F. Moore, Meryl Reise Louis, Craig C. Lundburg, and Joanne Martin, *Organizational Culture* (Beverly Hills, Calif.: Sage, 1985).

31. J. Barton Cunningham, "Approaches to the Evaluation of Organizational Effectiveness," *Academy of Management Review* 2 (1977): 463–74; Beckhard, *Organization Development.*

32. Frank Friedlander and Hal Pickle, "Components of Effectiveness in Small Organizations," *Administrative Science Quarterly* 13 (1968): 289–304.

33. Kim S. Cameron, "The Effectiveness of Ineffectiveness," in Barry M. Staw and L. L. Cummings, eds., *Research in Organizational Behavior* (Greenwich, Conn.: JAI Press, 1984), 235–86; Rosabeth Moss Kanter and Derick Brinkerhoff, "Organizational Performance: Recent Developments in Measurement," *Annual Review of Sociology* 7 (1981): 321–49.

34. Tusi, "A Multiple-Constituency Model of Effectiveness."

35. Fombrun and Shanley, "What's in a Name?"

Fundamentals of Organization Structure

*E*very organization wrestles with the problem of how to organize, and nearly every firm undergoes reorganization at some point. Structural changes are needed to reflect new strategies or respond to changes in other contingency factors introduced in Chapter 2: environment, technology, size and life cycle, and culture. For example, Xerox restructured into several horizontally aligned divisions to facilitate its differentiation strategy and speed innovative new products to market.

PURPOSE OF THIS CHAPTER

This chapter introduces basic concepts of organization structure and shows how to design structure as it appears on the organization chart. First we will define structure and provide an overview of structural design. Then, an information processing perspective explains how to design vertical and horizontal linkages to provide needed information flow. The chapter will next present basic design options, followed by strategies for grouping organizational activities into functional, divisional, or matrix structures. The final section will examine how the application of basic structures depends on the organization's situation and will outline the symptoms of structural misalignment.

ORGANIZATION STRUCTURE

The three key components in the definition of **organization structure** are:

1. Organization structure designates formal reporting relationships, including the number of levels in the hierarchy and the span of control of managers and supervisors.
2. Organization structure identifies the grouping together of individuals into departments and of departments into the total organization.
3. Organization structure includes the design of systems to ensure effective communication, coordination, and integration of effort across departments.[1]

These three elements of structure pertain to both vertical and horizontal aspects of organizing. For example, the first two elements are the structural *framework*, which is the vertical hierarchy.[2] The third element pertains to the pattern of *interactions* among organizational employees. An ideal structure encourages employees to provide horizontal information and coordination where and when it is needed.

Organization structure is reflected in the organization chart. It isn't possible to "see" the internal structure of an organization the way we might see its manufacturing tools, offices, or products. Although we might see employees going about their duties, performing different tasks, and working in different locations, the only way to actually see the structure underlying all this activity is through the organization chart.[3] The organization chart is the visual representation of a whole set of underlying activities and processes in an organization. Exhibit 3.1 shows a sample organization chart. The organization chart can be quite useful in understanding how a company works. It shows the various parts of an organization, how they are interrelated, and how each position and department fits into the whole.

The concept of an organization chart, showing what positions exist, how they are grouped, and who reports to whom, has been around for centuries. For example, diagrams outlining church hierarchy can be found in medieval churches in Spain. However, the use of the organization chart for business stems largely from the Industrial Revolution. As we discussed in Chapter 1, as work grew more complex and was performed by greater and greater numbers of workers, there was a pressing need to develop ways of managing and controlling organizations. The growth of the railroads provides an example. After the collision of two passenger trains in Massachusetts in 1841, the public demanded better control of the operation. As a result, the board of directors of the Western Railroad took steps to outline "definite responsibilities for each phase of the company's business, drawing solid lines of authority and command for the railroad's administration, maintenance, and operation."[4]

EXHIBIT 3.1   *A Sample Organization Chart*

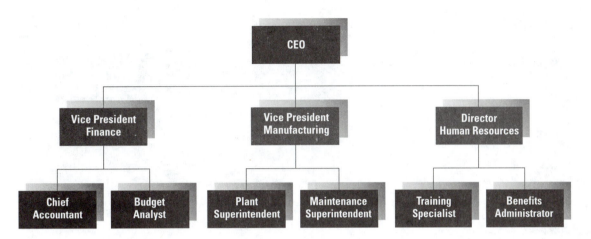

The type of organization structure that grew out of these efforts in the late nine-teenth and early twentieth centuries was one in which the CEO was placed at the top and everyone else was arranged in layers down below, as illustrated in Exhibit 3.1. The thinking and decision making is done by those at the top, and the physical work is per-formed by employees who are organized into distinct, functional departments. This structure was quite effective and became entrenched in the business world for most of the twentieth century. However, this type of vertical structure is not always effective, particularly in rapidly changing environments. Over the years, organizations have devel-oped other structural designs, many of them aimed at increasing horizontal coordina-tion and communication and encouraging adaptation to external changes. This chapter will examine four basic structural designs and show how they are reflected in the organ-ization chart.

INFORMATION-PROCESSING PERSPECTIVE ON STRUCTURE

The organization should be designed to provide both vertical and horizontal information flow as necessary to accomplish the organization's overall goals. If the structure doesn't fit the information requirements of the organization, people will have either too little infor-mation or will spend time processing information that is not vital to their tasks, thus reducing effectiveness.[5] However, there is an inherent tension between vertical and hori-zontal mechanisms in an organization. Whereas vertical linkages are designed primarily for control, horizontal linkages are designed for coordination and collaboration, which usu-ally means reducing control.

Organizations can choose whether to orient toward a traditional organization designed for efficiency, which emphasizes vertical communication and control, or toward a contemporary learning organization, which emphasizes horizontal communication and coordination. Exhibit 3.2 compares organizations designed for efficiency with those designed for learning. An emphasis on efficiency and control is associated with specialized tasks, hierarchy of authority, rules and regulations, formal reporting systems, few teams or task forces, and centralized decision making. Emphasis on learning is associated with shared tasks, relaxed hierarchy and few rules, face-to-face communication, many teams and task forces, and informal, decentralized decision making. All organizations need a mix of vertical and horizontal linkages. Managers have to find the right balance to fit the orga-nization's needs.

EXHIBIT 3.2   *The Relationship of Organization Design to Efficiency vs. Learning Outcomes*

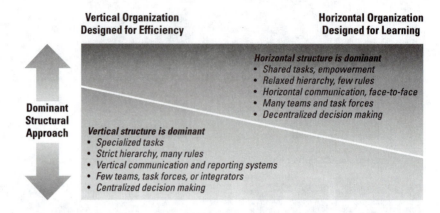

VERTICAL LINKAGES

Organization design should facilitate the communication among employees and departments that is necessary to accomplish the organization's overall task. *Linkage* is defined as the extent of communication and coordination among organizational elements. **Vertical linkages** are used to coordinate activities between the top and bottom of an organization and are designed primarily for control of the organization. Employees at lower levels should carry out activities consistent with top-level goals, and top executives must be informed of activities and accomplishments at the lower levels. Organizations may use any of a variety of structural devices to achieve vertical linkage, including hierarchical referral, rules, plans, and formal management information systems.[6]

Hierarchical Referral. The first vertical device is the hierarchy, or chain of command, which is illustrated by the vertical lines in Exhibit 3.1. If a problem arises that employees don't know how to solve, it can be referred up to the next level in the hierarchy. When the problem is solved, the answer is passed back down to lower levels. The lines of the organization chart act as communication channels.

Rules and Plans. The next linkage device is the use of rules and plans. To the extent that problems and decisions are repetitive, a rule or procedure can be established so employees know how to respond without communicating directly with their manager. Rules provide a standard information source enabling employees to be coordinated without actually communicating about every job. A plan also provides standing information for employees. The most widely used plan is the budget. With carefully designed budget plans, employees at lower levels can be left on their own to perform activities within their resource allotment.

Vertical Information Systems. Vertical information systems are another strategy for increasing vertical information capacity. **Vertical information systems** include the periodic reports, written information, and computer-based communications distributed to managers. Information systems make communication up and down the hierarchy more efficient. Cisco Systems has turned vertical information systems into a competitive advantage by using the Internet in virtually every aspect of its operations. Larry Carter, Cisco's CFO, can call up the company's revenues, profit margins, and order information from the previous day with just a few mouse clicks. Financial data that once took weeks to gather are collected and organized automatically.[7]

Managers may use a variety of these mechanisms to provide vertical linkage and control. The other major issue in organizing is horizontal linkages for coordination and collaboration.

HORIZONTAL LINKAGES

Horizontal communication overcomes barriers between departments and provides opportunities for coordination among employees to achieve unity of effort and organizational objectives. **Horizontal linkage** refers to the amount of communication and coordination horizontally across organizational departments. Its importance was discovered by Lee Iacocca when he took over Chrysler Corporation.

> What I found at Chrysler were thirty-five vice presidents, each with his own turf. . . . I couldn't believe, for example, that the guy running engineering departments wasn't in constant touch with his counterpart in manufacturing. But that's how it was. Everybody worked independently. I took one look at that system and I almost threw up. That's when I knew I was in really deep trouble.
>
> . . . Nobody at Chrysler seemed to understand that interaction among the different functions in a company is absolutely critical. People in engineering and manufacturing almost have to be sleeping together. These guys weren't even flirting![8]

During his tenure at Chrysler (now DaimlerChrysler), Iacocca pushed horizontal coordination to a high level. Everyone working on a specific vehicle project—designers, engineers, and manufacturers, as well as representatives from marketing, finance, purchasing, and even outside suppliers—worked together on a single floor so they could constantly communicate. Ford and General Motors have also enhanced horizontal communication and coordination through mechanisms such as teams, task forces, and information systems.

Horizontal linkage mechanisms often are not drawn on the organization chart, but nevertheless are part of organization structure. The following devices are structural alternatives that can improve horizontal coordination and information flow.[9] Each device enables people to exchange information.

Information Systems. A significant method of providing horizontal linkage in today's organizations is the use of cross-functional information systems. Computerized information systems can enable managers or front-line workers throughout the organization to routinely exchange information about problems, opportunities, activities, or decisions. For example, at Ford, every car and truck model has its own internal Web site to track design, production, quality control, and delivery processes. Ford's product-development system is updated hourly, enabling engineers, designers, suppliers, and other employees around the world to work from the same data, keeping the process moving and saving time and money.[10]

Direct Contact. A higher level of horizontal linkage is direct contact between managers or employees affected by a problem. One way to promote direct contact is to create a special **liaison role**. A liaison person is located in one department but has the responsibility for communicating and achieving coordination with another department. Liaison roles often exist between engineering and manufacturing departments because engineering has to develop and test products to fit the limitations of manufacturing facilities. Monsanto Co. found another way to use direct contact. To get the R&D and commercial staffs working together, Monsanto pairs a scientist with a marketing or financial specialist as co-managers. For example, Frederick Perlak, a noted geneticist, and Kevin Holloway, with a background in marketing and human resources, oversee the global cotton team as co-directors. They work in adjoining cubicles, share a secretary, spend hours talking with one another, and together make all the key decisions about Monsanto's global cotton business. Monsanto hopes this unique mechanism, known internally as *two in the box*, will help transform the company from a chemical conglomerate into a life-sciences powerhouse.[11]

Task Forces. Direct contact and liaison roles usually link only two departments. When linkage involves several departments, a more complex device such as a task force is required. A **task force** is a temporary committee composed of representatives from each department affected by a problem.[12] Each member represents the interest of a department and can carry information from the meeting back to that department.

Task forces are an effective horizontal linkage device for temporary issues. They solve problems by direct horizontal coordination and reduce the information load on the vertical hierarchy. Typically, they are disbanded after their tasks are accomplished.

Commercial Casework, a $10 million woodworking and cabinetry shop in Fremont, California, used a task force to research and design the company's bonus plan. The U.S. Department of Defense set up a task force to reengineer its cumbersome travel system and make it cheaper, more efficient, and more customer friendly. The task force reduced the steps in the pretravel process from thirteen to only four. Another task force brought together employees from various functional departments to tackle the issue of how to simplify the Defense Department's travel regulations. Within three months, 230 pages of regulations had been reduced to a 16-page pamphlet.[13]

Full-time Integrator. A stronger horizontal linkage device is to create a full-time position or department solely for the purpose of coordination. A **full-time integrator** frequently has a title, such as product manager, project manager, program manager, or brand manager. Unlike the liaison person described earlier, the integrator does not report to one of the functional departments being coordinated. He or she is located outside the departments and has the responsibility for coordinating several departments.

The brand manager for Planters Peanuts, for example, coordinates the sales, distribution, and advertising for that product. General Motors set up brand managers who are responsible for marketing and sales strategies for each of GM's new models.[14]

The integrator can also be responsible for an innovation or change project, such as developing the design, financing, and marketing of a new product. An organization chart that illustrates the location of project managers for new product development is shown in Exhibit 3.3. The project managers are drawn to the side to indicate their separation from other departments. The arrows indicate project members assigned to the new product development. New Product A, for example, has a financial accountant assigned to keep track of costs and budgets. The engineering member provides design advice, and purchasing and manufacturing members represent their areas. The project manager is responsible for the entire project. He or she sees that the new product is completed on time, is introduced to the market, and achieves other project goals. The horizontal lines in Exhibit 3.3 indicate that project managers do not have formal authority over team members with respect to giving pay raises, hiring, or firing. Formal authority rests with the managers of the functional departments, who have formal authority over subordinates.

Integrators need excellent people skills. Integrators in most companies have a lot of responsibility but little authority. The integrator has to use expertise and persuasion to achieve coordination. He or she spans the boundary between departments and must be able to get people together, maintain their trust, confront problems, and resolve conflicts and disputes in the interest of the organization.[15]

Teams. Project teams tend to be the strongest horizontal linkage mechanism. **Teams** are permanent task forces and are often used in conjunction with a full-time integrator. When activities among departments require strong coordination over a long period of time, a cross-functional team is often the solution. Special project teams may be used when organizations have a large-scale project, a major innovation, or a new product line.

Boeing used around 250 teams to design and manufacture the 777 aircraft. Some teams were created around sections of the plane, such as the wing, cockpit, or engines, while others were developed to serve specific customers, such as United Airlines or British Airways. Boeing's teams had to be tightly integrated and coordinated to accomplish this massive project. Even the U.S. Department of the Navy has discovered the power of cross-functional teams to improve horizontal coordination and increase productivity.[16]

The Rodney Hunt Company develops, manufactures, and markets heavy industrial equipment and uses teams to coordinate each product line across the manufacturing, engineering, and marketing departments. Members from each team meet the first thing each day as needed to resolve problems concerning customer needs, backlogs, engineering changes, scheduling conflicts, and any other problem with the product line.

EXHIBIT 3.3   *Project Manager Location in the Structure*

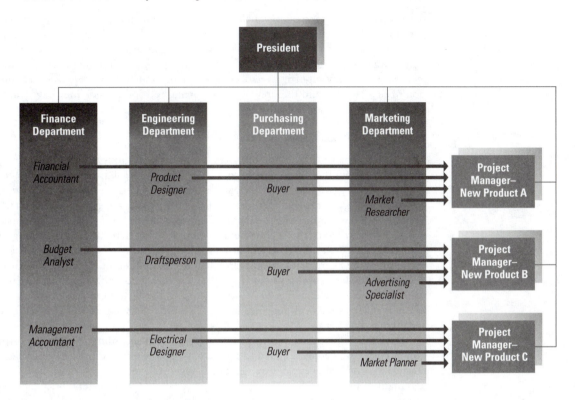

These devices represent alternatives that managers can select to increase horizontal coordination in any organization. The higher-level devices, such as full-time integrators or teams, provide more horizontal information capacity, although the cost to the organization in terms of time and human resources is greater. If horizontal communication is insufficient, departments will find themselves out of synchronization and will not contribute to the overall goals of the organization. When the amount of horizontal coordination required is high, managers should select higher-level mechanisms.

ORGANIZATION DESIGN ALTERNATIVES

The overall design of organization structure indicates three things—needed work activities, reporting relationships, and departmental groupings.

DEFINED WORK ACTIVITIES

Departments are created to perform tasks considered strategically important to the company. For example, when moving huge quantities of supplies in the Persian Gulf, the U.S. Army's logistics commander created a squad of fifteen soldiers called Ghostbusters who were charged with getting out among the troops, identifying logistics problems, and seeing that the problems got fixed. Richard H. Brown, CEO of Electronic Data Systems Corp. (EDS), has set a priority on reviving growth by helping companies launch e-commerce setups. Thus, Brown created an E-Business Solutions department to focus on the new business.[17] Defining a specific department is a way to accomplish tasks deemed valuable by the organization to accomplish its goals.

REPORTING RELATIONSHIPS

Reporting relationships, often called the chain of command, are represented by vertical lines on an organization chart. The chain of command should be an unbroken line of authority that links all persons in an organization and shows who reports to whom. In a large organization like EDS or Ford Motor Company, one hundred or more charts are required to identify reporting relationships among thousands of employees. The definition of departments and the drawing of reporting relationships defines how employees are to be grouped into departments.

DEPARTMENTAL GROUPING OPTIONS

Options for departmental grouping, including functional grouping, divisional grouping, geographic grouping, and multifocused grouping, are illustrated in Exhibit 3.4. **Departmental grouping** affects employees because they share a common supervisor and common resources, are jointly responsible for performance, and tend to identify and collaborate with one another.[18] For example, at Albany Ladder Company, the credit manager was shifted from the finance department to the marketing department. By being grouped with marketing, the credit manager started working with sales people to increase sales, thus becoming more liberal with credit than when he was located in the finance department.

Functional grouping places employees together who perform similar functions or work processes or who bring similar knowledge and skills to bear. For example, all marketing people would work together under the same supervisor, as would manufacturing and engineering people.

Divisional grouping means people are organized according to what the organization produces. All people required to produce toothpaste—including the marketing, manufacturing, and salespeople—are grouped together under one executive. In huge corporations such as EDS, some product or service lines may represent independent businesses, such as A. T. Kearney (management consulting), Centrobe (providing integrated customer care services), and Wendover Financial Services.

Geographic grouping means resources are organized to serve customers or clients in a particular geographical area. For example, all the activities required to serve Canada or Latin America or the eastern United States might be grouped together.

Multifocused grouping means an organization embraces two structural grouping alternatives simultaneously. This structural form is often called a *matrix* structure. The matrix will be discussed in more detail later in this chapter. An organization may need to group by function and product division simultaneously or perhaps by product division and geography.

The organizational forms described in Exhibit 3.4 provide the overall options within which the organization chart is drawn and the detailed structure is designed. Each structural design alternative has significant strengths and weaknesses, to which we now turn.

FUNCTIONAL, DIVISIONAL, AND GEOGRAPHICAL DESIGNS

Functional grouping and divisional grouping are the two most common approaches to structural design.

FUNCTIONAL STRUCTURE

In a **functional structure**, activities are grouped together by common function from the bottom to the top of the organization. All engineers are located in the engineering department, and the vice president of engineering is responsible for all engineering activities. An example of the functional organization structure was shown in Exhibit 3.1 earlier in this chapter.

With a functional structure, all human knowledge and skills with respect to specific activities are consolidated, providing a valuable depth of knowledge for the organization. This structure is most effective when in-depth expertise is critical to meeting organizational

EXHIBIT 3.4   *Structural Design Options for Grouping Employees into Departments*

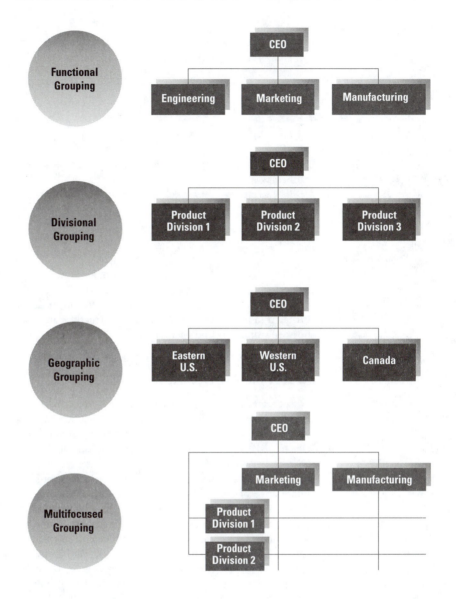

Source: Adapted from David Nadler and Michael Tushman, *Strategic Organization Design* (Glenview, Ill.: Scott Foresman, 1988), 68.

goals, when the organization needs to be controlled and coordinated through the vertical hierarchy, and when efficiency is important. The structure can be quite effective is there is little need for horizontal coordination. Exhibit 3.5 summarizes the strengths and weaknesses of the functional structure.

One strength of the functional structure is that it promotes economy of scale within functions. Economy of scale means all employees are located in the same place and can share facilities. Producing all products in a single plant, for example, enables the plant to acquire the latest machinery. Constructing only one facility instead of separate facilities for each product line reduces duplication and waste. The functional structure also promotes in-depth skill development of employees. Employees are exposed to a range of functional activities within their own department.[19]

EXHIBIT 3.5   *Strengths and Weaknesses of Functional Organization Structure*

Strengths
1. Allows economies of scale within functional departments
2. Enables in-depth knowledge and skill development
3. Enables organization to accomplish functional goals
4. Is best with only one or a few products

Weaknesses
1. Slow response time to environmental changes
2. May cause decisions to pile on top, hierarchy overload
3. Leads to poor horizontal coordination among departments
4. Results in less innovation
5. Involves restricted view of organizational goals

Source: Adapted from Robert Duncan, "What Is the Right Organization Structure? Decision Tree Analysis Provides the Answer," *Organizational Dynamics* (Winter 1979): 429.

The main weakness of the functional structure is a slow response to environmental changes that require coordination across departments. The vertical hierarchy becomes overloaded. Decisions pile up, and top managers do not respond fast enough. Other disadvantages of the functional structure are that innovation is slow because of poor coordination, and each employee has a restricted view of overall goals.

FUNCTIONAL STRUCTURE WITH HORIZONTAL LINKAGES

Today, there is a shift toward flatter, more horizontal structures. Very few of today's successful companies can maintain a strictly functional structure. Organizations compensate for the vertical functional hierarchy by installing horizontal linkages, as described earlier in this chapter. Managers improve horizontal coordination by using information systems, direct contact between departments, full-time integrators or project managers (illustrated in Exhibit 3.3), task forces, or teams. Not-for-profit organizations are also recognizing the importance of horizontal linkages. One interesting use of horizontal linkages occurred at Karolinska Hospital in Stockholm, Sweden, which had 47 functional departments. Even after top executives cut that down to eleven, coordination was still woefully inadequate. The team set about reorganizing workflow at the hospital around patient care. Instead of bouncing a patient from department to department, Karolinska now envisions the illness to recovery period as a process with pit stops in admissions, X-ray, surgery, and so forth. The most interesting aspect of the approach is the new position of nurse coordinator. Nurse coordinators serve as full-time integrators, looking for situations where the baton is dropped in the hand-off within or between departments. The improved horizontal coordination dramatically improved productivity and patient care at Karolinska.[20] Karolinska is effectively using horizontal linkages to overcome some of the disadvantages of the functional structure.

DIVISIONAL STRUCTURE

The term **divisional structure** is used here as the generic term for what is sometimes called a *product structure* or *strategic business units*. With this structure, divisions can be organized according to individual products, services, product groups, major projects or programs, divisions, businesses, or profit centers. The distinctive feature of a divisional structure is that grouping is based on organizational outputs.

The difference between a divisional structure and a functional structure is illustrated in Exhibit 3.6. The functional structure can be redesigned into separate product groups, and each group contains the functional departments of R&D, manufacturing, accounting, and marketing. Coordination across functional departments within each product group is

EXHIBIT 3.6   *Reorganization from Functional Structure to Divisional Structure at Info-Tech*

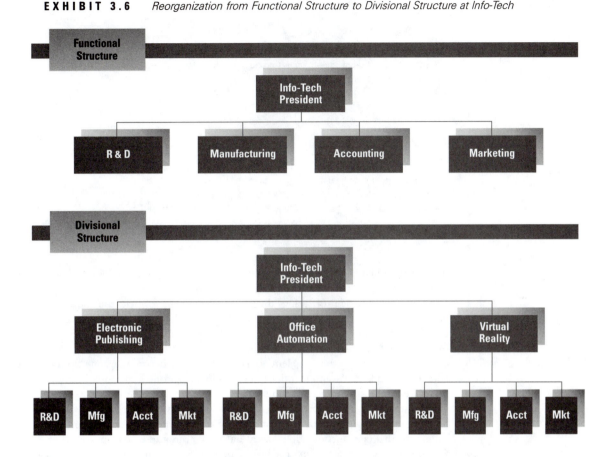

maximized. The divisional structure promotes flexibility and change because each unit is smaller and can adapt to the needs of its environment. Moreover, the divisional structure decentralizes decision making, because the lines of authority converge at a lower level in the hierarchy. The functional structure, by contrast, forces decisions all the way to the top before a problem affecting several functions can be resolved.

Strengths and weaknesses of the divisional structure are summarized in Exhibit 3.7. The divisional organization form of structure is excellent for achieving coordination across functional departments. It works well when organizations can no longer be adequately controlled through the traditional vertical hierarchy, and when goals are oriented toward adaptation and change. Giant, complex organizations such as General Electric, Nestlé, and Johnson & Johnson are subdivided into a series of smaller, self-contained organizations for better control and coordination. In these large companies, the units are sometimes called divisions, businesses, or strategic business units. The structure at Johnson & Johnson includes 180 separate operating units, including McNeil Consumer Products, makers of Tylenol; Ortho Pharmaceuticals, which makes Retin-A and birth control pills; and J & J Consumer Products, the company that brings us Johnson's Baby Shampoo and Band-Aids. Each division is a separately chartered, autonomous company operating under the guidance of Johnson & Johnson's corporate headquarters.[21]

The divisional structure has several strengths.[22] This structure is suited to fast change in an unstable environment and provides high product visibility. Since each product is a separate division, clients are able to contact the correct division and achieve satisfaction. Coordination across functions is excellent. Each product can adapt to requirements of individual customers or regions. The divisional structure typically works best in organizations that have multiple products or services and enough personnel to staff separate functional units. At corporations like Johnson & Johnson, PepsiCo, and Microsoft, decision

EXHIBIT 3.7   *Strengths and Weaknesses of Divisional Organization Structure*

Strengths
1. Suited to fast change in unstable environment
2. Leads to client satisfaction because product responsibility and contact points are clear
3. Involves high coordination across functions
4. Allows units to adapt to differences in products, regions, clients
5. Best in large organizations with several products
6. Decentralizes decision making

Weaknesses
1. Eliminates economies of scale in functional departments
2. Leads to poor coordination across product lines
3. Eliminates in-depth competence and technical specialization
4. Makes integration and standardization across product lines difficult

Source: Adapted from Robert Duncan, "What Is the Right Organization Structure? Decision Tree Analysis Provides the Answer," *Organization Dynamics* (Winter 1979): 431.

making is pushed down to the lowest levels. Each division is small enough to be quick on its feet, responding rapidly to changes in the market.

One disadvantage of using divisional structuring is that the organization loses economies of scale. Instead of fifty research engineers sharing a common facility in a functional structure, ten engineers may be assigned to each of five product divisions. The critical mass required for in-depth research is lost, and physical facilities have to be duplicated for each product line. Another problem is that product lines become separate from each other, and coordination across product lines can be difficult. As one Johnson & Johnson executive said, "We have to keep reminding ourselves that we work for the same corporation."[23]

Companies such as Hewlett-Packard and Xerox have a large number of divisions and have had real problems with horizontal coordination. The software division may produce programs that are incompatible with business computers sold by another division. Customers are frustrated when a sales representative from one division is unaware of developments in other divisions. Task forces and other linkage devices are needed to coordinate across divisions. A lack of technical specialization is also a problem in a divisional structure. Employees identify with the product line rather than with a functional specialty. R&D personnel, for example, tend to do applied research to benefit the product line rather than basic research to benefit the entire organization.

GEOGRAPHICAL STRUCTURE

Another basis for structural grouping is the organization's users or customers. The most common structure in this category is geography. Each region of the country may have distinct tastes and needs. Each geographic unit includes all functions required to produce and market products in that region. For multinational corporations, self-contained units are created for different countries and parts of the world.

Some years ago, Apple Computer reorganized from a functional to a geographical structure to facilitate manufacture and delivery of Apple computers to customers around the world. Exhibit 3.8 contains a partial organization structure illustrating the geographical thrust. Apple used this structure to focus managers and employees on specific geographical customers and sales targets. McDonald's divided its U.S. operations into five geographical divisions, each with its own president and staff functions such as human resources and legal.[24] The regional structure allows Apple and McDonald's to focus on the needs of customers in a geographical area.

The strengths and weaknesses of a geographic divisional structure are similar to the divisional organization characteristics listed in Exhibit 3.7. The organization can adapt to specific needs of its own region, and employees identify with regional goals rather than with national goals. Horizontal coordination within a region is emphasized rather than linkages across regions or to the national office.

EXHIBIT 3.8   *Geographical Structure for Apple Computer*

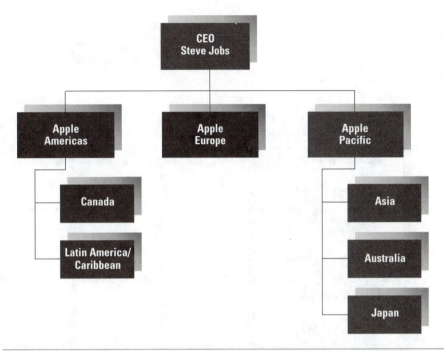

Source: Apple Computer, Inc. regions of the world. [Online] Available http://www.apple.com/find/areas. html, April 18, 2000.

MATRIX STRUCTURE

Sometimes, an organization's structure needs to be multifocused in that both product and function or product and geography are emphasized at the same time. One way to achieve this is through the **matrix structure**. The matrix can be used when both technical expertise and product innovation and change are important for meeting organizational goals. The matrix structure often is the answer when organizations find that neither the functional, divisional, nor geographical structures combined with horizontal linkage mechanisms will work.

The matrix is a strong form of horizontal linkage. The unique characteristic of the matrix organization is that both product division and functional structures (horizontal and vertical) are implemented simultaneously, as shown in Exhibit 3.9. The product managers and functional managers have equal authority within the organization, and employees report to both of them. The matrix structure is similar to the use of full-time integrators or product managers described earlier in this chapter (Exhibit 3.3), except that in the matrix structure the product managers (horizontal) are given formal authority equal to that of the functional managers (vertical).

CONDITIONS FOR THE MATRIX

A dual hierarchy may seem an unusual way to design an organization, but the matrix is the correct structure when the following conditions are met.[25]

- *Condition 1*. Pressure exists to share scarce resources across product lines. The organization is typically medium-sized and has a moderate number of product lines. It feels pressure for the shared and flexible use of people and equipment across those products. For example, the organization is not large enough to assign engineers full-time to each product line, so engineers are assigned part-time to several products or projects.

EXHIBIT 3.9   *Dual-Authority Structure in a Matrix Organization*

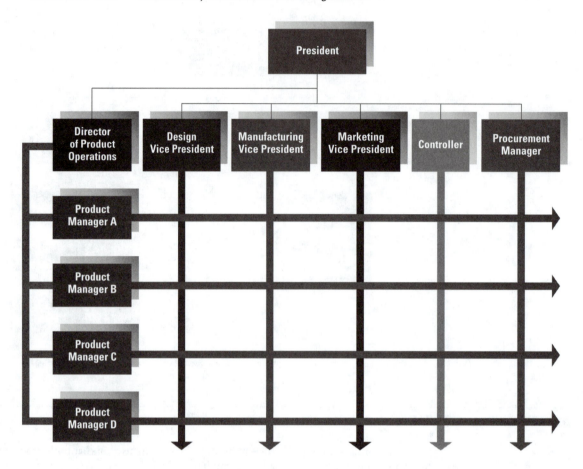

- *Condition 2.* Environmental pressure exists for two or more critical outputs, such as for in-depth technical knowledge (functional structure) and frequent new products (divisional structure). This dual pressure means a balance of power is needed between the functional and product sides of the organization, and a dual-authority structure is needed to maintain that balance.
- *Condition 3.* The environmental domain of the organization is both complex and uncertain. Frequent external changes and high interdependence between departments require a large amount of coordination and information processing in both vertical and horizontal directions.

Under these three conditions, the vertical and horizontal lines of authority must be given equal recognition. A dual-authority structure is thereby created so the balance of power between them is equal.

Referring again to Exhibit 3.9, assume the matrix structure is for a clothing manufacturer. Product A is footwear, product B is outerwear, product C is sleepwear, and so on. Each product line serves a different market and customers. As a medium-size organization, the company must effectively use people from manufacturing, design, and marketing to work on each product line. There are not enough designers to warrant a separate design department for each product line, so the designers are shared across product lines. Moreover, by keeping the manufacturing, design, and marketing functions intact, employees can develop the in-depth expertise to serve all product lines efficiently.

The matrix formalizes horizontal teams along with the traditional vertical hierarchy and tries to give equal balance to both. However, the matrix may shift one way or the other. Many companies have found a balanced matrix hard to implement and maintain because one side of the authority structure often dominates. Recognizing this tendency, two variations of matrix structure have evolved—the **functional matrix** and the **product matrix**. In a functional matrix, the functional bosses have primary authority and the project or product managers simply coordinate product activities. In a product matrix, by contrast, the project or product managers have primary authority and functional managers simply assign technical personnel to projects and provide advisory expertise as needed. For many organizations, one of these approaches works better than the balanced matrix with dual lines of authority.[26]

All kinds of organizations have experimented with the matrix, including hospitals, consulting firms, banks, insurance companies, government agencies, and many types of industrial firms.[27] This structure has been used successfully by organizations such as IBM and Unilever, which fine-tuned the matrix to suit their own particular goals and culture.

STRENGTHS AND WEAKNESSES

The matrix structure is best when environmental change is high and when goals reflect a dual requirement, such as for both product and functional goals. The dual-authority structure facilitates communication and coordination to cope with rapid environmental change and enables an equal balance between product and functional bosses. The matrix facilitates discussion and adaptation to unexpected problems. It tends to work best in organizations of moderate size with a few product lines. The matrix is not needed for only a single product line, and too many product lines make it difficult to coordinate both directions at once. Exhibit 3.10 summarizes the strengths and weaknesses of the matrix structure based on what we know of organizations that use it.[28]

The strength of the matrix is that it enables an organization to meet dual demands from customers in the environment. Resources (people, equipment) can be flexibly allocated across different products, and the organization can adapt to changing external requirements.[29] This structure also provides an opportunity for employees to acquire either functional or general management skills, depending on their interests.

One disadvantage of the matrix is that some employees experience dual authority, which is frustrating and confusing. They need excellent interpersonal and conflict-resolution skills, which may require special training in human relations. The matrix also forces managers to spend a great deal of time in meetings.[30] If managers do not adapt to the information and power sharing required by the matrix, the system will not work. Managers must collaborate with one another rather than rely on vertical authority in decision making.

EXHIBIT 3.10   *Strengths and Weaknesses of Matrix Organization Structure*

Strengths
1. Achieves coordination necessary to meet dual demands from customers
2. Flexible sharing of human resources across products
3. Suited to complex decisions and frequent changes in unstable environment
4. Provides opportunity for both functional and product skill development
5. Best in medium-sized organizations with multiple products

Weaknesses
1. Causes participants to experience dual authority, which can be frustrating and confusing
2. Means participants need good interpersonal skills and extensive training
3. Is time-consuming; involves frequent meetings and conflict resolution sessions
4. Will not work unless participants understand it and adopt collegial rather than vertical-type relationships
5. Requires great effort to maintain power balance

Source: Adapted from Robert Duncan, "What Is the Right Organization Structure? Decision Tree Analysis Provides the Answer," *Organizational Dynamics* (Winter 1979): 429.

APPLICATIONS OF STRUCTURAL DESIGN

Each type of structure is applied in different situations and meets different needs. In describing the various structures, we touched briefly on conditions such as environmental stability or change and organizational size that are related to structure. Each form of structure—functional, divisional, geographical, matrix—represents a tool that can help managers make an organization more effective, depending on the demands of its situation.

STRUCTURAL CONTINGENCIES

Recall the idea of "contingencies" from Chapter 2 and that managers design the organization to fit the contingency factors. As illustrated in Exhibit 3.11, structure is influenced by environment, strategy and goals, culture, technology, and size. Of these contextual variables, the connection between competitive strategy and structure is of particular interest and has been widely studied. Structure typically reflects organizational strategy, and a change in product or market strategy frequently leads to a change in structure.[31] Strategy and goals were discussed in detail in Chapter 2. Once a company formulates a strategy by which it plans to achieve a competitive advantage in the marketplace, leaders design or redesign the structure to coordinate organizational activities to best achieve that advantage.

The remaining contingency factors—environment, culture, technology, and size—will be discussed in subsequent chapters. Each variable influences the appropriate structural design. Moreover, environment, culture, technology, goals, and size may also

EXHIBIT 3.11   *Organization Contextual Variables that Influence Structure*

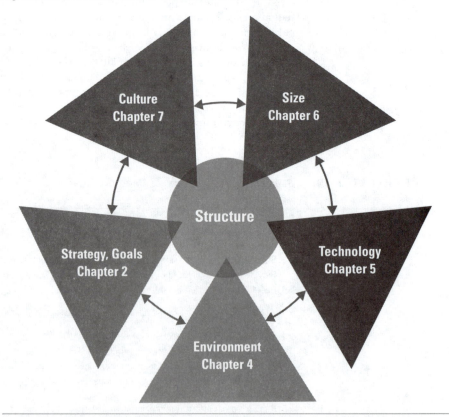

Sources: Adapted from Jay R. Galbraith, *Competing with Flexible Lateral Organizations,* 2nd ed. (Reading, Mass.: Addison-Wesley, 1994), ch. 1; Jay R. Galbraith, *Organization Design* (Reading, Mass.: Addison-Wesley, 1977), ch. 1.

influence one another, as illustrated by the connecting lines among these contextual variables in Exhibit 3.11.

SYMPTOMS OF STRUCTURAL DEFICIENCY

Top executives periodically evaluate organization structure to determine whether it is appropriate to changing organization needs. Many organizations try one organization structure, then reorganize to another structure in an effort to find the right fit between internal reporting relationships and the needs of the external environment. Compaq Computer Corporation, for example, switched from a functional structure to a divisional structure for about a year to develop new products and then switched back to a functional structure to reduce competition among its product lines.[32]

As a general rule, when organization structure is out of alignment with organization needs, one or more of the following **symptoms of structural deficiency** appear.[33]

- *Decision making is delayed or lacking in quality.* Decision makers may be overloaded because the hierarchy funnels too many problems and decisions to them. Delegation to lower levels may be insufficient. Another cause of poor quality decisions is that information may not reach the correct people. Information linkages in either the vertical or horizontal direction may be inadequate to ensure decision quality.
- *The organization does not respond innovatively to a changing environment.* One reason for lack of innovation is that departments are not coordinated horizontally. The identification of customer needs by the marketing department and the identification of technological developments in the research department must be coordinated. Organization structure also has to specify departmental responsibilities that include environmental scanning and innovation.
- *Too much conflict is evident.* Organization structure should allow conflicting departmental goals to combine into a single set of goals for the entire organization. When departments act at cross purposes or are under pressure to achieve departmental goals at the expense of organizational goals, the structure is often at fault. Horizontal linkage mechanisms are not adequate.

DISCUSSION QUESTIONS

1. What is the definition of *organization structure*? Does organization structure appear on the organization chart? Explain.
2. How do rules and plans help an organization achieve vertical integration?
3. When is a functional structure preferable to a divisional structure?
4. What is the difference between a task force and a team? Between liaison role and integrating role? Which of these provides the greatest amount of horizontal coordination?
5. What conditions usually have to be present before an organization should adopt a matrix structure?
6. The manager of a consumer products firm said, "We use the brand manager position to train future executives." Do you think the brand manager position is a good training ground? Discuss.
7. How can managers tell if structure is out of alignment with the organization's needs?

NOTES

1. John Child, *Organization* (New York: Harper & Row, 1984).
2. Stuart Ranson, Bob Hinings, and Royston Greenwood, "The Structuring of Organizational Structures," *Administrative Science Quarterly* 25 (1980): 1–17; Hugh Willmott, "The Structuring of Organizational Structure: A Note," *Administrative Science Quarterly* 26 (1981): 470–74.
3. This section is based on Frank Ostroff, *The Horizontal Organization: What the Organization of the Future Looks Like and How It Delivers Value to Customers* (New York: Oxford University Press, 1999).

4. Stephen Salsbury, *The State, the Investor, and the Railroad: The Boston & Albany, 1825-1867* (Cambridge: Harvard University Press, 1967), 186-187.

5. David Nadler and Michael Tushman, *Strategic Organization Design* (Glenview, Ill.: Scott Foresman, 1988).

6. Based on Jay R. Galbraith, *Designing Complex Organizations* (Reading, Mass.: Addison-Wesley, 1973), and *Organization Design* (Reading, Mass.: Addison-Wesley, 1977), 81-127.

7. Eryn Brown, "9 Ways to Win on the Web," *Fortune*, 24 May 1999, 112-125.

8. Lee Iacocca with William Novak, *Iacocca: An Autobiography* (New York: Phantom Books, 1984), 152–53.

9. Based on Galbraith, *Designing Complex Organizations*.

10. Mary J. Cronin, "Intranets Reach the Factory Floor," *Fortune*, 18 August 1997, 208; and Brown, "9 Ways to Win on the Web."

11. Timothy D. Schellhardt, "Monsanto Bets on 'Box Buddies'," *The Wall Street Journal*, 23 February 1999, B1, B10.

12. Walter Kiechel III, "The Art of the Corporate Task Force," *Fortune*, 28 January 1991, 104–5; William J. Altier, "Task Forces: An Effective Management Tool," *Management Review* (February 1987): 52–57.

13. Richard Koonce, "Reengineering the Travel Game," *Government Executive* (May 1995): 28-34, 69-70.

14. Keith Naughton and Kathleen Kerwin, "At GM, Two Heads May Be Worse Than One," *Business Week*, 14 August 1995, 46.

15. Paul R. Lawrence and Jay W. Lorsch, "New Managerial Job: The Integrator," *Harvard Business Review* (November-December 1967): 142–51.

16. Jay R. Galbraith, *Competing with Flexible Lateral Organizations*, 2nd ed. (Reading, Mass.: Addison-Wesley, 1994), 17–18; Laurie P. O'Leary, "Curing the Monday Blues: A U.S. Navy Guide for Structuring Cross-Functional Teams," *National Productivity Review* (Spring 1996): 43–51.

17. Wendy Zellner, "Can EDS Catch Up with the Net?" *Business Week*, 17 May 1999, 46.

18. Henry Mintzberg, *The Structuring of Organizations* (Englewood Cliffs, N.J.: Prentice-Hall, 1979).

19. Based on Robert Duncan, "What Is the Right Organization Structure?" *Organizational Dynamics* (Winter 1979): 59–80; W. Alan Randolph and Gregory G. Dess, "The Congruence Perspective of Organization Design: A Conceptual Model and Multivariate Research Approach," *Academy of Management Review* 9 (1984): 114–27.

20. Rahul Jacob, "The Struggle to Create an Organization for the 21st Century," *Fortune*, 3 April 1995, 90–99.

21. Joseph Weber, "A Big Company That Works," *Business Week*, 4 May 1992, 124–132; and Elyse Tanouye, "Johnson & Johnson Stays Fit by Shuffling Its Mix of Businesses," *The Wall Street Journal*, 22 December 1992, A1, A4.

22. Based on Duncan, "What Is the Right Organization Structure?"

23. Weber, "A Big Company That Works."

24. John Markoff, "John Sculley's Biggest Test," *New York Times*, 26 February 1989, sec. 3,1,26; and Shelly Branch, "What's Eating McDonald's?" *Fortune*, 13 October 1997, 122-125.

25. Stanley M. Davis and Paul R. Lawrence, *Matrix* (Reading, Mass.: Addison-Wesley, 1977): 11–24.

26. Eric W. Larson and David H. Gobeli, "Matrix Management: Contradictions and Insight," *California Management Review* 29 (Summer 1987): 126-138.

27. Davis and Lawrence, *Matrix*, 155-180.

28. Robert C. Ford and W. Alan Randolph, "Cross-Functional Structures: A Review and Integration of Matrix Organizations and Project Management," *Journal of Management* 18 (June 1992): 267–94; Duncan, "What Is the Right Organization Structure?"

29. Lawton R. Burns, "Matrix Management in Hospitals: Testing Theories of Matrix Structure and Development," *Administrative Science Quarterly* 34 (1989): 349–68.

30. Christopher A. Bartlett and Sumantra Ghoshal, "Matrix Management: Not a Structure, a Frame of Mind," *Harvard Business Review* (July-August 1990): 138–45.

31. Jay R. Galbraith, *Competing with Flexible Lateral Organizations*, 2d ed. (Reading, Mass.: Addison-Wesley, 1994): ch. 2; Terry L. Amburgey and Tina Dacin, "As the Left Foot Follows the Right? The Dynamics of Strategic and Structural Change," *Academy of Management Journal* 37, No. 6 (1994): 427-452; and Raymond E. Miles and W. E. Douglas Creed, "Organizational Forms and Managerial Philosophies: A Descriptive and Analytical Review," *Research in Organizational Behavior* 17 (1995): 333-372.

32. Jo Ellen Davis, "Who's Afraid of IBM?" *Business Week*, 29 June 1987, 68–74.

33. Based on Child, *Organization*, ch. 1.

PART 3

Open System Design Elements

The External Environment

*M*any companies are surprised by changes in the external environment. Perhaps the greatest tumult for today's organizations has been created by the rapid expansion of e-commerce. For example, Amazon.com was ringing up on-line book sales for more than a year before managers at Barnes & Noble even began thinking about a Web site. Barnes & Noble was highly successful with its book superstore concept, but its early efforts in e-commerce were marked by costly mistakes and missed opportunities. Even though the company burned through $100 million in an effort to "crush Amazon," Barnesandnoble.com was still selling only 15 percent of books bought online compared to Amazon's 75 percent.[1]

Firms in every industry, from auto manufacturing to telecommlunications, face similar uncertainty. Many factors in the external environment cause turbulence and uncertainty for organizations. Anheuser-Busch's CEO, for example, admits that his company was "five years late in recognizing that microbreweries were going to take as much market share as they did and five years late in recognizing that we should have joined them."[2] Small retailers have long suffered threats from huge discount stores such as Wal-Mart and Home Depot. Now, with electronics superstore Best Buy selling CDs for about half what they cost in traditional music stores, some record-selling chains have been forced into bankruptcy. In Western Europe, privatization of formerly state-owned enterprises has caused tremendous uncertainty for companies such as Swisscom, which seems to be thriving in the new environment, and Telecom Italia, which is not.[3] In the United States, the cattle industry has suffered declining prices because of increased imports of beef from Canada, Mexico, and Argentina. The list could go on and on. The external environment, including global competition, is the source of major threats facing today's organizations. The environment often imposes major constraints on the choices managers make for the organization.

PURPOSE OF THIS CHAPTER

The purpose of this chapter is to develop a framework for assessing environments and how organizations can respond to them. First, we will identify the organizational domain and the sectors that influence the organization. Then, we will explore two major environmental forces on the organization—the need for information and the need for resources. Organizations respond to these forces through structural design, planning systems, and attempts to change and control elements in the environment.

THE ENVIRONMENTAL DOMAIN

In a broad sense the environment is infinite and includes everything outside the organization. However, the analysis presented here considers only the aspects of the environment to which the organization is sensitive and must respond to survive. Thus, **organizational environment** is defined as all elements that exist outside the boundary of the organization and have the potential to affect all or part of the organization.

The environment of an organization can be understood by analyzing its domain within external sectors. An organization's **domain** is the chosen environmental field of action. It is the territory an organization stakes out for itself with respect to products, services, and markets served. Domain defines the organization's niche and defines those external sectors with which the organization will interact to accomplish its goals. Barnes & Noble ignored an important part of its domain when the bookselling environment changed. The company was slow to take advantage of new technology for e-commerce, allowing the competition to gain a huge advantage.

The environment comprises several **sectors** or subdivisions of the external environment that contain similar elements. Ten sectors can be analyzed for each organization: industry, raw materials, human resources, financial resources, market, technology, economic conditions, government, sociocultural, and international. The sectors and a hypothetical organizational domain are illustrated in Exhibit 4.1. For most companies, the sectors in Exhibit 4.1 can be further subdivided into the task environment and general environment.

TASK ENVIRONMENT

The **task environment** includes sectors with which the organization interacts directly and that have a direct impact on the organization's ability to achieve its goals. The task environment typically includes the industry, raw materials, and market sectors, and perhaps the human resources and international sectors.

The following examples illustrate how each of these sectors can affect organizations:

- In the *industry sector*, cola rivals Coke and Pepsi are intensifying their competition in local markets. For example, in New York City, one of the few markets where Pepsi-Cola outsells Coca-Cola Classic, each Coca-Cola marketing rep visits up to 120 small stores a week to push snazzier displays, better placement, and more promotions. In

EXHIBIT 4.1   *An Organization's Environment*

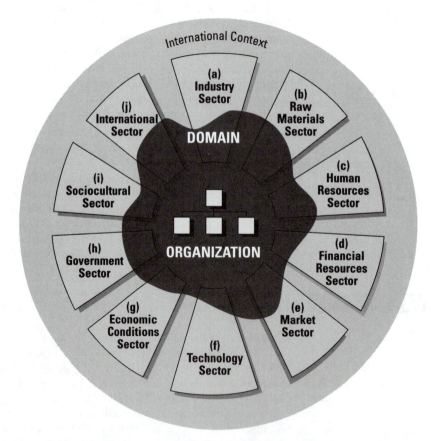

(a) Competitors, industry size and competitiveness, related industries
(b) Suppliers, manufacturers, real estate, services
(c) Labor market, employment agencies, universities, training schools, employees in other companies, unionization
(d) Stock markets, banks, savings and loans, private investors
(e) Customers, clients, potential users of products and services
(f) Techniques of production, science, computers, information technology, e-commerce

(g) Recession, unemployment rate, inflation rate, rate of investment, economics, growth
(h) City, state, federal laws and regulations, taxes, services, court system, political processes
(i) Age, values, beliefs, education, religion, work ethic, consumer and green movements
(j) Competition from and acquisition by foreign firms, entry into overseas markets, foreign customs, regulations, exchange rate

Harlem, where five convenience stores now sport red and white awnings thanks to Coca-Cola, small-store sales of Coke have doubled.[4]

- An interesting example in the *raw materials sector* concerns the beverage can industry. Steelmakers owned the beverage can market until the mid-1960s, when Reynolds Aluminum Company launched a huge aluminum recycling program to gain a cheaper source of raw materials and make aluminum cans price-competitive with steel.[5]

- In the *market sector*, changes in toy-buying patterns, with parents wanting more educational toys and electronics, have stalled growth rates for companies such as Mattel and Hasbro. Even Barbie and GI Joe are suffering sales declines. Toys "R" Us, once the giant of toy retailers, is reevaluating strategies and marketing plans to respond to changing customer desires.[6]

- The *human resources sector* has become of significant concern to almost every business because of the tightest labor market in thirty years. Well-educated, computer-literate young workers, sometimes called *gold-collar workers*, can often demand high salaries and generous benefits because companies have great difficulty finding qualified workers.[7]

- For U.S. automobile manufacturers, the *international sector* is part of the task environment because these companies face tough foreign competition, including an increasing number of foreign-owned manufacturing plants built on U.S. soil. The international sector as part of the general environment is discussed in more detail later in this chapter.

GENERAL ENVIRONMENT

The **general environment** includes those sectors that may not have a direct impact on the daily operations of a firm but will indirectly influence it. The general environment often includes the government, sociocultural, economic conditions, technology, and financial resources sectors. These sectors affect all organizations eventually. Consider the following examples:

- In response to well-publicized problems with medical devices such as heart valves and breast implants, the FDA introduced more stringent regulations that significantly slowed the rate of reviewing and approving new products. ISS, a small company that manufactures surgical assistant systems that use 3-D computer imaging and robotic tools, could once bring a new product to market in two or three years; it is now lucky to make it in six because of these changes in the *government sector*.[8]

- In the *sociocultural sector*, changing demographics are impacting numerous companies. The huge baby-boom generation is aging and losing some of its interest in high-cost, brand-name goods. Meanwhile, the sons and daughters of baby boomers, sometimes called "Generation Y," disdain such once-favored brands as Nike and Levi Strauss. Companies are struggling to build loyalty among this new generation, which rivals the baby boom in size and will soon rival it in buying clout.[9]

- General *economic conditions* often affect the way a company does business. To remain competitive in an era of low inflation, furniture maker Ethan Allen needed to keep prices low. To make a profit without raising prices, the company turned to making simpler furniture designs and increasing its technological efficiency.[10]

- The most overwhelming change in the *technology sector* is the rapid expansion of the Internet as a place for doing business. The World Wide Web and other advances in information technology have changed the whole face of business. For example, new formats for storing and transmitting music over the Internet could alter the entire recording industry. Although Val Azzoli, co-CEO of $700-million-plus-a-year Atlantic Group, views the Web primarily as a marketing tool for Atlantic's artists, a privately owned Web site called MP3.com is already giving away digitized music over the Web.[11]

- All businesses have to be concerned with *financial resources*, but this sector is often first and foremost in the minds of entrepreneurs starting a new business. Scott Blum started Buy.com, which resells computers and other products at or below cost over the Internet, with money out of his own savings. A couple of years later, Blum raised $60 million from Japanese tech company Softbank in return for a 20 percent equity stake in the company.[12]

INTERNATIONAL CONTEXT

The international sector can directly affect many organizations, and it has become extremely important in the last few years. In addition, all domestic sectors can be affected by international events. Despite the significance of international events for today's organizations, many students fail to appreciate the importance of international events and still think domestically. Think again. Even if you stay in your hometown, your company may be purchased tomorrow by the English, Canadians, Japanese, or Germans. For example, General Shale Brick, with headquarters in a small community in East Tennessee, was recently bought by Wienerberger Baustoffindustrie AG, a Vienna, Austria, company that is the world's largest brickmaker. The Japanese alone own more than one thousand U.S. companies, including steel mills, rubber and tire factories, automobile assembly plants, and auto parts suppliers. Nationwide, more than 350,000 Americans work for Japanese companies. People employed by Pillsbury, Shell Oil, Firestone, and CBS Records are working for foreign bosses.[13]

The impact of the international sector has grown rapidly with advances in technology and communications. The distinctions between domestic and foreign companies have become increasingly irrelevant as advances in transportation and electronic technology have reduced the impact of distance and time, as well as the differences among political and monetary systems, tastes, and standards. Global trade has tripled in the past twenty-five years, and today it is relatively easy for a firm of any size to operate on a global scale.[14] One small company, Montague Corporation, designs unique folding mountain bikes in Cambridge, Massachusetts, makes them in Taiwan, and sells most of them in Europe. Design changes are sent back and forth across three continents, sometimes on a daily basis. U.S.-based Coca-Cola, Canada's Northern Telecom, Switzerland's Nestlé, and France's Carrefour, the retailer that invented the *hypermarket* concept, all get a large percentage of their sales from outside their home countries.[15] In this global environment, it is no surprise that foreign-born people with international experience have been appointed to run such U.S. companies as Ford, Gerber, NCR, and Heinz. Consider the following trends:[16]

- The North American Free Trade Agreement is spurring many U.S. companies, including small businesses, to move into Canada and Mexico, affecting the market and human resources sectors.
- The European Union (EU) and Association of Southeast Asian Nations (ASEAN) may spawn large, powerful companies that compete easily with U.S. firms. These companies could reshape the industry and market sectors as we now know them.
- Despite recent economic woes, some analysts believe that in the twenty-first century, most of the economic activity in the world will take place in Asia and the Pacific Basin, sharply affecting the economic conditions and financial resources sectors.
- Newly industrialized countries such as Korea, Taiwan, Singapore, and Spain produce huge volumes of low-cost, high-quality commodities that will have an impact on the competitiveness of many industries, markets, and raw materials in North America.
- Eastern Europe, Russia, and China are all shifting toward market economies that also will affect markets, raw materials, industry competition, and worldwide economic conditions.
- Hundreds of partnerships are taking place between North American firms and firms in all parts of the world, facilitating the exchange of technology and production capability, thereby redefining the technology, raw materials, and industry sectors.
- Many companies in the United States build twin plants—one in Texas and one in Mexico. The Mexican plants provide component assembly, and that helps combat Mexico's high unemployment. Called *maquiladoras*, these plants reshape the human resources and raw materials sectors.

- All of these international connections are spawning new state and federal regulations, thereby affecting the government sector; and beliefs and values are becoming shared worldwide, shaping the sociocultural sector.

The increasing global interconnections have both positive and negative results for organizations. The recent economic turmoil in Asia and Eastern Europe blindsided many companies, creating great uncertainty for organizations doing business there. In addition, as the economic malaise spread to Latin America, it had an even greater impact on some U. S. companies based in Florida, since Southern Florida's economy is closely integrated with that of Latin America. CHS Electronics, a Miami-based firm with extensive ties to Latin America, has seen more and more of its Latin customers paying with local currency, and is finding debts harder to collect.[17]

Global interconnections also mean that competitiveness has reached a new level, as companies are competing on a broader scale than ever before. Less-developed countries are challenging mature countries in a number of industries. For example, India is becoming a major player in software development, and consumer electronics manufacturing, which long ago left the United States for Japan, is now rapidly leaving Japan for other countries in Asia.

Yet there is also a positive side. Domestic markets are saturated for many companies and the primary potential for growth lies overseas. Kimberly-Clark and Procter & Gamble, which spent years slugging it out in the now-flat U.S. diaper market, are targeting new markets in China, India, Brazil, Israel, and Russia. The demand for steel in China, India, and Brazil together is expected to grow 10 percent annually in the coming years—three times the U.S. rate. Nucor, a U.S.-based steel company, is opening a minimill in Thailand and partnering with a Brazilian company for a $700 million steel mill in northeastern Brazil. Other steel companies, such as LTV Corp. and North Star Steel, are moving into Asia, Europe, and Australia.[18] And, despite the economic convulsions there, large Western companies such as Ford, Procter & Gamble, and Coca-Cola continue to view Southeast Asia as the big market of the future. When companies think globally, the whole world is their marketplace.

The growing importance of the international sector means that the environment for all organizations has become extremely complex and extremely competitive. However, every organization faces uncertainty domestically as well as globally. In the following sections, we will discuss in greater detail how companies cope with and respond to environmental uncertainty and instability.

ENVIRONMENTAL UNCERTAINTY

How does the environment influence an organization? The patterns and events occurring across environmental sectors can be described along several dimensions, such as whether the environment is stable or unstable, homogeneous or heterogeneous, concentrated or dispersed, simple or complex; the extent of turbulence; and the amount of resources available to support the organization.[19] These dimensions boil down to two essential ways the environment influences organizations: (1) the need for information about the environment and (2) the need for resources from the environment. The environmental conditions of complexity and change create a greater need to gather information and to respond based on that information. The organization also is concerned with scarce material and financial resources and with the need to ensure availability of resources. Each sector can be analyzed relative to these three analytical categories. The remainder of this section will discuss the information perspective, which is concerned with the uncertainty that environmental complexity and change create for the organization. Later in the chapter, we will discuss how organizations control the environment to acquire needed resources.

Organizations must cope with and manage uncertainty to be effective. **Uncertainty** means that decision makers do not have sufficient information about environmental factors, and they have a difficult time predicting external changes. Uncertainty increases the risk of failure for organizational responses and makes it difficult to compute costs and probabilities associated with decision alternatives.[20] Characteristics of the environmental domain that influence uncertainty are the extent to which the external domain is simple or complex and the extent to which events are stable or unstable.[21]

SIMPLE–COMPLEX DIMENSION

The **simple–complex dimension** concerns environmental complexity, which refers to heterogeneity, or the number and dissimilarity of external elements relevant to an organization's operations. In a complex environment, many diverse external elements interact with and influence the organization. In a simple environment, as few as three or four similar external elements influence the organization.

Telecommunications firms such as AT&T and British Telecom have a complex environment, as do universities. Universities span a large number of technologies and are a focal point for cultural and value changes. Government regulatory and granting agencies interact with a university, and so do a variety of professional and scientific associations, alumni, parents, foundations, legislators, community residents, international agencies, donors, corporations, and athletic teams. A large number of external elements thus make up the organization's domain, creating a complex environment. On the other hand, a family-owned hardware store in a suburban community is in a simple environment. The only external elements of any real importance are a few competitors, suppliers, and customers. Government regulation is minimal, and cultural change has little impact. Human resources are not a problem because the store is run by family members or part-time help.

STABLE–UNSTABLE DIMENSION

The **stable–unstable dimension** refers to whether elements in the environment are dynamic. An environmental domain is stable if it remains the same over a period of months or years. Under unstable conditions, environmental elements shift abruptly. Instability may occur when competitors react with aggressive moves and countermoves regarding advertising and new products. For example, aggressive advertising and introduction of new products can create instability for companies, such as Coke's giving away 2 million Coca-Cola cards to build its teen market in New York City and the introduction of Surge to compete with Pepsi's Mountain Dew. Sometimes specific, unpredictable events–such as reports of syringes in cans of Pepsi or glass shards in Gerber's baby foods, the poisoning of Tylenol, or the Church of Scientology's attack on the antidepressant drug Prozac–create unstable conditions. Today, "hate sites" on the World Wide Web, such as Ihatemcdonalds.com and Walmartsucks.com, are an important source of instability for scores of companies, from Allstate Insurance to Toys "R" Us. Microsoft critics can visit more than twenty hate sites.[22]

Although environments are becoming more unstable for most organizations today, an example of a traditionally stable environment is a public utility.[23] In the rural Midwest, demand and supply factors for a public utility are stable. A gradual increase in demand may occur, which is easily predicted over time. Toy companies, by contrast, have an unstable environment. Hot new toys are difficult to predict, a problem compounded by the fact that toys are subject to fad buying. Coleco Industries, makers of the once-famous Cabbage Patch Kids, and Worlds of Wonder, creators of Teddy Ruxpin, went bankrupt because of the unstable nature of the toy environment, their once-winning creations replaced by Bandai's Mighty Morphin Power Rangers or Playmate Toys' Teenage Mutant Ninja Turtles.[24] Those toys, in turn, were replaced by fads such as Furby, Beanie Babies, Star Wars figures, and Pokémon.

FRAMEWORK

The simple-complex and stable-unstable dimensions are combined into a framework for assessing environmental uncertainty in Exhibit 4.2. In the *simple, stable* environment, uncertainty is low. There are only a few external elements to contend with, and they tend

EXHIBIT 4.2   *Framework for Assessing Environmental Uncertainty*

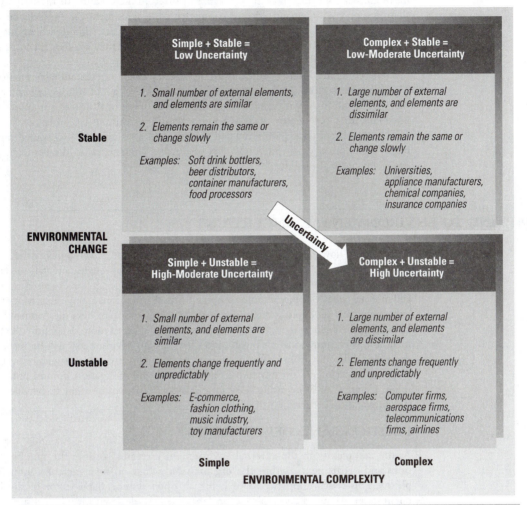

Source: Adapted and reprinted from "Characteristics of Perceived Environments and Perceived Environmental Uncertainty" by Robert B. Duncan, published in *Administrative Science Quarterly* 17 (1972): 313–27, by permission of *The Administrative Science Quarterly*. Copyright © 1972 by Cornell University.

to remain stable. The *complex, stable* environment represents somewhat greater uncertainty. A large number of elements have to be scanned, analyzed, and acted upon for the organization to perform well. External elements do not change rapidly or unexpectedly in this environment.

Even greater uncertainty is felt in the *simple, unstable* environment.[25] Rapid change creates uncertainty for managers. Even though the organization has few external elements, those elements are hard to predict, and they react unexpectedly to organizational initiatives. The greatest uncertainty for an organization occurs in the *complex, unstable* environment. A large number of elements impinge upon the organization, and they shift frequently or react strongly to organizational initiatives. When several sectors change simultaneously, the environment becomes turbulent.[26]

A beer distributor functions in a simple, stable environment. Demand for beer changes only gradually. The distributor has an established delivery route, and supplies of beer arrive on schedule. State universities, appliance manufacturers, and insurance companies are in somewhat stable, complex environments. A large number of external elements are present, but although they change, changes are gradual and predictable.

Toy manufacturers are in simple, unstable environments. Organizations that design, make, and sell toys, as well as those that are involved in the clothing or music industry, face shifting supply and demand. Most e-commerce companies focus on a specific competitive niche and, hence, operate in simple but unstable environments. Although there may be few elements to contend with—e.g., technology, competitors—they are difficult to predict and change abruptly and unexpectedly.

The computer industry and the airline industry face complex, unstable environments. Many external sectors are changing simultaneously. In the case of airlines, in just a few years they were confronted with deregulation, the growth of regional airlines, surges in fuel costs, price cuts from competitors such as Southwest Airlines, shifting customer demand, an air-traffic controller shortage, overcrowded airports, and a reduction of scheduled flights.[27] A recent series of major air traffic disasters has further contributed to the complex, unstable environment for the industry.

ADAPTING TO ENVIRONMENTAL UNCERTAINTY

Once you see how environments differ with respect to change and complexity, the next question is, "How do organizations adapt to each level of environmental uncertainty?" Environmental uncertainty represents an important contingency for organization structure and internal behaviors. Recall from Chapter 3 that organizations facing uncertainty generally encourage cross-functional communication and collaboration to help the company adapt to changes in the environment. In this section we will discuss in more detail how the environment affects organizations. An organization in a certain environment will be managed and controlled differently from an organization in an uncertain environment with respect to positions and departments, organizational differentiation and integration, control processes, and future planning and forecasting. Organizations need to have the right fit between internal structure and the external environment.

POSITIONS AND DEPARTMENTS

As the complexity in the external environment increases, so does the number of positions and departments within the organization, which in turn increases internal complexity. This relationship is part of being an open system. Each sector in the external environment requires an employee or department to deal with it. The human resources department deals with unemployed people who want to work for the company. The marketing department finds customers. Procurement employees obtain raw materials from hundreds of suppliers. The finance group deals with bankers. The legal department works with the courts and government agencies. Today, many companies are adding e-business departments to handle electronic commerce and information technology departments to deal with the increasing complexity of computerized information and knowledge management systems.

BUFFERING AND BOUNDARY SPANNING

The traditional approach to coping with environmental uncertainty was to establish buffer departments. The **buffering role** is to absorb uncertainty from the environment.[28] The technical core performs the primary production activity of an organization. Buffer departments surround the technical core and exchange materials, resources, and money between the environment and the organization. They help the technical core function efficiently. The purchasing department buffers the technical core by stockpiling supplies and raw materials. The human resources department buffers the technical core by handling the uncertainty associated with finding, hiring, and training production employees.

A newer approach some organizations are trying is to drop the buffers and expose the technical core to the uncertain environment. These organizations no longer create buffers because they believe being well connected to customers and suppliers is more important than internal efficiency. For example, John Deere has assembly-line workers visiting local farms to determine and respond to customer concerns. Whirlpool pays hundreds of customers to test computer-simulated products and features.[29] Opening up the organization to the environment makes it more fluid and adaptable.

Boundary-spanning roles link and coordinate an organization with key elements in the external environment. Boundary spanning is primarily concerned with the exchange of information to (1) detect and bring into the organization information about changes in the environment and (2) send information into the environment that presents the organization in a favorable light.[30]

Organizations have to keep in touch with what is going on in the environment so that managers can respond to market changes and other developments. A survey of high-tech firms found that 97 percent of competitive failures resulted from lack of attention to market changes or the failure to act on vital information.[31] To detect and bring important information into the organization, boundary personnel scan the environment. For example, a market research department scans and monitors trends in consumer tastes. Boundary spanners in engineering and research and development (R&D) departments scan new technological developments, innovations, and raw materials. Boundary spanners prevent the organization from stagnating by keeping top managers informed about environmental changes. Often, the greater the uncertainty in the environment, the greater the importance of boundary spanners.[32]

One of the fastest growing areas of boundary spanning is competitive intelligence. Companies large and small are setting up competitive intelligence departments or hiring outside specialists to gather information on competitors. Competitive intelligence gives top executives a systematic way to collect and analyze public information about rivals and use it to make better decisions.[33] Using techniques that range from Internet surfing to digging through trash cans, intelligence professionals dig up information on competitors' new products, manufacturing costs, or training methods and share it with top leaders. For example, Nutrasweet's competitive intelligence department helped the company delay a costly advertising campaign when it learned that a rival sweetener was at least five years away from FDA approval.[34] In today's uncertain environment, competitive intelligence is a trend that is likely to increase. In addition, companies such as UtiliTech Inc. of Stratford, Connecticut, and WavePhore Inc. of Phoenix, Arizona, regularly monitor the Internet for large corporations to see what is being said about them on the Web. This provides important information to top executives about how the company is perceived in the environment.

The boundary task of sending information into the environment to represent the organization is used to influence other people's perception of the organization. In the marketing department, advertising and sales people represent the organization to customers. Purchasers may call on suppliers and describe purchasing needs. The legal department informs lobbyists and elected officials about the organization's needs or views on political matters. Many companies set up their own Web pages to present the organization in a favorable light. To counteract hate sites that criticize their labor practices in Third World countries, Nike and Unocal both created Web sites specifically to tell their side of the story.[35]

DIFFERENTIATION AND INTEGRATION

Another response to environmental uncertainty is the amount of differentiation and integration among departments. Organization **differentiation** is "the differences in cognitive and emotional orientations among managers in different functional departments, and the difference in formal structure among these departments."[36] When the external environment is complex and rapidly changing, organizational departments become highly specialized to handle the uncertainty in their external sector. Success in each sector requires special expertise and behavior. Employees in a research and development department thus have unique attitudes, values, goals, and education that distinguish them from employees in manufacturing or sales departments.

A study by Paul Lawrence and Jay Lorsch examined three organizational departments—manufacturing, research, and sales—in ten corporations.[37] This study found that each department evolved toward a different orientation and structure to deal with specialized parts of the external environment. The market, scientific, and manufacturing subenvironments identified by Lawrence and Lorsch are illustrated in Exhibit 4.3. Each department interacted with different external groups. The differences that evolved among departments within the organizations are shown in Exhibit 4.4. To work effectively with the scientific subenvironment, R&D had a goal of quality work, a long time horizon (up to five years), an informal structure, and task-oriented employees. Sales was at the opposite extreme. It had a goal of customer satisfaction, was oriented toward the short term (two weeks or so), had a very formal structure, and was socially oriented.

One outcome of high differentiation is that coordination among departments becomes difficult. More time and resources must be devoted to achieving coordination when attitudes, goals, and work orientation differ so widely. **Integration** is the quality of collaboration among departments.[38] Formal integrators are often required to coordinate departments. When the environment is highly uncertain, frequent changes require more information processing to achieve horizontal coordination, so integrators become a necessary addition to the organization structure. Sometimes integrators are called liaison personnel, project managers, brand managers, or coordinators. As illustrated in Exhibit 4.5, organizations with highly uncertain environments and a highly differentiated structure assign about 22 percent of management personnel to integration activities, such

EXHIBIT 4.3   *Organizational Departments Differentiate to Meet Needs of Subenvironments*

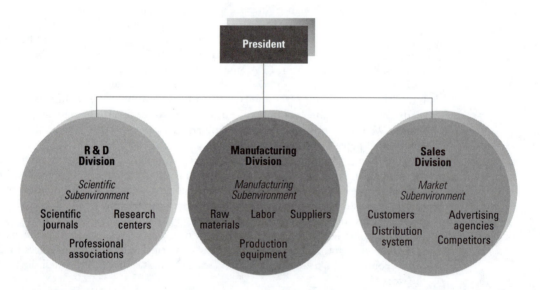

EXHIBIT 4.4   *Differences in Goals and Orientations Among Organizational Departments*

	R&D Department	Manufacturing Department	Sales Department
Goals	New developments, quality	Efficient production	Customer satisfaction
Time horizon	Long	Short	Short
Interpersonal orientation	Mostly task	Task	Social
Formality of structure	Low	High	High

Source: Based on Paul R. Lawrence and Jay W. Lorsch, *Organization and Environment* (Homewood, Ill.: Irwin, 1969), 23–29.

EXHIBIT 4.5   *Environmental Uncertainty and Organizational Integrators*

	Plastics	Industry Foods	Container
Environmental uncertainty	High	Moderate	Low
Departmental differentiation	High	Moderate	Low
Percent management in integrating roles	22%	17%	0%

Source: Based on Jay W. Lorsch and Paul R. Lawrence, "Environmental Factors and Organizational Integration," *Organizational Planning: Cases and Concepts* (Homewood, Ill.: Irwin and Dorsey, 1972), 45.

as serving on committees, on task forces, or in liaison roles.[39] In organizations characterized by very simple, stable environments, almost no managers are assigned to integration roles. Exhibit 4.5 shows that, as environmental uncertainty increases, so does differentiation among departments; hence, the organization must assign a larger percentage of managers to coordinating roles.

Lawrence and Lorsch's research concluded that organizations perform better when the levels of differentiation and integration match the level of uncertainty in the environment. Organizations that performed well in uncertain environments had high levels of both differentiation and integration, while those performing well in less uncertain environments had lower levels of differentiation and integration.

ORGANIC VERSUS MECHANISTIC MANAGEMENT PROCESSES

Another response to environmental uncertainty is the amount of formal structure and control imposed on employees. Tom Burns and G. M. Stalker observed twenty industrial firms in England and discovered that external environment was related to internal management structure.[40] When the external environment was stable, the internal organization was characterized by rules, procedures, and a clear hierarchy of authority. Organizations were formalized. They were also centralized, with most decisions made at the top. Burns and Stalker called this a **mechanistic** organization system.

In rapidly changing environments, the internal organization was much looser, free-flowing, and adaptive. Rules and regulations often were not written down or, if written down, were ignored. People had to find their own way through the system to figure out what to do. The hierarchy of authority was not clear. Decision-making authority was decentralized. Burns and Stalker used the term **organic** to characterize this type of management structure.

Exhibit 4.6 summarizes the differences in organic and mechanistic systems. As environmental uncertainty increases, organizations tend to become more organic, which means decentralizing authority and responsibility to lower levels, encouraging employees

EXHIBIT 4.6   *Mechanistic and Organic Forms*

Mechanistic	Organic
1. Tasks are broken down into specialized separate parts.	1. Employees contribute to the common tasks of the department.
2. Tasks are rigidly defined.	2. Tasks are adjusted and redefined through employee teamwork.
3. There is a strict hierarchy of authority and control, and there are many rules.	3. There is less hierarchy of authority and control, and there are few rules.
4. Knowledge and control of tasks are centralized at the top of organization.	4. Knowledge and control of tasks are located anywhere in the organization.
5. Communication is vertical.	5. Communication is horizontal.

Source: Adapted from Gerald Zaltman, Robert Duncan, and Johnny Holbek, *Innovations and Organizations* (New York: Wiley, 1973), 131.

to take care of problems by working directly with one another, encouraging teamwork, and taking an informal approach to assigning tasks and responsibility. Thus, the organization is more fluid and is able to adapt continually to changes in the external environment.[41]

PLANNING AND FORECASTING

The final organizational response to uncertainty is to increase planning and environmental forecasting. When the environment is stable, the organization can concentrate on current operational problems and day-to-day efficiency. Long-range planning and forecasting are not needed because environmental demands in the future will be the same as they are today.

With increasing environmental uncertainty, planning and forecasting become necessary.[42] Planning can soften the adverse impact of external shifting. Organizations that have unstable environments often establish a separate planning department. In an unpredictable environment, planners scan environmental elements and analyze potential moves and countermoves by other organizations. Planning can be extensive and may forecast various scenarios for environmental contingencies. As time passes, plans are updated through replanning. However, planning does not substitute for other actions, such as boundary spanning. Indeed, under conditions of extraordinarily high uncertainty, formal planning may not be helpful because the future is so difficult to predict.

RESOURCE DEPENDENCE

Thus far, this chapter has described several ways in which organizations adapt to the lack of information and to the uncertainty caused by environmental change and complexity. We turn now to the third characteristic of the organization-environment relationship that affects organizations, which is the need for material and financial resources. The environment is the source of scarce and valued resources essential to organizational survival. Research in this area is called the resource dependence perspective. **Resource dependence** means that organizations depend on the environment but strive to acquire control over resources to minimize their dependence.[43] Organizations are vulnerable if vital resources are controlled by other organizations, so they try to be as independent as possible. Organizations do not want to become too vulnerable to other organizations because of negative effects on performance. For example, several years ago the supplier for more than half of Mattress Warehouse's stock decided to open a factory-direct store in the same market. Mattress Warehouse had only a week's notice that the supplier relationship was terminated, leaving the company scrambling to find another bedding vendor. It was a wake-up call for Mattress Warehouse owner Kimberly Brown Knopf, who diversified her supplier base to prevent the loss of one supplier from jeopardizing her business in the future.[44]

When costs and risks are high, however, companies also team up to reduce resource dependence and the possibility of bankruptcy. In today's volatile environment, companies are collaborating as never before to share scarce resources and be more competitive on a global scale.

Formal relationships with other organizations, however, present a dilemma to managers. North American organizations seek to reduce vulnerability with respect to resources by developing links with other organizations, but they also like to maximize their own autonomy and independence. Organizational linkages require coordination,[45] and they reduce the freedom of each organization to make decisions without concern for the needs and goals of other organizations. Interorganizational relationships thus represent a tradeoff between resources and autonomy. To maintain autonomy, organizations that already have abundant resources will tend not to establish new linkages. Organizations that need resources will give up independence to acquire those resources.

Dependence on shared resources gives power to other organizations. Once an organization relies on others for valued resources, those other organizations can influence managerial decision making. When a large company like DuPont, Motorola, or Xerox forges a partnership with a supplier for parts, both sides benefit, but each loses a small amount of autonomy. For example, some of these large companies are now putting strong pressure on vendors to lower costs, and the vendors have few alternatives but to go along.[46] In much the same way, dependence on shared resources gives advertisers power over print and electronic media companies. For example, as newspapers face increasingly tough financial times, they are less likely to run stories that are critical of advertisers. Though newspapers insist advertisers don't get special treatment, some editors admit there is growing talk around the country of the need for "advertiser-friendly" newspapers.[47]

In another industry, Microsoft is so large and powerful that it has a virtual monopoly in personal computer operating systems, so its every technical change adversely affects producers of application software. Microsoft has been accused of abusing this power and of squashing small competitors that would like to link up with it.[48]

CONTROLLING ENVIRONMENTAL RESOURCES

In response to the need for resources, organizations try to maintain a balance between linkages with other organizations and their own independence. Organizations maintain this balance through attempts to modify, manipulate, or control other organizations.[49] To survive, the focal organization often tries to reach out and change or control elements in the environment. Two strategies can be adopted to manage resources in the external environment: (1) establish favorable linkages with key elements in the environment and (2) shape the environmental domain.[50] Techniques to accomplish each of these strategies are summarized in Exhibit 4.7. As a general rule, when organizations sense that valued resources are scarce, they will use the strategies in Exhibit 4.7 rather than go it alone.

ESTABLISHING INTERORGANIZATIONAL LINKAGES

Ownership. Companies use ownership to establish linkages when they buy a part of or a controlling interest in another company. This gives the company access to technology, products, or other resources it doesn't currently have. The communications and information technology industry has become particularly complex, and many companies have been teaming up worldwide.

A greater degree of ownership and control is obtained through acquisition or merger. An *acquisition* involves the purchase of one organization by another so that the buyer assumes control. A *merger* is the unification of two or more organizations into a single unit.[51] In the world of e-business, USWeb and CKS Group merged to create a company that pulls in more than a quarter of a billion dollars by helping companies set up and run Internet divisions. Its clients include the dot-com divisions of companies such as Apple, NBC, and Levi Strauss.[52] The creation of Pharmacia & Upjohn Inc. from the Upjohn Co. of Kalamazoo, Michigan, and Sweden's Pharmacia was a merger. Acquisition occurred when Hewlett-Packard bought VeriFone and when America Online purchased Netscape Communications. These forms of ownership reduce uncertainty in an area important to the acquiring company.

EXHIBIT 4.7   *Organizing Strategies for Controlling the External Environment*

Establishing Interorganizational Linkages	Controlling the Environmental Domain
1. Ownership	1. Change of domain
2. Contracts, joint ventures	2. Political activity, regulation
3. Cooptation, interlocking directorates	3. Trade associations
4. Executive recruitment	4. Illegitimate activities
5. Advertising, public relations	

Formal Strategic Alliances. When there is a high level of complementarity between the business lines, geographical positions, or skills of two companies, the firms often go the route of a strategic alliance rather than ownership through merger or acquisition.[53] Such alliances are formed through contracts and joint ventures.

Contracts and joint ventures reduce uncertainty through a legal and binding relationship with another firm. Contracts come in the form of *license agreements* that involve the purchase of the right to use an asset (such as a new technology) for a specific time and *supplier arrangements* that contract for the sale of one firm's output to another. Contracts can provide long-term security by tying customers and suppliers to specific amounts and prices. For example, McDonald's contracts for an entire crop of russet potatoes to be certain of its supply of french fries. McDonald's also gains influence over suppliers through these contracts and has changed the way farmers grow potatoes and the profit margins they earn, which is consistent with the resource dependence perspective.[54] Large retailers such as Wal-Mart, Kmart, Toys 'R' Us, and Home Depot are gaining so much clout that they can almost dictate contracts telling manufacturers what to make, how to make it, and how much to charge for it. For example, CD companies edit songs and visual covers to cut out "offensive material" in order to get their products on the shelves of Wal-Mart, which sells more than 50 million CDs annually. As one manufacturing rep put it, "Most suppliers would do absolutely anything to sell Wal-Mart."[55] *Joint ventures* result in the creation of a new organization that is formally independent of the parents, although the parents will have some control.[56] In a joint venture, organizations share the risk and cost associated with large projects or innovations. For example, Barnesandnoble.com is a joint venture between Barnes & Noble and Germany's Bertelsmann AG. Barnes & Noble and Bertelsmann have agreed to invest $100 million each and share the risks of the joint venture as it battles Amazon.com in the world of online bookselling.

Cooptation, Interlocking Directorates. Cooptation occurs when leaders from important sectors in the environment are made part of an organization. It takes place, for example, when influential customers or suppliers are appointed to the board of directors, such as when the senior executive of a bank sits on the board of a manufacturing company. As a board member, the banker may become psychologically coopted into the interests of the manufacturing firm. Community leaders also can be appointed to a company's board of directors or to other organizational committees or task forces. These influential people are thus introduced to the needs of the company and are more likely to include the company's interests in their decision making.

An **interlocking directorate** is a formal linkage that occurs when a member of the board of directors of one company sits on the board of directors of another company. The individual is a communications link between companies and can influence policies and decisions. Internet startups, such as the Seattle-based companies TechWave, AccountingNet, and Honkworm International, often use this strategy to share advice and resources.[57] When one individual is the link between two companies, this is typically referred to as a **direct interlock**. An **indirect interlock** occurs when a director of company A and a director of company B are both directors of company C. They have access to one another but do not have direct influence over their respective companies.[58] Recent research shows that, as a firm's financial fortunes decline, direct interlocks with financial institutions increase. Financial uncertainty facing an industry also has been associated with greater indirect interlocks between competing companies.[59]

Executive Recruitment. Transferring or exchanging executives also offers a method of establishing favorable linkages with external organizations. For example, each year the aerospace industry hires retired generals and executives from the Department of Defense. These generals have personal friends in the department, so the aerospace companies obtain better information about technical specifications, prices, and dates for new weapon systems. They can learn the needs of the defense department and are able to present their case for defense contracts in a more effective way. Companies without personal contacts find it nearly impossible to get a defense contract. Having channels of influence and communication between organizations serves to reduce financial uncertainty and dependence for an organization.

Advertising and Public Relations. A traditional way of establishing favorable relationships is through advertising. Organizations spend large amounts of money to influence the taste of consumers. Advertising is especially important in highly competitive consumer industries and in industries that experience variable demand. In the fashion industry, once-stodgy JCPenney turned its Arizona Jeans into one of the hottest brands around through hip advertising featuring rock music and Internet imagery. A recent ad campaign shows teens mocking ads that attempt to speak their language, ending with the tagline "Just show me the jeans."[60]

Public relations is similar to advertising, except that stories often are free and aimed at public opinion. Public relations people cast an organization in a favorable light in speeches, in press reports, and on television. Public relations attempts to shape the company's image in the minds of customers, suppliers, and government officials. For example, in an effort to survive in this antismoking era, tobacco companies have launched an aggressive public relations campaign touting smokers' rights and freedom of choice.

Summary. Organizations can use a variety of techniques to establish favorable linkages that ensure the availability of scarce resources. Linkages provide control over vulnerable environmental elements. Strategic alliances, interlocking directorates, and outright ownership provide mechanisms to reduce resource dependency on the environment. U.S. companies such as IBM, Apple, AT&T, and Motorola have been quick in recent years to turn rivalry into partnership. Perhaps surprisingly, Japan's electronics companies have been slower to become involved in joint ventures and other strategic alliances.

CONTROLLING THE ENVIRONMENTAL DOMAIN

In addition to establishing favorable linkages to obtain resources, organizations often try to change the environment. There are four techniques for influencing or changing a firm's environmental domain.

Change of Domain. The ten sectors described earlier in this chapter are not fixed. The organization decides which business it is in, the market to enter, and the suppliers, banks, employees, and location to use, and this domain can be changed.[61] An organization can seek new environmental relationships and drop old ones. An organization may try to find a domain where there is little competition, no government regulation, abundant suppliers, affluent customers, and barriers to keep competitors out.

Acquisition and divestment are two techniques for altering the domain. Canada's Bombardier, maker of Ski-Doo snowmobiles, began a series of acquisitions to alter its domain when the energy crisis of the mid–1970s nearly wiped out the snowmobile industry. CEO Laurent Beaudoin gradually moved the company into the aerospace industry by negotiating deals to purchase Canadair, Boeing's deHaviland unit, business-jet pioneer Learjet, and Short Brothers of Northern Ireland. Deere & Co. felt vulnerable with the declining customer base for agricultural machinery, so Chairman and CEO Hans Becherer began reallocating resources into other lines of business, such as health care and financial services. Entering these new domains is helping Deere weather uncertain times and take some pressure off the machinery business.[62] An example of divestment is when Sears redefined its domain by selling off its financial services divisions, including Coldwell Banker, Allstate, and Dean Witter, to focus the company on retailing.

Political Activity, Regulation. Political activity includes techniques to influence government legislation and regulation. For example, General Motors used political activity to successfully settle a battle with the U.S. Transportation Department over the safety of some of its pickup trucks. The settlement requires that GM spend $51 million on safety programs over a five-year period but saved the company the cost of a $1 billion recall.[63]

In one technique, organizations pay lobbyists to express their views to members of federal and state legislatures. In the telecommunications industry, the Baby Bells hired powerful lobbyists to influence a sweeping new telecommunications bill giving local phone companies access to new markets.[64] Many CEOs, however, believe they should do their own lobbying. CEOs have easier access than lobbyists and can be especially effective when they do the politicking. Political activity is so important that "informal lobbyist" is an unwritten part of almost any CEO's job description.[65]

Political strategy can be used to erect regulatory barriers against new competitors or to squash unfavorable legislation. Corporations also try to influence the appointment to agencies of people who are sympathetic to their needs. The value of political activity is illustrated by the efforts of Sun Microsystems and Netscape to persuade the Justice Department to break up Microsoft, arguing that Microsoft had acted as a monopoly in controlling the software industry and now threatens to extend that power to Internet access. Some observers noted that if Microsoft had paid more attention to political lobbying earlier, it could have avoided Justice Department investigation.

Trade Associations. Much of the work to influence the external environment is accomplished jointly with other organizations that have similar interests. Most manufacturing companies are part of the National Association of Manufacturers and also belong to associations in their specific industry. By pooling resources, these organizations can pay people to carry out activities such as lobbying legislators, influencing new regulations, developing public relations campaigns, and making campaign contributions. For example, the National Tooling and Machining Association (NTMA) devotes a quarter of a million dollars each year to lobbying, mainly on issues that affect small business, such as taxes, health insurance, or government mandates. NTMA also gives its members statistics and information that help them become more competitive in the global marketplace.[66]

Illegitimate Activities. Illegitimate activities represent the final technique companies sometimes use to control their environmental domain. Certain conditions, such as low profits, pressure from senior managers, or scarce environmental resources, may lead managers to adopt behaviors not considered legitimate.[67] Many well-known companies have been found guilty of behavior considered unlawful. Example behaviors include payoffs to foreign governments, illegal political contributions, promotional gifts, and wiretapping. Intense competition among cement producers and in the oil business during a period of decline led to thefts and illegal kickbacks.[68] In the defense industry, the intense competition for declining contracts for major weapon systems led some companies to do almost anything to get an edge, including schemes to peddle inside information and to pay off officials.[69] One study found that companies in industries with low demand, shortages, and strikes were more likely to be convicted for illegal activities, implying that illegal acts are an attempt to cope with resource scarcity.[70] In another study, social movement organizations such as Earth First! and the AIDS Coalition to Unleash Power (ActUp) were found to have acted in ways considered illegitimate or even illegal to bolster their visibility and reputation.[71]

ORGANIZATION-ENVIRONMENT INTEGRATIVE FRAMEWORK

The relationships illustrated in Exhibit 4.8 summarize the two major themes about organization-environment relationships discussed in this chapter. One theme is that the amount of complexity and change in an organization's domain influences the need for information and hence the uncertainty felt within an organization. Greater information uncertainty is resolved through greater structural flexibility, and the assignment of additional departments and boundary roles. When uncertainty is low, management structures can be more mechanistic, and the number of departments and boundary roles can be fewer. The second theme pertains to the scarcity of material and financial resources. The more dependent an organization is on other organizations for those resources, the more important it is to either establish favorable linkages with those organizations or control entry into the domain. If dependence on external resources is low, the organization can maintain autonomy and does not need to establish linkages or control the external domain.

EXHIBIT 4.8   *Relationship Between Environmental Characteristics and Organizational Actions*

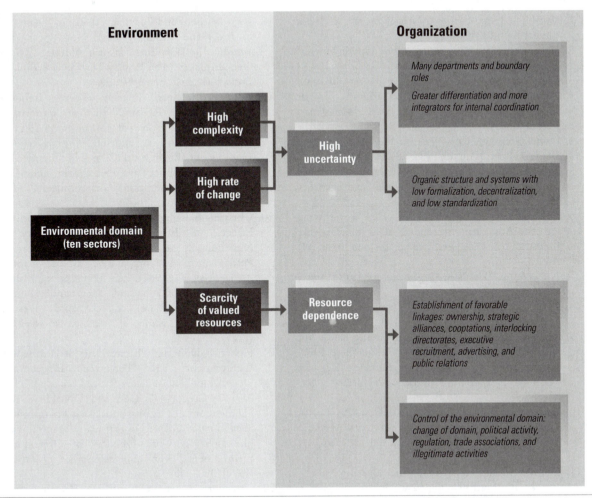

Source: Adapted from Gerald Zaltman, Robert Duncan, and Johnny Holbek, Innovations and Organizations (New York: Wiley, 1973), 131.

DISCUSSION QUESTIONS

1. Define *organizational environment*. Would the task environment for a new Internet-based company be the same as that of a government welfare agency? Discuss.

2. What are some forces that influence environmental uncertainty? Which typically has the greatest impact on uncertainty—environmental complexity or environmental change? Why?

3. Why does environmental complexity lead to organizational complexity? Explain.

4. Discuss the importance of the international sector for today's organizations, compared to domestic sectors. What are some ways in which the international sector affects organizations in your city or community?

5. Describe differentiation and integration. In what type of environmental uncertainty will differentiation and integration be greatest? Least?

6. What is an organic organization? A mechanistic organization? How does the environment influence organic and mechanistic structures?

7. Why do organizations become involved in interorganizational relationships? Do these relationships affect an organization's dependency? Performance?

8. Is changing the organization's domain a feasible strategy for coping with a threatening environment? Explain.

NOTES

1. Warren St. John, "Barnes & Noble's Epiphany," *Wired* (June 1999): 132-144.

2. Gary Hamel, "Turning Your Business Upside Down," *Fortune,* 23 June 1997, 87-88.

3. Tim Carvell, "These Prices Really Are Insane," *Fortune,* 4 August 1997, 109-116; and Trevor Merriden, "Europe's Privatized Stars," *Management Review* June 1999, 16-23.

4. David Greising, "Cola Wars on the Mean Streets," *Business Week,* 3 August 1998, 78-79.

5. Dana Milbank, "Aluminum Producers, Aggressive and Agile, Outfight Steelmakers," *The Wall Street Journal,* 1 July 1992, A1.

6. Joseph Pereira and William M. Buckley, "Toy-Buying Patterns Are Changing and That Is Shaking the Industry," *The Wall Street Journal,* 16 June 1998, A1, A8.

7. Nina Munk, "The New Organization Man," *Fortune,* 16 March 1998, 63-74.

8. Bela L. Musits, "When Big Changes Happen to Small Companies," *Inc.* (August 1994): 27–28.

9. Michael Hickins, "Brand Names Losing Luster for Affluent Customers," *Management Review* (June 1999) 9; and Ellen Neuborne with Kathleen Kerwin, "Generation Y," *Business Week,* 15 February 1999, 80-88.

10. Lucinda Harper and Fred R. Bleakley, "An Era of Low Inflation Changes the Calculus for Buyers and Sellers," *The Wall Street Journal,* 14 January 1994, A1, A3.

11. Jodi Mardesich, "How the Internet Hits Big Music," *Fortune,* 10 May 1999, 96-102.

12. Eric Nee, "Meet Mister buy(everything).com," *Fortune,* 29 May 1999, 119-124.

13. Andrew Kupfer, "How American Industry Stacks Up," *Fortune,* 9 March 1992, 36–46.

14. Fred L. Steingraber, "How to Succeed in the Global Marketplace," *USA Today Magazine (*November 1997): 30-31.

15. Alan Farnham, "Global—or Just Globaloney?" *Fortune,* 27 June 1994, 97–100; William C. Symonds, Brian Bremner, Stewart Toy, and Karen Lowry Miller, "The Globetrotters Take Over," *Business Week,* 8 July 1996, 46–48; Carla Rapoport, "Nestlé's Brand Building Machine," *Fortune,* 19 September 1994, 147–156; "Execs with Global Vision," *USA Today,* International Edition, 9 February 1996, 12B.

16. Tom Peters, "Prometheus Barely Unbound," *Academy of Management Executive* 4 (1990): 70–84; and Clifford C. Hebard, "Managing Effectively in Asia," *Training & Development* (April 1996): 35–39.

17. Marlene Piturro, "What Are You Doing About the New Global Realities?" *Management Review (*March 1999): 16-22.

18. Raju Narisetti and Jonathan Friedland, "Diaper Wars of P&G and Kimberly-Clark Now Heat Up in Brazil," *The Wall Street Journal,* 4 June 1997; and Stephen Baker, "The Bridges That Steel is Building," *Business Week,* 2 June 1997, 39.

19. Allen C. Bluedorn, "Pilgrim's Progress: Trends and Convergence in Research on Organizational Size and Environment," *Journal of Management* 19 (1993): 163–91; Howard E. Aldrich, *Organizations and Environments* (Englewood, Cliffs, N.J.: Prentice-Hall, 1979); Fred E. Emery and Eric L. Trist, "The Casual Texture of Organizational Environments," *Human Relations* 18 (1965): 21–32.

20. Christine S. Koberg and Gerardo R. Ungson, "The Effects of Environmental Uncertainty and Dependence on Organizational Structure and Performance: A Comparative Study," *Journal of Management* 13 (1987): 725–37; Frances J. Milliken, "Three Types of Perceived Uncertainty About the Environment: State, Effect, and Response Uncertainty," *Academy of Management Review* 12 (1987): 133–43.

21. Robert B. Duncan, "Characteristics of Organizational Environment and Perceived Environmental Uncertainty," *Administrative Science Quarterly* 17 (1972): 313–27; Gregory G. Dess and Donald W. Beard, "Dimensions of Organizational Task Environments," *Administrative Science Quarterly* 29 (1984): 52–73; Ray Jurkovich, "A Core Typology of Organizational Environments," *Administrative Science Quarterly* 19 (1974): 380–94.

22. Greising, "Cola Wars on the Mean Streets"; and Mike France with Joann Muller, "A Site for Soreheads," *Business Week,* 12 April 1999, 86-90.

23. J. A. Litterer, *The Analysis of Organizations,* 2d ed. (New York: Wiley, 1973), 335.

24. Joseph Pereira, "Toy Industry Finds It Harder and Harder to Pick the Winners," *The Wall Street Journal,* 21 December 1993, A1, A5.

25. Rosalie L. Tung, "Dimensions of Organizational Environments: An Exploratory Study of Their Impact on Organizational Structure," *Academy of Management Journal* 22 (1979): 672–93.

26. Joseph E. McCann and John Selsky, "Hyperturbulence and the Emergence of Type 5 Environments," *Academy of Management Review* 9 (1984): 460–70.

27. Judith Valente and Asra Q. Nomani, "Surge in Oil Price has Airlines Struggling, Some Just to Hang on," *The Wall Street Journal,* 10 August 1990, A1, A4.

28. James D. Thompson, *Organizations in Action* (New York: McGraw-Hill, 1967), 20–21.

29. Sally Solo, "Whirlpool: How to Listen to Consumers," *Fortune,* 11 January 1993, 77–79.

30. David B. Jemison, "The Importance of Boundary Spanning Roles in Strategic Decision-Making," *Journal of Management Studies* 21 (1984): 131–52; Mohamed Ibrahim Ahmad At-Twaijri and John R. Montanari, "The Impact of Context and Choice on the Boundary-Spanning Process: An Empirical Extension," *Human Relations* 40 (1987): 783–98.

31. Michelle Cook, "The Intelligentsia," *Business 2.0* (July 1999): 135-136.

32. Robert C. Schwab, Gerardo R. Ungson, and Warren B. Brown, "Redefining the Boundary-Spanning Environment Relationship," *Journal of Management* 11 (1985): 75–86.

33. Ken Western, "Ethical Spying," *Business Ethics* (September/October 1995): 22–23; Stan Crock, Geoffrey Smith, Joseph Weber, Richard A. Melcher, and Linda Himelstein, "They Snoop to Conquer," *Business Week,* 28 October 1996, 172–176; Kenneth A. Sawka, "Demystifying Business Intelligence," *Management Review* (October 1996): 47–51.

34. Crock, et. al, "They Snoop to Conquer."

35. France with Muller, "A Site for Soreheads."

36. Jay W. Lorsch, "Introduction to the Structural Design of Organizations," in Gene W. Dalton, Paul R. Lawrence, and Jay W. Lorsch, eds., *Organizational Structure and Design* (Homewood, Ill.: Irwin and Dorsey, 1970), 5.

37. Paul R. Lawrence and Jay W. Lorsch, *Organization and Environment* (Homewood, Ill.: Irwin, 1969).

38. Lorsch, "Introduction to the Structural Design of Organizations," 7.

39. Jay W. Lorsch and Paul R. Lawrence, "Environmental Factors and Organizational Integration," in J. W. Lorsch and Paul R. Lawrence, eds., *Organizational Planning: Cases and Concepts* (Homewood, Ill.: Irwin and Dorsey, 1972), 45.

40. Tom Burns and G. M. Stalker, *The Management of Innovation* (London: Tavistock, 1961).

41. John A. Courtright, Gail T. Fairhurst, and L. Edna Rogers, "Interaction Patterns in Organic and Mechanistic Systems," *Academy of Management Journal* 32 (1989): 773–802.

42. Thomas C. Powell, "Organizational Alignment as Competitive Advantage," *Strategic Management Journal* 13 (1992): 119–34. Mansour Javidan, "The Impact of Environmental Uncertainty on Long-Range Planning Practices of the U.S. Savings and Loan Industry," *Strategic Management Journal* 5 (1984): 381–92; Tung, "Dimensions of Organizational Environments," 672–93; Thompson, *Organizations in Action.*

43. David Ulrich and Jay B. Barney, "Perspectives in Organizations: Resource Dependence, Efficiency, and Population," *Academy of Management Review* 9 (1984): 471–81; Jeffrey Pfeffer and Gerald Salancik, *The External Control of Organizations: A Resource Dependent Perspective* (New York: Harper & Row, 1978).

44. Lana J. Chandler, "Something to Sleep On," *Nation's Business,* February 1998, 57-58.

45. Andrew H. Van de Ven and Gordon Walker, "The Dynamics of Interorganizational Coordination," *Administrative Science Quarterly* (1984): 598–621; Huseyin Leblebici and Gerald R. Salancik, "Stability in Interorganizational Exchanges: Rulemaking Processes of the Chicago Board of Trade," *Administrative Science Quarterly* 27 (1982): 227–42.

46. Kevin Kelly and Zachary Schiller with James B. Treece, "Cut Costs or Else: Companies Lay Down the Law to Suppliers," *Business Week,* 22 March 1993, 28–29.

47. G. Pascal Zachary, "Many Journalists See a Growing Reluctance to Criticize Advertisers," *The Wall Street Journal,* 6 February 1992, A1, A9.

48. Richard Brandt, "Microsoft Is Like an Elephant Rolling around, Squashing Ants," *Business Week,* 30 October 1989, 148–52.

49. Judith A. Babcock, *Organizational Responses to Resource Scarcity and Munificence: Adaptation and Modification in Colleges within a University* (Ph.D. diss., Pennsylvania State University, 1981).

50. Peter Smith Ring and Andrew H. Van de Ven, "Developmental Processes of Corporative Interorganizational Relationships," *Academy of Management Review* 19 (1994): 90–118; Jeffrey Pfeffer, "Beyond Management and the Worker: The Institutional Function of Management," *Academy of Management Review* 1 (April 1976): 36–46; John P. Kotter, "Managing External Dependence," *Academy of Management Review* 4 (1979): 87–92.

51. Bryan Borys and David B. Jemison, "Hybrid Arrangements as Strategic Alliances: Theoretical Issues in Organizational Combinations," *Academy of Management Review* 14 (1989): 234–49.

52. William R. Pape, "Little Giant," *Inc. Tech* (1999): No. 1, 27-28.

53. Julie Cohen Mason, "Strategic Alliances: Partnering for Success," *Management Review* (May 1993): 10–15.

54. John F. Love, *McDonald's: Behind the Arches* (New York: Bantam Books, 1986).

55. Zachary Schiller and Wendy Zellner with Ron Stodghill II and Mark Maremont, "Clout! More and More, Retail Giants Rule the Marketplace," *Business Week,* 21 December 1992, 66–73.

56. Borys and Jemison, "Hybrid Arrangements as Strategic Alliances."

57. Edward O. Welles, "Not Your Father's Industry," *Inc.* (January 1999): 25-28.

58. Donald Palmer, "Broken Ties: Interlocking Directorates and Intercorporate Coordination," *Administrative Science Quarterly* 28 (1983): 40–55;

F. David Shoorman, Max H. Bazerman, and Robert S. Atkin, "Interlocking Directorates: A Strategy for Reducing Environmental Uncertainty," *Academy of Management Review* 6 (1981): 243–51; Ronald S. Burt, *Toward a Structural Theory of Action* (New York: Academic Press, 1982).

59. James R. Lang and Daniel E. Lockhart, "Increased Environmental Uncertainty and Changes in Board Linkage Patterns," *Academy of Management Journal* 33 (1990): 106–28; Mark S. Mizruchi and Linda Brewster Stearns, "A Longitudinal Study of the Formation of Interlocking Directorates," *Administrative Science Quarterly* 33 (1988): 194–210.

60. Neuborne with Kerwin, "Generation Y."

61. Kotter, "Managing External Dependence."

62. William C. Symonds, with Farah Nayeri, Geri Smith, and Ted Plafker, "Bombardier's Blitz," *Business Week*, 6 February 1995, 62-66; Joseph Weber, with Wendy Zellner and Geri Smith, "Loud Noises at Bombardier," *Business Week*, 26 January 1998, 94-95; and Anita Lienert, "Plowing Ahead in Uncertain Times," *Management Review*, December 1998, 16–21.

63. Daniel Pearl and Gabriella Stern, "How GM Managed to Wring Pickup Pact and Keep on Truckin'," *The Wall Street Journal*, 5 December 1994, A1.

64. Rick Wartzman and John Harwood, "For the Baby Bells, Government Lobbying Is Hardly Child's Play," *The Wall Street Journal*, 15 March 1994, A1.

65. David B. Yoffie, "How an Industry Builds Political Advantage," *Harvard Business Review* (May-June

1988): 82–89; Jeffrey H. Birnbaum, "Chief Executives Head to Washington to Ply the Lobbyist's Trade," *The Wall Street Journal*, 19 March 1990, A1, A16.

66. David Whitford, "Built By Association," *Inc.* (July 1994): 71–75.

67. Anthony J. Daboub, Abdul M. A. Rasheed, Richard L. Priem, and David A. Gray, "Top Management Team Characteristics and Corporate Illegal Activity," *Academy of Management Review* 20, no. 1 (1995): 138–70.

68. Bryan Burrough, "Oil-Field Investigators Say Fraud Flourishes from Wells to Offices," *The Wall Street Journal*, 15 January 1985, 1, 20; Irwin Ross, "How Lawless Are Big Companies?" *Fortune*, 1 December 1980, 57–64.

69. Stewart Toy, "The Defense Scandal," *Business Week*, 4 July 1988, 28–30.

70. Barry M. Staw and Eugene Szwajkowski, "The Scarcity-Munificence Component of Organizational Environments and the Commission of Illegal Acts," *Administrative Science Quarterly* 20 (1975): 345–54.

71. Kimberly D. Elsbach and Robert I. Sutton, "Acquiring Organizational Legitimacy through Illegitimate Actions: A Marriage of Institutional and Impression Management Theories," *Academy of Management Journal* 35 (1992): 699–738.

CHAPTER 5

Manufacturing and Service Technologies

his chapter explores both service and manufacturing technologies and how technology is related to organizational structure. **Technology** refers to the tools, techniques, machines, and actions used to transform organizational inputs (materials, information, ideas) into outputs (products and services).[1] Technology is an organization's production process and includes work procedures as well as machinery.

Organization technology begins with raw materials of some type (for example, unfinished steel castings in a valve manufacturing plant). Employees take action on the raw material to make a change in it (they machine steel castings), which transforms the raw material into the output of the organization (control valves ready for shipment to oil refineries). For a service organization like Federal Express, the production technology includes the equipment and procedures for delivering overnight mail.

Exhibit 5.1 features an example of production technology for a manufacturing plant. Note how the technology consists of raw material inputs, a transformation process that changes and adds value to these items, and the ultimate product or service output that is sold to consumers in the environment. In today's large, complex organizations, it can be hard to pinpoint technology. Technology can be partly assessed by examining the raw materials flowing into the organization,[2] the variability of work activities,[3] the degree to which the production process is mechanized,[4] the extent to which one task depends upon another in the work flow,[5] or the number of new product or service outputs.[6]

Recall from Chapter 1 that organizations have a technical core that reflects the organization's primary purpose. The technical core contains the transformation process that represents the organization's technology. As today's organizations try to become more flexible in a changing environment, new technology may influence organizational structure, but decisions about organizational structure may also shape or limit technology. Thus, the interaction between core technology and structure leads to a patterned relationship in many organizations.[7]

Organizations are made up of many departments, each of which may use a different technology to produce its outputs and meet departmental goals. Thus, research and development transforms ideas into new product proposals, and marketing transforms inventory into sales, each using a different technology. Moreover, the administrative technology used by managers to run the organization represents yet another technology. New information technology has a tremendous impact on the administrative arena.

PURPOSE OF THIS CHAPTER

In this chapter, we will explore the nature of organizational technologies and the relationship between technology and organization structure. Chapter 4 described how the environment influences organization design. The question addressed in this chapter is, "How should the organization structure be designed to accommodate and facilitate the production process?" Form usually follows function, so the form of the organization's structure should be tailored to fit the needs of the production technology.

The remainder of the chapter will unfold as follows. First, we will examine how the technology for the organization as a whole influences organization structure and design. This discussion will include both manufacturing and service technologies. Next, we will examine differences in departmental technologies and how the technologies influence the design and management of organizational subunits. Third, we will explore how interdependence—flow of materials and information—among departments affects structure.

ORGANIZATION-LEVEL MANUFACTURING TECHNOLOGY

Manufacturing technologies include traditional manufacturing processes and new computer-based manufacturing systems.

EXHIBIT 5.1   *Transformation Process for a Manufacturing Company*

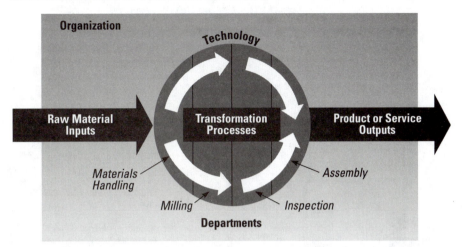

MANUFACTURING FIRMS

Woodward's Study. The first and most influential study of manufacturing technology was conducted by Joan Woodward, a British industrial sociologist. Her research began as a field study of management principles in south Essex. The prevailing management wisdom at the time (1950s) was contained in what was known as universal principles of management. These principles were "one best way" prescriptions that effective organizations were expected to adopt. Woodward surveyed one hundred manufacturing firms firsthand to learn how they were organized.[8] She and her research team visited each firm, interviewed managers, examined company records, and observed the manufacturing operations. Her data included a wide range of structural characteristics (span of control, levels of management) and dimensions of management style (written versus verbal communications, use of rewards) and the type of manufacturing process. Data were also obtained that reflected commercial success of the firms.

Woodward developed a scale and organized the firms according to technical complexity of the manufacturing process. **Technical complexity** represents the extent of mechanization of the manufacturing process. High technical complexity means most of the work is performed by machines. Low technical complexity means workers play a larger role in the production process. Woodward's scale of technical complexity originally had ten categories, as summarized in Exhibit 5.2. These categories were further consolidated into three basic technology groups:

- *Group I: Small-batch and unit production.* These firms tend to be job shop operations that manufacture and assemble small orders to meet specific needs of customers. Custom work is the norm. **Small-batch production** relies heavily on the human operator; it is thus not highly mechanized. Steinway & Sons is an example of small-batch production. Although computerized machines are now used to cut wood more precisely than human hands, much of the work of building a Steinway piano is done by craftsmen in much the same way it was done a century ago. Compared to competitors, who turn out hundreds of thousands of pianos annually, Steinway's artisans build only 2,500 in the United States and 2,000 in Germany each year.[9]
- *Group II: Large-batch and mass production.* **Large-batch production** is a manufacturing process characterized by long production runs of standardized parts. Output often goes into inventory from which orders are filled, because customers do not have special needs. Examples include most assembly lines, such as for automobiles or trailer homes.
- *Group III: Continuous process production.* In **continuous process production** the entire process is mechanized. There is no starting and stopping. This represents mechanization and standardization one step beyond those in an assembly line. Automated

EXHIBIT 5.2   *Woodward's Classification of One Hundred British Firms According to Their Systems of Production*

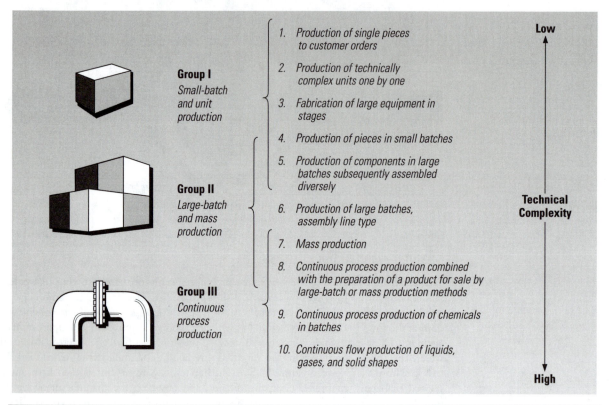

1. Production of single pieces to customer orders
2. Production of technically complex units one by one
3. Fabrication of large equipment in stages

Group I
Small-batch and unit production

4. Production of pieces in small batches
5. Production of components in large batches subsequently assembled diversely
6. Production of large batches, assembly line type

Group II
Large-batch and mass production

7. Mass production
8. Continuous process production combined with the preparation of a product for sale by large-batch or mass production methods
9. Continuous process production of chemicals in batches
10. Continuous flow production of liquids, gases, and solid shapes

Group III
Continuous process production

Low ↑
Technical Complexity
↓ **High**

Source: Adapted from Woodward, *Management and Technology* (London: Her Majesty's Stationery Office, 1958). Used with permission of Her Britannic Majesty's Stationery Office.

machines control the continuous process, and outcomes are highly predictable. Examples would include chemical plants, oil refineries, liquor producers, and nuclear power plants.

Using this classification of technology, Woodward's data made sense. A few of her key findings are given in Exhibit 5.3. The number of management levels and the manager/total personnel ratio, for example, show definite increases as technical complexity increases from unit production to continuous process. This indicates that greater management intensity is needed to manage complex technology. Direct/indirect labor ratio decreases with technical complexity because more indirect workers are required to support and maintain complex machinery. Other characteristics, such as span of control, formalized procedures, and centralization, are high for mass production technology but low for other technologies because the work is standardized. Unit production and continuous process technologies require highly skilled workers to run the machines and verbal communication to adapt to changing conditions. Mass production is standardized and routinized, so few exceptions occur, little verbal communication is needed, and employees are less skilled.

Overall, the management systems in both unit production and continuous process technology are characterized as organic, as defined in Chapter 4. They are more free-flowing and adaptive, with fewer procedures and less standardization. Mass production, however, is mechanistic, with standardized jobs and formalized procedures. Woodward's discovery about technology thus provided substantial new insight into the causes of organization structure. In Joan Woodward's own words, "Different technologies impose different kinds of demands on individuals and organizations, and those demands had to be met through an appropriate structure."[10]

EXHIBIT 5.3   *Relationship Between Technical Complexity and Structural Characteristics*

Structural Characteristic	Technology		
	Unit Production	Mass Production	Continuous Process
Number of management levels	3	4	6
Supervisor span of control	23	48	15
Direct/indirect labor ratio	9:1	4:1	1:1
Manager/total personnel ratio	Low	Medium	High
Workers' skill level	High	Low	High
Formalized procedures	Low	High	Low
Centralization	Low	High	Low
Amount of verbal communication	High	Low	High
Amount of written communication	Low	High	Low
Overall structure	Organic	Mechanistic	Organic

Source: Joan Woodward, *Industrial Organization: Theory and Practice* (London: Oxford University Press, 1965). Used with permission.

Strategy, Technology, and Performance. Another portion of Woodward's study examined the success of the firms along dimensions such as profitability, market share, stock price, and reputation. As indicated in Chapter 2, the measurement of effectiveness is not simple or precise, but Woodward was able to rank firms on a scale of commercial success according to whether they displayed above-average, average, or below-average performance on strategic objectives.

Woodward compared the structure-technology relationship against commercial success and discovered that successful firms tended to be those that had complementary structures and technologies. Many of the organizational characteristics of the successful firms were near the average of their technology category, as shown in Exhibit 5.3. Below-average firms tended to depart from the structural characteristics for their technology type. Another conclusion was that structural characteristics could be interpreted as clustering into organic and mechanistic management systems. Successful small-batch and continuous process organizations had organic structures, and successful mass production organizations had mechanistic structures. Subsequent research has replicated her findings.[11]

What this illustrates for today's companies is that strategy, structure, and technology need to be aligned, especially when competitive conditions change.[12] Some insurance companies in the United States are currently realigning strategy, structure, and technology because of increased competition in the insurance business. Companies such as Geico and USAA are growing rapidly through the use of direct mail and phone solicitation, avoiding the costs associated with doing business through independent insurance agents. Agency-based companies like State Farm and Allstate have had to put new emphasis on a low-cost strategy and are adopting efficiency-oriented information technology to cut costs and more effectively serve customers. Another example is the Madame Alexander doll factory in Harlem, where a new production system led to a restructuring of employees into teams. Now, instead of individually producing parts such as wigs, shoes, and all the other tiny bits that go into a doll, employees work in teams that each produce about three hundred complete doll or wardrobe assemblies a day.[13]

Failing to adopt appropriate new technologies to support strategy, or adopting a new technology and failing to realign strategy to match it, can lead to poor performance. Today's increased global competition means more volatile markets, shorter product life cycles, and more sophisticated and knowledgeable consumers; and flexibility to meet these new demands has become a strategic imperative for many companies.[14] Companies can adopt new technologies to support the strategy of flexibility. However, organization structures and management processes must also be realigned, as a highly mechanistic structure hampers flexibility and prevents the company from reaping the benefits of the new technology.[15]

COMPUTER-INTEGRATED MANUFACTURING

In the years since Woodward's research, new developments have occurred in manufacturing technology. New manufacturing technologies include robots, numerically controlled machine tools, and computerized software for product design, engineering analysis, and remote control of machinery. The ultimate technology is called **computer-integrated manufacturing** (CIM).[16] Also called *advanced manufacturing technology, agile manufacturing, the factory of the future, smart factories,* or *flexible manufacturing systems,* CIM links together manufacturing components that previously stood alone. Thus, robots, machines, product design, and engineering analysis are coordinated by a single computer.

The result has already revolutionized the shop floor, enabling large factories to deliver a wide range of custom-made products at low mass production costs.[17] Computer-integrated manufacturing also enables small companies to go toe-to-toe with large factories and low-cost foreign competitors. Techknits, Inc., a small manufacturer located in New York City, competes successfully against low-cost sweater-makers in the Far East by using $8 million worth of computerized looms and other machinery. The work of designing sweaters, which once took two days, can now be accomplished in two hours. Looms operate round-the-clock and crank out 60,000 sweaters a week, enabling Techknits to fill customer orders faster than foreign competitors.[18]

Computer-integrated manufacturing is typically the result of three subcomponents.

- *Computer-aided design (CAD).* Computers are used to assist in the drafting, design, and engineering of new parts. Designers guide their computers to draw specified configurations on the screen, including dimensions and component details. Hundreds of design alternatives can be explored, as can scaled-up or scaled-down versions of the original.[19]
- *Computer-aided manufacturing (CAM).* Computer-controlled machines in materials handling, fabrication, production, and assembly greatly increase the speed at which items can be manufactured. CAM also permits a production line to shift rapidly from producing one product to any variety of other products by changing the instruction tapes or software in the computer. CAM enables the production line to quickly honor customer requests for changes in product design and product mix.[20]
- *Integrated Information Network.* A computerized system links all aspects of the firm—including accounting, purchasing, marketing, inventory control, design, production, and so forth. This system, based on a common data and information base, enables managers to make decisions and direct the manufacturing process in a truly integrated fashion.

The combination of CAD, CAM, and integrated information systems represents the highest level of computer-integrated manufacturing. A new product can be designed on the computer, and a prototype can be produced untouched by human hands. The ideal factory can switch quickly from one product to another, working fast and with precision, without paperwork or recordkeeping to bog down the system.[21]

A company can adopt CAD in its engineering design department and/or CAM in its production area and make substantial improvements in efficiency and quality. However, when all three components are brought together in a truly advanced plant, the results are breathtaking. Companies such as Xerox, Texas Instruments, Hewlett-Packard, and Boeing are leading the way. Boeing's 777, the largest twin-engine plane ever built, has been called the first "paperless" jetliner. The company designed the plane with eight IBM mainframe computers supporting 2,200 workstations that eventually handled 3,500 billion bits of information. The digital design system reduced the possibility of human error and cut engineering changes and reworking of ill-fitting components by more than 50 percent over previous plane projects.[22]

This ultra-advanced system is not achieved piecemeal. CIM reaches its ultimate level to improve quality, customer service, and cost-cutting when all parts are used interdependently. The integration of CIM and flexible work processes is changing the face of manufacturing. The wave of the manufacturing future is **mass customization**, whereby factories are able to mass-produce products designed to exact customer specification. Today, you can buy a computer assembled to your exact specifications, jeans customized for your body, glasses molded to precisely fit and flatter your face, CDs with music tracks that you select, and pills with the exact blend of vitamins and minerals you want. Acumin, for example, is an Internet-based company that blends vitamins, herbs, and minerals according to each customer's instructions, compressing up to ninety-five ingredients into three to five pills. At Custom Foot stores, customers mix and match design components such as style, color, and material. A high-tech electronic scanner measures the customer's foot, then the complete order is sent by modem to the company's headquarters in Florence, Italy. Shoes are generally ready in about three weeks and often cost less than many premium brands sold off the shelf.[23] Even automobiles are moving toward mass customization, and 60 percent of the cars BMW sells in Europe are built to order.[24] Although so far, most U.S. customers have not been willing to wait the several months it takes for a custom-ordered vehicle, some business leaders envision a time in the near future when cars can be custom made in as little as three days.[25]

Performance. The awesome advantage of CIM is that products of different sizes, types, and customer requirements freely intermingle on the assembly line. Bar codes imprinted on a part enable machines to make instantaneous changes—such as putting a larger screw in a different location—without slowing the production line. A manufacturer can turn out an infinite variety of products in unlimited batch sizes, as illustrated in Exhibit 5.4. In traditional

EXHIBIT 5.4   *Relationship of Computer-Integrated Manufacturing Technology to Traditional Technologies*

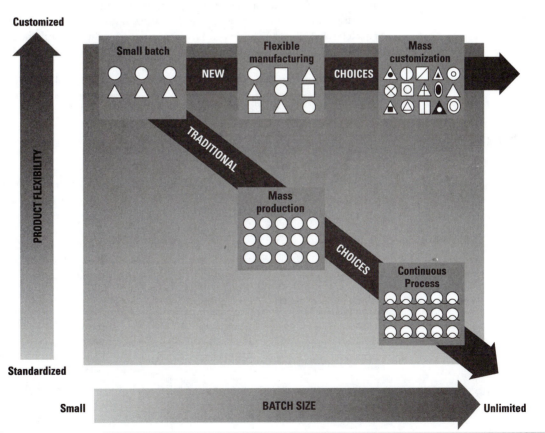

Source: Based on Jack Meredith, "The Strategic Advantages of New Manufacturing Technologies for Small Firms," *Strategic Management Journal* 8 (1987): 249–58; Paul Adler, "Managing Flexible Automation," *California Management Review* (Spring 1988): 34–56; and Otis Port, "Custom-made Direct from the Plant," *Business Week/21st Century Capitalism,* 18 November 1994, 158–59.

manufacturing systems studied by Woodward, choices were limited to the diagonal. Small batch allowed for high product flexibility and custom orders, but because of the "craftsmanship" involved in custom-making products, batch size was necessarily small. Mass production could have large-batch size, but offered limited product flexibility. Continuous process could produce a single standard product in unlimited quantities. Computer-integrated manufacturing allows plants to break free of this diagonal and to increase both batch size and product flexibility at the same time. When taken to its ultimate level, CIM allows for mass customization, with each specific product tailored to customer specification. This high-level use of CIM has been referred to as *computer-aided craftsmanship* because computers tailor each product to meet a customer's exact needs.[26] The Internet plays an important role in the trend toward mass customization because it enables companies to keep in close touch with each individual customer in addition to making it easier and faster to coordinate customer orders with factory tooling and supply requirements.

Studies suggest that with CIM, machine utilization is more efficient, labor productivity increases, scrap rates decrease, and product variety and customer satisfaction increase.[27] Many U.S. manufacturing companies are reinventing the factory using CIM and associated management systems to increase productivity.

Structural Implications. Research into the relationship between CIM and organizational characteristics is beginning to emerge, and the patterns are summarized in Exhibit 5.5. Compared with traditional mass production technologies, CIM has a narrow span of control, few hierarchical levels, adaptive tasks, low specialization, decentralization, and the overall environment is characterized as organic and self-regulative. Employees need the skills to participate in teams, training is broad (so workers are not overly specialized) and frequent (so workers are up to date). Expertise tends to be cognitive so workers can process abstract ideas and solve problems. Interorganizational relationships in CIM firms are characterized by changing demand from customers—which is easily handled with the new technology—and close relationships with a few suppliers that provide top-quality raw materials.[28]

Technology alone cannot give organizations the benefits of flexibility, quality, increased production, and greater customer satisfaction. Research suggests that CIM can become a

EXHIBIT 5.5   *Comparison of Organizational Characteristics Associated with Mass Production and Computer Integrated Manufacturing*

Characteristic	Mass Production	CIM
Structure		
Span of control	Wide	Narrow
Hierarchical levels	Many	Few
Tasks	Routine, repetitive	Adaptive, craftlike
Specialization	High	Low
Decision making	Centralized	Decentralized
Overall	Bureaucratic, mechanistic	Self-regulating, organic
Human Resources		
Interactions	Stand alone	Teamwork
Training	Narrow, one time	Broad, frequent
Expertise	Manual, technical	Cognitive, social Solve problems
Interorganizational		
Customer demand	Stable	Changing
Suppliers	Many, arm's length	Few, close relations

Source: Based on Patricia L. Nemetz and Louis W. Fry, "Flexible Manufacturing Organizations: Implications for Strategy Formulation and Organization Design," *Academy of Management Review* 13 (1988): 627–38; Paul S. Adler, "Managing Flexible Automation," *California Management Review* (Spring 1988): 34–56; and Jeremy Main, "Manufacturing the Right Way," *Fortune*, 21 May 1990, 54–64.

competitive burden rather than a competitive advantage unless organizational structures and management processes are redesigned to take advantage of the new technology.[29] However, when top managers make a commitment to implement new structures and processes that empower workers and support a learning and knowledge-creating environment, CIM can help companies be more competitive.

ORGANIZATION-LEVEL SERVICE TECHNOLOGY

One of the biggest changes occurring in the technology of organizations is the growing service sector. The percentage of the work force employed in manufacturing continues to decline, not only in the United States, but in Canada, France, Germany, the United Kingdom, and Sweden as well. In the United States, services now generate 74 percent of the gross domestic product and account for 79 percent of all jobs.[30] Service technologies are different from manufacturing technologies and, in turn, require a specific organization structure.

SERVICE FIRMS

Definition. Whereas manufacturing organizations achieve their primary purpose through the production of products, service organizations accomplish their primary purpose through the production and provision of services, such as education, health care, transportation, banking, and hospitality. Studies of service organizations have focused on the unique dimensions of service technologies. The characteristics of **service technology** are compared to those of manufacturing technology in Exhibit 5.6.

The most obvious difference is that service technology produces an *intangible output*, rather than a tangible product, such as a refrigerator produced by a manufacturing firm. A service is abstract and often consists of knowledge and ideas rather than a physical product.

EXHIBIT 5.6   *Differences Between Manufacturing and Service Technologies*

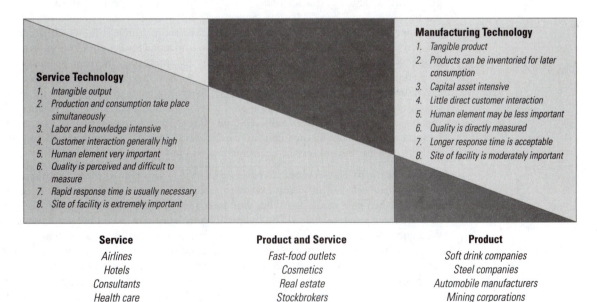

Manufacturing Technology
1. Tangible product
2. Products can be inventoried for later consumption
3. Capital asset intensive
4. Little direct customer interaction
5. Human element may be less important
6. Quality is directly measured
7. Longer response time is acceptable
8. Site of facility is moderately important

Service Technology
1. Intangible output
2. Production and consumption take place simultaneously
3. Labor and knowledge intensive
4. Customer interaction generally high
5. Human element very important
6. Quality is perceived and difficult to measure
7. Rapid response time is usually necessary
8. Site of facility is extremely important

Service	Product and Service	Product
Airlines	Fast-food outlets	Soft drink companies
Hotels	Cosmetics	Steel companies
Consultants	Real estate	Automobile manufacturers
Health care	Stockbrokers	Mining corporations
Law firms	Retail stores	Food processing plants

Sources: Based on F. F. Reichheld and W. E. Sasser, Jr., "Zero Defections: Quality Comes to Services," *Harvard Business Review* 68 (September–October 1990): 105–11; and David E. Bowen, Caren Siehl, and Benjamin Schneider, "A Framework for Analyzing Customer Service Orientations in Manufacturing," *Academy of Management Review* 14 (1989): 75–95.

Thus, whereas manufacturers' products can be inventoried for later sale, services are characterized by *simultaneous production and consumption*. A client meets with a doctor or attorney, for example, and students and teachers come together in the classroom. A service is an intangible product that does not exist until it is requested by the customer. It cannot be stored, inventoried, or viewed as a finished good. If a service is not consumed immediately upon production, it disappears.[31] This typically means that service firms are *labor and knowledge intensive*, with many employees needed to meet the needs of customers, whereas manufacturing firms tend to be capital intensive, relying on mass production, continuous process, and advanced manufacturing technologies.[32]

Direct interaction between customer and employee is generally very high with services, while there is little direct interaction between customers and employees in the technical core of a manufacturing firm. This direct interaction means that the *human element* (employees) becomes extremely important in service firms. Whereas most people never meet the workers who manufactured their cars, they interact directly with the salesperson who sold them their Subaru or Pontiac Grand Am. The treatment received from the salesperson—or by a doctor, lawyer, or hairstylist—affects the perception of the service received and the customer's level of satisfaction. The *quality of a service is perceived* and cannot be directly measured and compared in the same way that the quality of a product can. Another characteristic that affects customer satisfaction and perception of quality service is *rapid response time*. A service must be provided when the customer wants and needs it. When you take a friend to dinner, you want to be seated and served in a timely manner; you would not be very satisfied if the hostess or manager told you to come back tomorrow when there would be more tables or servers available to accommodate you.

The final defining characteristic of service technology is that *site selection is often much more important* than with manufacturing. Because services are intangible, they have to be located where the customer wants to be served. Services are dispersed and located geographically close to customers. For example, fast-food franchises usually disperse their facilities into local stores. Most towns of even moderate size today have two or more McDonald's restaurants rather than one huge one in order to provide service where customers want it.

In reality, it is difficult to find organizations that reflect 100 percent service or 100 percent manufacturing characteristics. Some service firms take on characteristics of manufacturers, and vice versa. Many manufacturing firms are placing a greater emphasis on customer service to differentiate themselves and be more competitive, which is one reason for the increased use of computer-integrated manufacturing. In addition, manufacturing organizations have departments such as purchasing, human resources, and marketing that are based on service technology. On the other hand, organizations such as gas stations, stockbrokers, retail stores, and fast-food restaurants may belong to the service sector, even though the provision of a product is a significant part of the transaction. The vast majority of organizations involve some combination of products and services. The important point is that all organizations can be classified along a continuum that includes both manufacturing and service characteristics, as illustrated in Exhibit 5.6.

New Directions in Services. Service firms have always tended toward providing *customized output*—that is, providing exactly the service each customer wants and needs. For example, when you visit a hairstylist, you don't automatically get the same cut the stylist gave the three previous clients. The stylist cuts your hair the way you request it. However, the trend toward mass customization that is revolutionizing manufacturing has had a significant impact on the service sector as well. Customer expectations of what constitutes good service are rising.[33] Service companies such as the Ritz-Carlton Hotels, USAA, an insurance and financial services company, and Wells Fargo Bank are using new technology to keep customers coming back. All Ritz-Carlton hotels are linked to a database filled with the preferences of half-a-million guests, allowing any desk clerk or bellhop to find out what your favorite wine is, whether you're allergic to feather pillows, and how many extra towels you want in your room. At Wells Fargo, customers can apply over the Internet and get a three-second decision on a loan structured specifically for them.[34]

DESIGNING THE SERVICE ORGANIZATION

The feature of service technologies with a distinct influence on organizational structure and control systems is the need for technical core employees to be close to the customer.[35] The differences between service and product organizations necessitated by customer contact are summarized in Exhibit 5.7.

The impact of customer contact on organization structure is reflected in the use of boundary roles and structural disaggregation.[36] Boundary roles are used extensively in manufacturing firms to handle customers and to reduce disruptions for the technical core. They are used less in service firms because a service is intangible and cannot be passed along by boundary spanners, so service customers must interact directly with technical employees, such as doctors or brokers.

A service firm deals in information and intangible outputs and does not need to be large. Its greatest economies are achieved through disaggregation into small units that can be located close to customers. Stockbrokers, doctors' clinics, consulting firms, and banks disperse their facilities into regional and local offices. Some fast-food chains, such as Taco Bell, are taking this a step further, selling chicken tacos and bean burritos anywhere people gather—airports, supermarkets, college campuses, or street corners. Manufacturing firms, on the other hand, tend to aggregate operations in a single area that has raw materials and an available work force. A large manufacturing firm can take advantage of economies derived from expensive machinery and long production runs.

Service technology also influences internal organization characteristics used to direct and control the organization. For one thing, the skills of technical core employees need to be higher. These employees need enough knowledge and awareness to handle customer problems rather than just enough to perform a single, mechanical task. Some service organizations give their employees the knowledge and freedom to make decisions and do whatever is needed to satisfy customers, whereas others, such as McDonald's, have set rules and procedures for customer service. Yet in all cases, service employees need social and interpersonal skills as well as technical skills.[37] Because of higher skills and structural dispersion, decision making often tends to be decentralized in service firms, and formalization tends to be low. Many Taco Bell outlets operate with no manager on the premises. Self-directed teams manage inventory, schedule work, order supplies, and train new employees.

Understanding the nature of service technology helps managers align strategy, structure, and management processes that may be quite different from those for a product-based or traditional manufacturing technology. In addition, as mentioned earlier, manufacturing organizations are placing greater emphasis on service, and managers can use these concepts and ideas to strengthen their company's service orientation.

Now let's turn to another perspective on technology, that of production activities within specific organizational departments. Departments often have characteristics similar to those of service technology, providing services to other departments within the organization.

EXHIBIT 5.7   *Configuration and Structural Characteristics of Service Organizations Versus Product Organizations*

Structure	Service	Product
1. Separate boundary roles	Few	Many
2. Geographical dispersion	Much	Little
3. Decision making	Decentralized	Centralized
4. Formalization	Lower	Higher
Human Resources		
1. Employee skill level	Higher	Lower
2. Skill emphasis	Interpersonal	Technical

DEPARTMENTAL TECHNOLOGY

This section shifts to the department level of analysis for departments not necessarily within the technical core. Each department in an organization has a production process that consists of a distinct technology. General Motors has departments for engineering, R&D, human resources, advertising, quality control, finance, and dozens of other functions. This section analyzes the nature of departmental technology and its relationship with departmental structure.

The framework that has had the greatest impact on the understanding of departmental technologies was developed by Charles Perrow.[38] Perrow's model has been useful for a broad range of technologies, which made it ideal for research into departmental activities.

VARIETY

Perrow specified two dimensions of departmental activities that were relevant to organization structure and process. The first is the number of exceptions in the work. This refers to task **variety**, which is the frequency of unexpected and novel events that occur in the conversion process. When individuals encounter a large number of unexpected situations, with frequent problems, variety is considered high. When there are few problems, and when day-to-day job requirements are repetitious, technology contains little variety. Variety in departments can range from repeating a single act, such as on an assembly line, to working on a series of unrelated problems or projects.

ANALYZABILITY

The second dimension of technology concerns the **analyzability** of work activities. When the conversion process is analyzable, the work can be reduced to mechanical steps and participants can follow an objective, computational procedure to solve problems. Problem solution may involve the use of standard procedures, such as instructions and manuals, or technical knowledge, such as that in a textbook or handbook. On the other hand, some work is not analyzable. When problems arise, it is difficult to identify the correct solution. There is no store of techniques or procedures to tell a person exactly what to do. The cause of or solution to a problem is not clear, so employees rely on accumulated experience, intuition, and judgment. The final solution to a problem is often the result of wisdom and experience and not the result of standard procedures. Philippos Poulos, a tone regulator at Steinway & Sons, has an unanalyzable technology. Tone regulators carefully check each piano's hammers to be sure they produce the proper Steinway sound.[39] These quality control tasks require years of experience and practice. Standard procedures will not tell a person how to do such tasks.

FRAMEWORK

The two dimensions of technology and examples of departmental activities on Perrow's framework are shown in Exhibit 5.8. The dimensions of variety and analyzability form the basis for four major categories of technology: routine, craft, engineering, and nonroutine.

Routine technologies are characterized by little task variety and the use of objective, computational procedures. The tasks are formalized and standardized. Examples include an automobile assembly line and a bank teller department.

Craft technologies are characterized by a fairly stable stream of activities, but the conversion process is not analyzable or well understood. Tasks require extensive training and experience because employees respond to intangible factors on the basis of wisdom, intuition, and experience. Although advances in machine technologies seem to have reduced the number of craft technologies in organizations, a few craft technologies remain. For example, steel furnace engineers continue to mix steel based on intuition and experience, pattern makers at apparel firms still convert rough designers' sketches into salable garments, and gas and oil explorationists use their internal divining rod to determine where millions will be spent on drilling operations.

EXHIBIT 5.8   *Framework for Department Technologies*

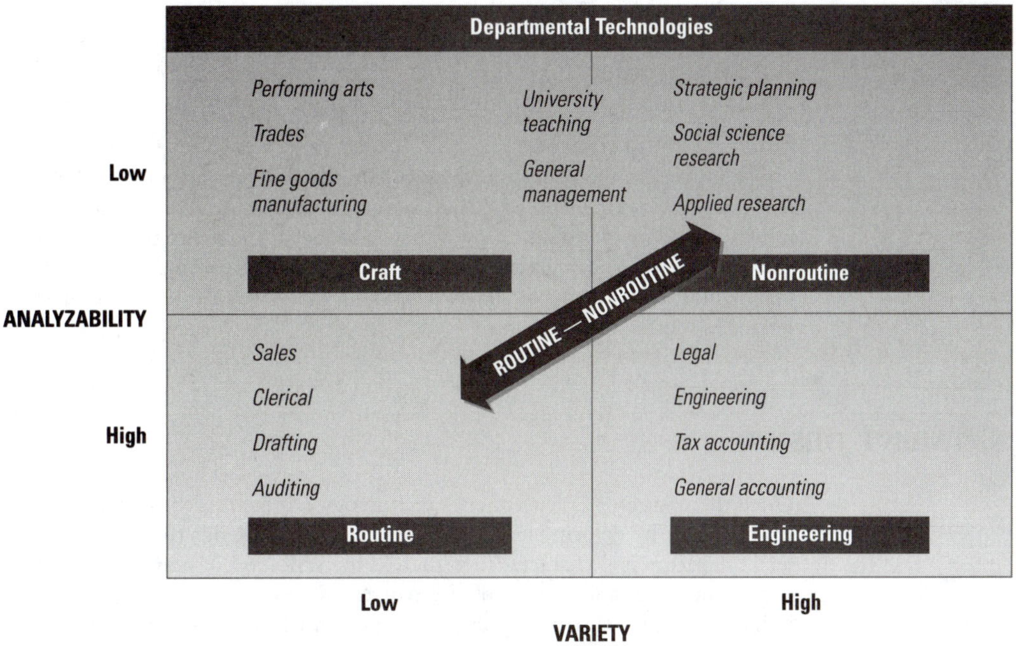

Framework showing Departmental Technologies across dimensions of Analyzability (Low/High) and Variety (Low/High):

- **Craft** (Low variety, Low analyzability): Performing arts, Trades, Fine goods manufacturing
- **Nonroutine** (High variety, Low analyzability): Strategic planning, Social science research, Applied research
- Center top: University teaching, General management
- **Routine** (Low variety, High analyzability): Sales, Clerical, Drafting, Auditing
- **Engineering** (High variety, High analyzability): Legal, Engineering, Tax accounting, General accounting
- Diagonal arrow: ROUTINE — NONROUTINE

Source: Adapted with permission from Richard Daft and Norman Macintosh, "A New Approach to Design and Use of Management Information," *California Management Review* 21 (1978): 82–92. Copyright © 1978 by the Regents of the University of California. Reprinted by permission of the Regents.

Engineering technologies tend to be complex because there is substantial variety in the tasks performed. However, the various activities are usually handled on the basis of established formulas, procedures, and techniques. Employees normally refer to a well-developed body of knowledge to handle problems. Engineering and accounting tasks usually fall in this category.

Nonroutine technologies have high task variety, and the conversion process is not analyzable or well understood. In nonroutine technology, a great deal of effort is devoted to analyzing problems and activities. Several equally acceptable options typically can be found. Experience and technical knowledge are used to solve problems and perform the work. Basic research, strategic planning, and other work that involves new projects and unexpected problems are nonroutine.

Routine Versus Nonroutine. Exhibit 5.8 also illustrates that variety and analyzability can be combined into a single dimension of technology. This dimension is called routine versus nonroutine technology, and it is the diagonal line in Exhibit 5.8. The analyzability and variety dimensions are often correlated in departments, meaning that technologies high in variety tend to be low in analyzability, and technologies low in variety tend to be analyzable. Departments can be evaluated along a single dimension of routine versus nonroutine that combines both analyzability and variety, which is a useful shorthand measure for analyzing departmental technology.

The following questions show how departmental technology can be analyzed for determining its placement on Perrow's technology framework in Exhibit 5.8.[40] Employees normally circle a number from one to seven in response to each question.

Variety
1. To what extent would you say your work is routine?
2. Does most everyone in this unit do about the same job in the same way most of the time?
3. Are unit members performing repetitive activities in doing their jobs?

Analyzability

1. To what extent is there a clearly known way to do the major types of work you normally encounter?
2. To what extent is there an understandable sequence of steps that can be followed in doing your work?
3. To do your work, to what extent can you actually rely on established procedures and practices?

If answers to the above questions indicate high scores for analyzability and low scores for variety, the department would have a routine technology. If the opposite occurs, the technology would be nonroutine. Low variety and low analyzability indicate a craft technology, and high variety and high analyzability indicate an engineering technology. As a practical matter, most departments fit somewhere along the diagonal and can be most easily characterized as routine or nonroutine.

DEPARTMENT DESIGN

Once the nature of a department's technology has been identified, then the appropriate structure can be determined. Department technology tends to be associated with a cluster of departmental characteristics, such as the skill level of employees, formalization, and pattern of communication. Definite patterns do exist in the relationship between work unit technology and structural characteristics, which are associated with departmental performance.[41] Key relationships between technology and other dimensions of departments are described in this section and are summarized in Exhibit 5.9.

The overall structure of departments may be characterized as either organic or mechanistic. Routine technologies are associated with a mechanistic structure and processes, with formal rules and rigid management processes. Nonroutine technologies are associated with an organic structure, and department management is more flexible and free-flowing. The specific design characteristics of formalization, centralization, worker skill level, span of control, and communication and coordination vary, depending on work unit technology.

1. *Formalization.* Routine technology is characterized by standardization and division of labor into small tasks that are governed by formal rules and procedures. For nonroutine tasks, the structure is less formal and less standardized. When variety is high, as in a research department, fewer activities are covered by formal procedures.[42]
2. *Decentralization.* In routine technologies, most decision making about task activities is centralized to management.[43] In engineering technologies, employees with technical training tend to acquire moderate decision authority because technical knowledge is important to task accomplishment. Production employees who have long experience obtain decision authority in craft technologies because they know how to respond to problems. Decentralization to employees is greatest in nonroutine settings, where many decisions are made by employees.
3. *Worker skill level.* Work staff in routine technologies typically require little education or experience, which is congruent with repetitive work activities. In work units with greater variety, staff are more skilled and often have formal training in technical schools or universities. Training for craft activities, which are less analyzable, is more likely to be through job experience. Nonroutine activities require both formal education and job experience.[44]
4. *Span of control.* Span of control is the number of employees who report to a single manager or supervisor. This characteristic is normally influenced by departmental technology. The more complex and nonroutine the task, the more problems arise in which the supervisor becomes involved. Although the span of control may be influenced by other factors, such as skill level of employees, it typically should be smaller for complex tasks because on such tasks the supervisor and subordinate must interact frequently.[45]

EXHIBIT 5.9   *Relationship of Department Technology to Structural and Management Characteristics*

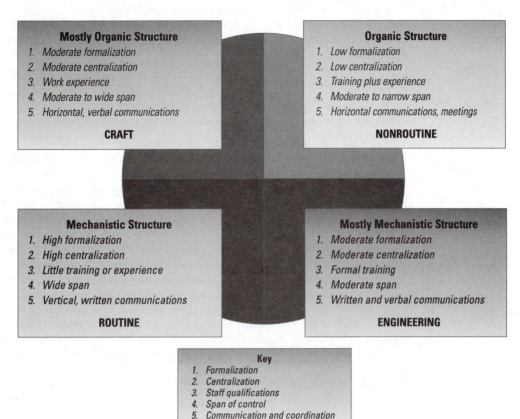

Mostly Organic Structure
1. *Moderate formalization*
2. *Moderate centralization*
3. *Work experience*
4. *Moderate to wide span*
5. *Horizontal, verbal communications*

CRAFT

Organic Structure
1. *Low formalization*
2. *Low centralization*
3. *Training plus experience*
4. *Moderate to narrow span*
5. *Horizontal communications, meetings*

NONROUTINE

Mechanistic Structure
1. *High formalization*
2. *High centralization*
3. *Little training or experience*
4. *Wide span*
5. *Vertical, written communications*

ROUTINE

Mostly Mechanistic Structure
1. *Moderate formalization*
2. *Moderate centralization*
3. *Formal training*
4. *Moderate span*
5. *Written and verbal communications*

ENGINEERING

Key
1. *Formalization*
2. *Centralization*
3. *Staff qualifications*
4. *Span of control*
5. *Communication and coordination*

5. *Communication and coordination.* Communication activity and frequency increase as task variety increases.[46] Frequent problems require more information sharing to solve problems and ensure proper completion of activities. The direction of communication is typically horizontal in nonroutine work units and vertical in routine work units.[47] The form of communication varies by task analyzability.[48] When tasks are highly analyzable, statistical and written forms of communication (memos, reports, rules, and procedures) are frequent. When tasks are less analyzable, information typically is conveyed face-to-face, over the telephone, or in group meetings.

Two important points are reflected in Exhibit 5.9. First, departments do differ from one another and can be categorized according to their workflow technology.[49] Second, structural and management processes differ based on departmental technology. Managers should design their departments so that requirements based on technology can be met. Design problems are most visible when the design is clearly inconsistent with technology. Studies have found that when structure and communication characteristics did not reflect technology, departments tended to be less effective.[50] Employees could not communicate with the frequency needed to solve problems.

WORKFLOW INTERDEPENDENCE AMONG DEPARTMENT

So far, this chapter has explored how organization and department technologies influence structural design. The final characteristic of technology that influences structure is called interdependence. **Interdependence** means the extent to which departments depend on each other for resources or materials to accomplish their tasks. Low interdependence means that departments can do their work independently of each other and have little need for interaction, consultation, or exchange of materials. High interdependence means departments must constantly exchange resources.

TYPES

James Thompson defined three types of interdependence that influence organization structure.[51] These interdependencies are illustrated in Exhibit 5.10 and are discussed in the following sections.

Pooled. Pooled interdependence is the lowest form of interdependence among departments. In this form, work does not flow between units. Each department is part of the organization and contributes to the common good of the organization, but works independently. McDonald's restaurants or branch banks are examples of pooled interdependence. An outlet in Chicago need not interact with an outlet in Urbana. Pooled interdependence may be associated with the relationships within a *divisional structure*, defined in Chapter 3. Divisions or branches share financial resources from a common pool, and the success of each division contributes to the success of the overall organization.

Thompson proposed that pooled interdependence would exist in firms with what he called a mediating technology. A **mediating technology** provides products or services that mediate or link clients from the external environment and, in so doing, allows each department to work independently. Banks, brokerage firms, and real estate offices all mediate between buyers and sellers, but the offices work independently within the organization.

The management implications associated with pooled interdependence are quite simple. Thompson argued that managers should use rules and procedures to standardize activities across departments. Each department should use the same procedures and financial

EXHIBIT 5.10   *Thompson's Classification of Interdependence and Management Implications*

Form of Interdependence	Demands on Horizontal Communication, Decision Making	Type of Coordination Required	Priority for Locating Units Close Together
Pooled (bank)	Low communication	Standardization, rules, procedures	Low
Sequential (assembly line)	Medium communication	Plans, schedules, feedback	Medium
Reciprocal (hospital)	High communication	Mutual adjustment, cross-departmental meetings, teamwork	High

statements so the outcomes of all departments can be measured and pooled. Very little day-to-day coordination is required among units.

Sequential. When interdependence is of serial form, with parts produced in one department becoming inputs to another department, then it is called **sequential interdependence**. The first department must perform correctly for the second department to perform correctly. This is a higher level of interdependence than pooled, because departments exchange resources and depend upon others to perform well. Sequential interdependence creates a greater need for horizontal mechanisms such as integrators or task forces.

Sequential interdependence occurs in what Thompson called **long-linked technology**, which "refers to the combination in one organization of successive stages of production; each stage of production uses as its inputs the production of the preceding stage and produces inputs for the following stage."[52] Large organizations that use assembly line production, such as in the automobile industry, use long-linked technologies and are characterized by sequential interdependence between plants or departments. For example, a United Auto Workers' strike at two General Motors parts plants in the summer of 1998 eventually halted production at all but one of GM's assembly plants in North America. Assembly plants were unable to continue work because they could not get the parts they needed.

The management requirements for sequential interdependence are more demanding than for pooled interdependence. Coordination among the linked plants or departments is required. Since the interdependence implies a one-way flow of materials, extensive planning and scheduling are generally needed. Plant B needs to know what to expect from Plant A so both can perform effectively. Some day-to-day communication among plants is also needed to handle unexpected problems and exceptions that arise.

Reciprocal. The highest level of interdependence is **reciprocal interdependence**. This exists when the output of operation A is the input to operation B, and the output of operation B is the input back again to operation A. The outputs of departments influence those departments in reciprocal fashion.

Reciprocal interdependence tends to occur in organizations with what Thompson called **intensive technologies**, which provide a variety of products or services in combination to a client. Hospitals are an excellent example because they provide coordinated services to patients. A patient may move back and forth between X ray, surgery, and physical therapy as needed to be cured. A firm developing new products is another example. Intense coordination is needed between design, engineering, manufacturing, and marketing to combine all their resources to suit the customer's product need.

Management requirements are greatest in the case of reciprocal interdependence. Reciprocal interdependence requires that departments work together intimately and be closely coordinated. The structure must allow for frequent horizontal communication and adjustment, perhaps through the use of permanent teams. Extensive planning is required in hospitals, for example, but plans will not anticipate or solve all problems. Daily interaction and mutual adjustment among departments are required. Managers from several departments are jointly involved in face-to-face coordination, teamwork, and decision making. Reciprocal interdependence is the most complex interdependence for organizations to handle.

STRUCTURAL PRIORITY

As indicated in Exhibit 5.10, since decision making, communication, and coordination problems are greatest for reciprocal interdependence, reciprocal interdependence should receive first priority in organization structure. New product development is one area of reciprocal interdependence that is of growing concern to managers as companies face increasing pressure to get new products to market fast. Many firms are revamping the design-manufacturing relationship by closely integrating computer-aided design (CAD) and computer-aided manufacturing (CAM) technologies discussed earlier in this chapter.[53] Activities that are reciprocally interdependent should be grouped close together in the organization so managers have easy access to one another for mutual adjustment. These units should report to the same person on the organization chart and should be physically close so the time and effort for coordination can be minimized. Poor coordination will result in poor performance for the organization. If reciprocally interdependent units are not located close together, the organization should design mechanisms for coordination, such as daily meetings between departments or an intranet to facilitate communication. The next priority is given to sequential interdependencies, and finally to pooled interdependencies.

This strategy of organizing keeps the communication channels short where coordination is most critical to organizational success. For example, Boise Cascade Corporation experienced poor service to customers because customer service reps located in New York City were not coordinating with production planners in Oregon plants. Customers couldn't get delivery as needed. Boise was reorganized, and the two groups were consolidated under one roof, reporting to the same supervisor at division headquarters. Now customer needs are met because customer service reps work with production planning to schedule customer orders.

STRUCTURAL IMPLICATIONS

Most organizations experience various levels of interdependence, and structure can be designed to fit these needs, as illustrated in Exhibit 5.11.[54] In a manufacturing firm, new product development entails reciprocal interdependence among the design, engineering, purchasing, manufacturing, and sales departments. Perhaps cross-functional teams could be used to handle the back-and-forth flow of information and resources. Once a product is designed, its actual manufacture would be sequential interdependence, with a flow of goods from one department to another, such as among purchasing, inventory, production control, manufacturing, and assembly. The actual ordering and delivery of products is

EXHIBIT 5.11   *Primary Means to Achieve Coordination for Different Levels of Task Interdependence in a Manufacturing Firm*

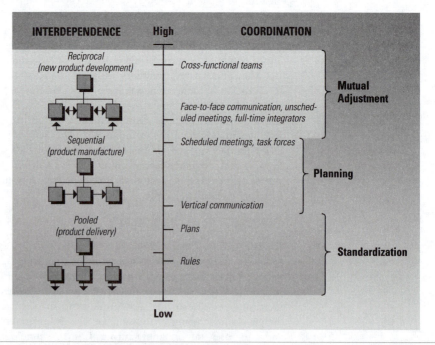

Source: Adapted from Andrew H. Van de Ven, Andre Delbecq, and Richard Koenig, "Determinants of Communication Modes Within Organizations," *American Sociological Review* 41 (1976): 330.

pooled interdependence, with warehouses working independently. Customers could place an order with the nearest facility, which would not require coordination among warehouses, except in unusual cases such as a stock outage.

When consultants analyzed NCR to learn why the development of new products was so slow, they followed the path from initial idea to implementation. The problem was that the development, production, and marketing of products took place in separate divisions, and communication across the three interdependent groups was difficult. NCR broke up its traditional organization structure and created several stand-alone units of about five hundred people, each with its own development, production, and marketing people. The new structure enabled new products to be introduced in record time.

IMPACT OF TECHNOLOGY ON JOB DESIGN

So far, this chapter has described models for analyzing how manufacturing, service, and department technologies influence structure and management processes. The relation between a new technology and organization seems to follow a pattern, beginning with immediate effects on the content of jobs followed (after a longer period) by impact on design of the organization. The ultimate impact of technology on employees can be partially understood through the concepts of job design and sociotechnical systems.

JOB DESIGN

Job design includes the assignment of goals and tasks to be accomplished by employees. Managers may consciously change job design to improve productivity or worker motivation. For example, when workers are involved in performing boring, repetitive tasks, managers may introduce **job rotation**, which means moving employees from job to job to give them a greater variety of tasks. However, managers may also unconsciously influence job design through the introduction of new technologies, which can change how jobs are done and the very nature of jobs.[55] Managers should understand how the introduction of a new technology may affect employees' jobs. The common theme of new technologies in the workplace is that they in some way substitute machinery for human labor in transforming inputs into outputs. Automated teller machines (ATMs) have replaced thousands of human bank tellers, for example.

In addition to actually replacing human workers, technology may have several different effects on the human jobs that remain. Research has indicated that mass production technologies tend to produce **job simplification**, which means that the variety and difficulty of tasks performed by a single person is reduced. The consequence is boring, repetitive jobs that generally provide little satisfaction. More advanced technology, on the other hand, tends to cause **job enrichment**, meaning that the job provides greater responsibility, recognition, and opportunities for growth and development. These technologies create a greater need for employee training and education because workers need higher-level skills and greater competence to master their tasks. For example, ATMs took most the routine tasks (deposits and withdrawals) away from bank tellers and left them with the more complex tasks that require higher-level skills. Studies of computer-integrated manufacturing found that it produces three noticeable results for employees: more opportunities for intellectual mastery and enhanced cognitive skills for workers; more worker responsibility for results; and greater interdependence among workers, enabling more social interaction and the development of teamwork and coordination skills.[56] Advanced manufacturing technology may also contribute to **job enlargement**, which is an expansion of the number of different tasks performed by an employee. Because fewer workers are needed with the new technology, each employee has to be able to perform a greater number and variety of tasks.

With advanced technology, workers have to keep learning new skills because technology is changing so rapidly. Advances in *information technology* are having a significant effect on jobs in the service industry, including doctors' offices and medical clinics, law firms, financial planners, and libraries. Workers may find that their jobs change almost daily because of new software programs, increased use of the Internet, and other advances in information technology.

Advanced technology does not always have a positive effect on employees, but research findings in general are encouraging, suggesting that jobs for workers are enriched rather than simplified, engaging their higher mental capacities, offering opportunities for learning and growth, and providing greater job satisfaction.

SOCIOTECHNICAL SYSTEMS

The **sociotechnical systems approach** recognizes the interaction of technical and human needs in effective job design, combining the needs of people with the organization's need for technical efficiency. The *socio* portion of the approach refers to the people and groups who work in organizations and how work is organized and coordinated. The *technical* portion refers to the materials, tools, machines, and processes used to transform organizational inputs into outputs.

The goal of the sociotechnical systems approach is to design the organization for **joint optimization**, which means that an organization functions best only when the social and technical systems are designed to fit the needs of one another. Designing the organization to meet human needs while ignoring the technical systems, or changing technology to improve efficiency while ignoring human needs, may inadvertently cause performance problems. The sociotechnical systems approach attempts to find a balance between what workers want and need and the technical requirements of the organization's production system.[57]

Sociotechnical principles evolved from the work of the Tavistock Institute, a research organization in England, during the 1950s and 1960s.[58] Examples of organizational change using sociotechnical systems principles have occurred in numerous organizations, including General Motors, Volvo, the Tennessee Valley Authority (TVA), and Procter & Gamble.[59] Although there have been failures, in many of these applications, the joint optimization of changes in technology and structure to meet the needs of people as well as efficiency improved performance, safety, quality, absenteeism, and turnover. In some cases, work design was not the most efficient based on technical and scientific principles, but worker involvement and commitment more than made up for the difference. Thus, once again research shows that new technologies need not have a negative impact on workers, because the technology often requires higher-level mental and social skills and can be organized to encourage the involvement and commitment of employees, thereby benefiting both the employee and the organization.

The sociotechnical systems principle that people should be viewed as resources and provided with appropriate skills, meaningful work, and suitable rewards becomes even more important in today's world of growing technological complexity.[60] One study found that organizations that put too much faith in machines and technology and pay little attention to the appropriate management of people do not achieve advances in productivity and flexibility. Today's most successful companies strive to find the right mix of machines, computer systems, and people and the most effective way to coordinate them.[61]

DISCUSSION QUESTIONS

1. Where would your university or college department be located on Perrow's technology framework? Look for the underlying variety and analyzability characteristics when making your assessment. Would a department devoted exclusively to teaching be put in a different quadrant from a department devoted exclusively to research?
2. Explain Thompson's levels of interdependence. Identify an example of each level of interdependence in the university or college setting. What kinds of coordination mechanisms should an administration develop to handle each level of interdependence?
3. Describe Woodward's classification of organizational technologies. Explain why each of the three technology groups is related differently to organization structure and management processes.

4. What relationships did Woodward discover between supervisor span of control and technological complexity?
5. How does computer-integrated manufacturing differ from other manufacturing technologies? What is the primary advantage of CIM?
6. Mass customization of products has become a common approach in manufacturing organizations. Discuss ways in which mass customization can be applied to service firms as well.
7. In what primary ways does the design of service firms typically differ from that of product firms? Why?
8. A top executive claimed that top-level management is a craft technology because the work contains intangibles, such as handling personnel, interpreting the environment, and coping with unusual situations that have to be learned through experience. If this is true, is it appropriate to teach management in a business school? Does teaching management from a textbook assume that the manager's job is analyzable, and hence that formal training rather than experience is most important?
9. In which quadrant of Perrow's framework would a mass production technology be placed? Where would small batch and continuous process technologies be placed? Why? Would Perrow's framework lead to the same recommendation about organic versus mechanistic structures that Woodward made?

NOTES

1. Charles Perrow, "A Framework for the Comparative Analysis of Organizations," *American Sociological Review* 32 (1967): 194–208; R. J. Schonberger, *World Class Manufacturing: The Next Decade*, (New York: The Free Press, 1996).
2. Linda Argote, "Input Uncertainty and Organizational Coordination in Hospital Emergency Units," *Administrative Science Quarterly* 27 (1982): 420–34; Charles Perrow, *Organizational Analysis: A Sociological Approach* (Belmont, Calif.: Wadsworth, 1970); William Rushing, "Hardness of Material as Related to the Division of Labor in Manufacturing Industries," *Administrative Science Quarterly* 13 (1968): 229–45.
3. Lawrence B. Mohr, "Organizational Technology and Organization Structure," *Administrative Science Quarterly* 16 (1971): 444–59; David Hickson, Derek Pugh, and Diana Pheysey, "Operations Technology and Organization Structure: An Empirical Reappraisal," *Administrative Science Quarterly* 14 (1969): 378–97.
4. Joan Woodward, *Industrial Organization: Theory and Practice* (London: Oxford University Press, 1965); Joan Woodward, *Management and Technology* (London: Her Majesty's Stationery Office, 1958).
5. Hickson, Pugh, and Pheysey, "Operations Technology and Organization Structure"; James D. Thompson, *Organizations in Action* (New York: McGraw-Hill, 1967).
6. Edward Harvey, "Technology and the Structure of Organizations," *American Sociological Review* 33 (1968): 241–59.
7. Wanda J. Orlikowski, "The Duality of Technology: Rethinking the Concept of Technology in Organizations," *Organization Science* 3 (1992): 398–427.
8. Based on Woodward, *Industrial Organization and Management and Technology.*
9. Jim Morrison, "Grand Tour. Making Music: The Craft of the Steinway Piano," *Spirit*, February 1997, 42–49, 100.
10. Woodward, *Industrial Organization*, vi.
11. William L. Zwerman, *New Perspectives on Organizational Theory* (Westport, Conn.: Greenwood, 1970); Harvey, "Technology and the Structure of Organizations," 241–59.
12. Dean M. Schroeder, Steven W. Congden, and C. Gopinath, "Linking Competitive Strategy and Manufacturing Process Technology," *Journal of Management Studies* 32, no. 2 (March 1995): 163–89.
13. Alex Taylor III, "It Worked for Toyota. Can It Work for Toys?" *Fortune*, 11 January 1999, 36.
14. Fernando F. Suarez, Michael A. Cusumano, and Charles H. Fine, "An Empirical Study of Flexibility in Manufacturing," *Sloan Management Review* (Fall 1995): 25–32.
15. Raymond F. Zammuto and Edward J. O'Connor, "Gaining Advanced Manufacturing Technologies' Benefits: The Roles of Organization Design and Culture," *Academy of Management Review* 17, no. 4 (1992): 701–28; Dean Schroeder, Steven W. Congden, and C. Gopinath, "Linking Competitive Strategy and Manufacturing Process Technology."
16. Jack R. Meredith, "The Strategic Advantages of the Factory of the Future," *California Management Review* 29 (Spring 1987): 27–41; Jack Meredith, "The Strategic Advantages of the New Manufacturing Technologies for Small Firms," *Strategic Management*

Journal 8 (1987): 249–58; Althea Jones and Terry Webb, "Introducing Computer Integrated Manufacturing," *Journal of General Management* 12 (Summer 1987): 60–74.

17. Raymond F. Zammuto and Edward J. O'Connor, "Gaining Advanced Manufacturing Technologies' Benefits: The Roles of Organization Design and Culture," *Academy of Management Review* 17 (1992): 701–28.

18. John S. DeMott, "Small Factories' Big Lessons," *Nation's Business* (April 1995): 29–30.

19. Paul S. Adler, "Managing Flexible Automation," *California Management Review* (Spring 1988): 34–56.

20. Bela Gold, "Computerization in Domestic and International Manufacturing," *California Management Review* (Winter 1989): 129–43.

21. Graham Dudley and John Hassard, "Design Issues in the Development of Computer Integrated Manufacturing (CIM)," *Journal of General Management* 16 (1990): 43–53.

22. John Holusha, "Can Boeing's New Baby Fly Financially?" *New York Times,* 27 March 1994, Section 3, 1, 6.

23. Joel D. Goldhar and David Lei, "Variety is Free: Manufacturing In the Twenty-First Century," *Academy of Management Executive* 9, no. 4 (1995): 73–86; and Justin Martin, "Give 'Em *Exactly* What They Want," *Fortune,* 10 October 1997, 283-285.

24. Erick Schonfeld, "The Customized, Digitized, Have-It-Your-Way Economy," *Fortune,* 28 September 1998, 115-124.

25. Len Estrin, "The Dawn of Manufacturing," *Enterprise* (April 1994): 31–35; Otis Port, "The Responsive Factory," *Business Week/Enterprise* (1993): 48–52.

26. Goldhar and Lei, "Variety is Free: Manufacturing In the Twenty-First Century."

27. Meredith, "Strategic Advantages of the Factory of the Future."

28. Patricia L. Nemetz and Louis W. Fry, "Flexible Manufacturing Organizations: Implementations for Strategy Formulation and Organization Design," *Academy of Management Review* 13 (1988): 627–38; Paul S. Adler, "Managing Flexible Automation," *California Management Review* (Spring 1988): 34–56; Jeremy Main, "Manufacturing the Right Way," *Fortune,* 21 May 1990, 54–64; Frank M. Hull and Paul D. Collins, "High-Technology Batch Production Systems: Woodward's Missing Type," *Academy of Management Journal* 30 (1987): 786–97.

29. Goldhar and Lei, "Variety Is Free: Manufacturing In The Twenty-First Century"; P. Robert Duimering, Frank Safayeni, and Lyn Purdy, "Integrated Manufacturing: Redesign the Organization before Implementing Flexible Technology," *Sloan Management*

Review (Summer 1993): 47–56; Zammuto and O'Connor, "Gaining Advanced Manufacturing Technologies' Benefits."

30. "Manufacturing's Decline," *Johnson City Press*, 17 July 1999, 9; Ronald Henkoff, "Service Is Everybody's Business," *Fortune,* 27 June 1994, 48–60; Ronald Henkoff, "Finding, Training, and Keeping the Best Service Workers," *Fortune,* 3 October 1994, 110–22.

31. Byron J. Finch and Richard L. Luebbe, *Operations Management: Competing in a Changing Environment* (Fort Worth, Tex.: The Dryden Press, 1995), 51.

32. David E. Bowen, Caren Siehl, and Benjamin Schneider, "A Framework for Analyzing Customer Service Orientations in Manufacturing," *Academy of Management Review* 14 (1989): 79–95; Peter K. Mills and Newton Margulies, "Toward a Core Typology of Service Organizations," *Academy of Management Review* 5 (1980): 255–65; Peter K. Mills and Dennis J. Moberg, "Perspectives on the Technology of Service Operations," *Academy of Management Review* 7 (1982): 467–78; G. Lynn Shostack, "Breaking Free from Product Marketing," *Journal of Marketing* (April 1977): 73–80.

33. Ron Zemke, "The Service Revolution: Who Won?" *Management Review (*March 1997): 10-15; and Wayne Wilhelm and Bill Rossello, "The Care and Feeding of Customers," *Management Review* (March 1997): 19-23.

34. Schonfeld, "The Customized, Digitized, Have-It-Your-Way Economy."

35. Richard B. Chase and David A. Tansik, "The Customer Contact Model for Organization Design," *Management Science* 29 (1983): 1037–50.

36. Ibid.

37. David E. Bowen and Edward E. Lawler III, "The Empowerment of Service Workers: What, Why, How, and When," *Sloan Management Review* (Spring 1992): 31–39: Gregory B. Northcraft and Richard B. Chase, "Managing Service Demand at the Point of Delivery," *Academy of Management Review* 10 (1985): 66–75; Roger W. Schmenner, "How Can Service Businesses Survive and Prosper?" *Sloan Management Review* 27 (Spring 1986): 21–32.

38. Perrow, "Framework for Comparative Analysis" and *Organizational Analysis.*

39. Morrison, "Grand Tour."

40. Michael Withey, Richard L. Daft, and William C. Cooper, "Measures of Perrow's Work Unit Technology: An Empirical Assessment and a New Scale," *Academy of Management Journal* 25 (1983): 45–63.

41. Christopher Gresov, "Exploring Fit and Misfit with Multiple Contingencies," *Administrative Science*

Quarterly 34 (1989): 431–53; Dale L. Goodhue and Ronald L. Thompson, "Task-Technology Fit and Individual Performance," *MIS Quarterly* (June 1995): 213–36.

42. Gresov, "Exploring Fit and Misfit with Multiple Contingencies"; Charles A. Glisson, "Dependence of Technological Routinization on Structural Variables in Human Service Organizations," *Administrative Science Quarterly* 23 (1978): 383–95; Jerald Hage and Michael Aiken, "Routine Technology, Social Structure and Organizational Goals," *Administrative Science Quarterly* 14 (1969): 368–79.

43. Gresov, "Exploring Fit and Misfit with Multiple Contingencies"; A.J. Grimes and S.M. Kline, "The Technological Imperative: The Relative Impact of Task Unit, Modal Technology, and Hierarchy on Structure," *Academy of Management Journal* 16 (1973): 583–97; Lawrence G. Hrebiniak, "Job Technologies, Supervision and Work Group Structure," *Administrative Science Quarterly* 19 (1974): 395–410; Jeffrey Pfeffer, *Organizational Design* (Arlington Heights, Ill.: AHM, 1978), ch. 1.

44. Patrick E. Connor, *Organizations: Theory and Design* (Chicago: Science Research Associates, 1980); Richard L. Daft and Norman B. Macintosh, "A Tentative Exploration into Amount and Equivocality of Information Processing in Organizational Work Units," *Administrative Science Quarterly* 26 (1981): 207–24.

45. Paul D. Collins and Frank Hull, "Technology and Span of Control: Woodward Revisited," *Journal of Management Studies* 23 (1986): 143–64; Gerald D. Bell, "The Influence of Technological Components of Work upon Management Control," *Academy of Management Journal* 8 (1965): 127–32; Peter M. Blau and Richard A. Schoenherr, *The Structure of Organizations* (New York: Basic Books, 1971).

46. W. Alan Randolph, "Matching Technology and the Design of Organization Units," *California Management Review* 22–23 (1980–81): 39–48; Daft and Macintosh, "Tentative Exploration into Amount and Equivocality of Information Processing"; Michael L. Tushman, "Work Characteristics and Subunit Communication Structure: A Contingency Analysis," *Administrative Science Quarterly* 24 (1979): 82–98.

47. Andrew H. Van de Ven and Diane L. Ferry, *Measuring and Assessing Organizations* (New York: Wiley, 1980); Randolph, "Matching Technology and the Design of Organization Units."

48. Richard L. Daft and Robert H. Lengel, "Information Richness: A New Approach to Managerial Behavior and Organization Design," in Barry Staw and Larry L. Cummings, eds., *Research in Organizational Behavior,* vol. 6 (Greenwich, Conn.: JAI Press, 1984), 191–233; Richard L. Daft and Norman B. Macintosh,

"A New Approach into Design and Use of Management Information," *California Management Review* 21 (1978): 82–92; Daft and Macintosh, "Tentative Exploration in Amount and Equivocality of Information Processing"; W. Alan Randolph, "Organizational Technology and the Media and Purpose Dimensions of Organizational Communication," *Journal of Business Research* 6 (1978): 237–59; Linda Argote, "Input Uncertainty and Organizational Coordination in Hospital Emergency Units," *Administrative Science Quarterly* 27 (1982): 420–34; Andrew H. Van de Ven and Andre Delbecq, "A Task Contingent Model of Work Unit Structure," *Administrative Science Quarterly* 19 (1974): 183–97.

49. Peggy Leatt and Rodney Schneck, "Criteria for Grouping Nursing Subunits in Hospitals," *Academy of Management Journal* 27 (1984): 150–65; Robert T. Keller, "Technology-Information Processing," *Academy of Management Journal* 37, no. 1 (1994): 167–79.

50. Gresov, "Exploring Fit and Misfit with Multiple Contingencies"; Michael L. Tushman, "Technological Communication in R&D Laboratories: The Impact of Project Work Characteristics," *Academy of Management Journal* 21 (1978): 624–45; Robert T. Keller, "Technology-Information Processing Fit and the Performance of R&D Project Groups: A Test of Contingency Theory," *Academy of Management Journal* 37, no. 1 (1994): 167–79.

51. James Thompson, *Organizations in Action* (New York: McGraw-Hill, 1967).

52. *Ibid.*, 40.

53. Paul S. Adler, "Interdepartmental Interdependence and Coordination: The Case of the Design/ Manufacturing Interface," *Organization Science* 6, no. 2 (March–April 1995): 147–67.

54. Christopher Gresov, "Effects of Dependence and Tasks on Unit Design and Efficiency," *Organization Studies* 11 (1990): 503–29; Andrew H. Van de Ven, Andre Delbecq, and Richard Koenig, "Determinants of Coordination Modes within Organizations," *American Sociological Review* 41 (1976): 322–38; Linda Argote, "Input Uncertainty and Organizational Coordination in Hospital Emergency Units"; Jack K. Ito and Richard B. Peterson, "Effects of Task Difficulty and Interdependence on Information Processing Systems," *Academy of Management Journal* 29 (1986): 139–49; Joseph L. C. Cheng, "Interdependence and Coordination in Organizations: A Role-System Analysis," *Academy of Management Journal* 26 (1983): 156–62.

55. Michele Liu, Héléné Denis, Harvey Kolodny, and Benjt Stymne, "Organization Design for Technological Change," *Human Relations* 43 (January 1990): 7–22.

56. Gerald I. Susman and Richard B. Chase, "A Sociotechnical Analysis of the Integrated Factory,"

Journal of Applied Behavioral Science 22 (1986): 257–70; Paul Adler, "New Technologies, New Skills," *California Management Review* 29 (Fall 1986): 9–28.

57. F. Emery, "Characteristics of Sociotechnical Systems," Tavistock Institute of Human Relations, document 527, 1959; Passmore, Francis, and Haldeman, "Sociotechnical Systems"; and William M. Fox, "Sociotechnical System Principles and Guidelines: Past and Present," *Journal of Applied Behavioral Science* 31, no. 1 (March 1995): 91–105.

58. Eric Trist and Hugh Murray, eds., *The Social Engagement of Social Science: A Tavistock Anthology,* Vol. 11, (Philadelphia: University of Pennsylvania Press, 1993); and William A. Pasmore, "Social Science Transformed: The Socio-Technical Perspective," *Human Relations* 48, No. 1 (1995) 1-21.

59. R. E. Walton, "From Control to Commitment in the Workplace," *Harvard Business Review* 63, No. 2 (1985), 76-84; E. W. Lawler, III, *High Involvement Management* (London: Jossey-Bass, 1986), 84; and Hellriegel, Slocum, and Woodman, *Organizational Behavior,* 491.

60. William A. Pasmore, "Social Science Transformed: The Socio-Technical Perspective," *Human Relations* 48, no. 1 (1995) 1–21.

61. David M. Upton, "What Really Makes Factories Flexible?" *Harvard Business Review* (July-August 1995): 74–84.

PART 4

Internal Design Elements

CHAPTER **6**

Organization Size, Life Cycle, and Control

ost entrepreneurs want their organizations to grow. However, as a company grows larger and more complex, managers have to develop systems and procedures that can help them guide and control the organization. During the twentieth century, large organizations became widespread, and over the past few decades, bureaucracy has been a major topic of study in organization theory.[1] Today, many organizations are trying to reduce bureaucracy to be more flexible and responsive in a rapidly changing marketplace.

However, although bureaucracy has been accused of many sins, including inefficiency, rigidity, and demeaning, routinized work that alienates both employees and customers, bureaucratic characteristics also bring many positive effects. Most large organizations have bureaucratic characteristics. These organizations provide us with abundant goods and services and surprise us with astonishing feats that are testimony to their effectiveness.

PURPOSE OF THIS CHAPTER

In this chapter, we will explore the question of large versus small organization and how size is related to structure and control. Organization size is a contextual variable that influences organizational design and functioning just as do the contextual variables—technology, environment, goals—discussed in previous chapters. In the first section, we will look at the advantages of large versus small size. Then, we will examine the historical need for bureaucracy as a means to control large organizations and how managers today attack bureaucracy in some large organizations. Next, we will explore what is called an organization's life cycle and the structural characteristics at each stage. Finally, we will examine mechanisms for organizational control and how managers determine the best means for controlling the organization. By the end of this chapter, you should understand the nature of bureaucracy and its strengths and weaknesses. You should be able to recognize when bureaucratic control can make an organization effective, as well as when other types of control are more appropriate.

ORGANIZATION SIZE: IS BIGGER BETTER?

The question of big versus small begins with the notion of growth and the reasons so many organizations feel the need to grow large.

PRESSURES FOR GROWTH

In the early 1990s, America's management guru, Peter Drucker, declared that "the *Fortune* 500 is over"; yet the dream of practically every businessperson is still to have his or her company become a member of the *Fortune* 500 list—to grow fast and to grow large.[2] Sometimes this goal is more urgent than to make the best products or show the greatest profits. Some observers believe the United States is entering a new era of "bigness," as companies strive to acquire the size and resources to compete on a global scale, to invest in new technology and to control distribution channels and guarantee access to markets. For example, more than $1.6 trillion in mergers took place worldwide in 1997 alone, with over half of that activity in the United States.[3]

There are other pressures for organizations to grow. Many executives have found that firms must grow to stay economically healthy. To stop growing is to stagnate. To be stable means that customers may not have their demands met fully or that competitors will increase market share at the expense of your company. Scale is crucial to economic health in marketing-intensive companies such as Coca-Cola and Anheuser-Busch. Greater size gives these companies power in the marketplace and thus increased revenues.[4] In addition, growing organizations are vibrant, exciting places to work, which enables these companies to attract and keep quality employees. When the number of employees is expanding, the company can offer many challenges and opportunities for advancement.

LARGE VERSUS SMALL

Organizations feel compelled to grow, but how much and how large? What size organization is better poised to compete in a global environment? The arguments are summarized in Exhibit 6.1.

Large. Huge resources and economies of scale are needed for many organizations to compete globally. Only large organizations can build a massive pipeline in Alaska. Only a large corporation like Boeing can afford to build a 747, and only a large American Airlines can buy it. Only a large Johnson & Johnson can invest hundreds of millions in new products such as bifocal contact lenses and a birth control patch that delivers contraceptives through the skin.

Large companies also are standardized, often mechanistically run, and complex. The complexity offers hundreds of functional specialties within the organization to perform complex tasks and to produce complex products. Moreover, large organizations, once established, can be a presence that stabilizes a market for years. Managers can join the company and expect a career reminiscent of the "organization men" of the 1950s and 1960s. The organization can provide longevity, raises, and promotions.

Small. The competing argument says small is beautiful because the crucial requirements for success in a global economy are responsiveness and flexibility in fast-changing markets. While the U.S. economy contains many large organizations, research shows that as global trade has accelerated, smaller organizations have become the norm. Since the mid-1960s, most of the then-existing large businesses have lost market share worldwide.[5] Today, fully 96 percent of exporters are small businesses.[6] The economic vitality of the United States, as well as most of the rest of the developed world, is tied to small and mid-sized businesses. Although many large companies have become even larger

EXHIBIT 6.1   *Differences Between Large and Small Organizations*

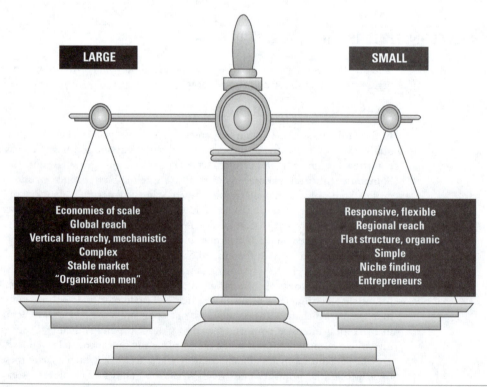

Source: Based on John A. Byrne, "Is Your Company Too Big?" *Business Week,* 27 March 1989, 84–94.

through merger, they are also less numerous as a result. Countless small businesses have sprang up to fill specialized niches and serve targeted markets.[7] The development of the Internet has provided fertile ground for the growth of small firms. In addition, the rapidly growing service sector, as discussed in Chapter 5, also contributes to a decrease in average organization size, since most service companies remain small to be more responsive to customers.[8]

ORGANIZATIONAL LIFE CYCLE

A useful way to think about organizational growth and change is the concept of an organizational **life cycle**,[9] which suggests that organizations are born, grow older, and eventually die. Organization structure, leadership style, and administrative systems follow a fairly predictable pattern through stages in the life cycle. Stages are sequential in nature and follow a natural progression.

STAGES OF LIFE CYCLE DEVELOPMENT

Recent work on organizational life cycle suggests that four major stages characterize organizational development.[10] These stages are illustrated in Exhibit 6.2 along with the problems associated with transition to each stage. Growth is not easy. Each time an organization enters

EXHIBIT 6.2   *Organizational Life Cycle*

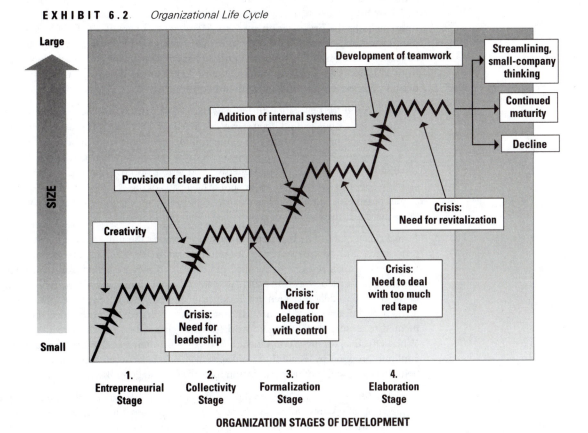

Source: Adapted from Robert E. Quinn and Kim Cameron, "Organizational Life Cycles and Shifting Criteria of Effectiveness: Some Preliminary Evidence," *Management Science* 29 (1983): 33–51; and Larry E. Greiner, "Evolution and Revolution as Organizations Grow," *Harvard Business Review* 50 (July–August 1972): 37–46.

a new stage in the life cycle, it enters a whole new ballgame with a new set of rules for how the organization functions internally and how it relates to the external environment.[11]

1. *Entrepreneurial Stage.* When an organization is born, the emphasis is on creating a product and surviving in the marketplace. The founders are entrepreneurs, and they devote their full energies to the technical activities of production and marketing. The organization is informal and nonbureaucratic. The hours of work are long. Control is based on the owners' personal supervision. Growth is from a creative new product or service. Apple Computer was in the **entrepreneurial stage** when it was created by Steve Jobs and Stephen Wozniak in Wozniak's parents' garage. Small Internet-based companies such as HomeRuns, Peapod, and ShopLink, which sell groceries online, are currently in the entrepreneurial stage.

    Crisis: Need for Leadership. As the organization starts to grow, the larger number of employees causes problems. The creative and technically oriented owners are confronted with management issues, but they may prefer to focus their energies on making and selling the product or inventing new products and services. At this time of crisis, entrepreneurs must either adjust the structure of the organization to accommodate continued growth or else bring in strong managers who can do so. When Apple began a period of rapid growth, A. C. Markkula was brought in as a leader because neither Jobs nor Wozniak was qualified or cared to manage the expanding company.

2. *Collectivity Stage.* If the leadership crisis is resolved, strong leadership is obtained and the organization begins to develop clear goals and direction. Departments are established along with a hierarchy of authority, job assignments, and a beginning division of labor. Employees identify with the mission of the organization and spend long hours helping the organization succeed. Members feel part of a collective, and communication and control are mostly informal although a few formal systems begin to appear. Apple Computer was in the **collectivity stage** during the rapid growth years from 1978 to 1981. Employees threw themselves into the business as the major product line was established and more than two thousand dealers signed on.

    Crisis: Need for Delegation. If the new management has been successful, lower-level employees gradually find themselves restricted by the strong top-down leadership. Lower-level managers begin to acquire confidence in their own functional areas and want more discretion. An autonomy crisis occurs when top managers, who were successful because of their strong leadership and vision, do not want to give up responsibility. Top managers want to make sure that all parts of the organization are coordinated and pulling together. The organization needs to find mechanisms to control and coordinate departments without direct supervision from the top.

3. *Formalization Stage.* The **formalization stage** involves the installation and use of rules, procedures, and control systems. Communication is less frequent and more formal. Engineers, human resource specialists, and other staff may be added. Top management becomes concerned with issues such as strategy and planning, and leaves the operations of the firm to middle management. Product groups or other decentralized units may be formed to improve coordination. Incentive systems based on profits may be implemented to ensure that managers work toward what is best for the overall company. When effective, the new coordination and control systems enable the organization to continue growing by establishing linkage mechanisms between top management and field units. Apple Computer was in the formalization stage in the mid-1980s.

    Crisis: Too Much Red Tape. At this point in the organization's development, the proliferation of systems and programs may begin to strangle middle-level executives. The organization seems bureaucratized. Middle management may resent the intrusion of staff people. Innovation may be restricted. The organization seems too large and complex to be managed through formal programs. It was at this stage of Apple's growth that Jobs resigned from the company and CEO John Sculley took full control to face his own management challenges.

4. *Elaboration Stage.* The solution to the red tape crisis is a new sense of collaboration and teamwork. Throughout the organization, managers develop skills for confronting problems and working together. Bureaucracy may have reached its limit. Social control and self-discipline reduce the need for additional formal controls. Managers learn to work within the bureaucracy without adding to it. Formal systems may be simplified and replaced by manager teams and task forces. To achieve collaboration, teams are often formed across functions or divisions of the company. The organization may also be split into multiple divisions to maintain a small-company philosophy. Apple Computer is currently in the **elaboration stage** of the life cycle, as are such large companies as Caterpillar and Motorola.

> Crisis: Need for Revitalization. After the organization reaches maturity, it may enter periods of temporary decline.[12] A need for renewal may occur every ten to twenty years. The organization shifts out of alignment with the environment or perhaps becomes slow moving and overbureaucratized and must go through a stage of streamlining and innovation. Top managers are often replaced during this period. At Apple, the top spot has changed hands a number of times as the company struggles to revitalize. CEOs John Sculley, Michael Spindler, and Gilbert Amelio were each ousted by the board as Apple's problems deepened. Now, Stephen Jobs—who had returned to the company as a special advisor to Amelio—is serving as CEO of the company he founded almost 25 years ago. Many believe Jobs has gained the management skills needed to help Apple weather the crisis at this stage and move forward into a new era. He has reorganized the company, weeded out inefficiencies, and refocused Apple on the consumer market. The sleek, jelly-bean colored iMac, one of the hottest computer launches ever, has Apple's sales growing faster than the industry average for the first time in years.[13] However, although Jobs has brought life back to Apple, he also must be able to sustain it. If mature organizations do not go through periodic revitalizations, they will decline, as shown in the last stage of Exhibit 6.2.

Summary. Eighty-four percent of businesses that make it past the first year still fail within five years because they can't make the transition from the entrepreneurial stage.[14] The transitions become even more difficult as organizations progress through future stages of the life cycle. Organizations that do not successfully resolve the problems associated with these transitions are restricted in their growth and may even fail.

ORGANIZATIONAL CHARACTERISTICS DURING THE LIFE CYCLE

As organizations evolve through the four stages of the life cycle, changes take place in structure, control systems, innovation, and goals. The organizational characteristics associated with each stage are summarized in Exhibit 6.3.

Entrepreneurial. Initially, the organization is small, nonbureaucratic, and a one-person show. The top manager provides the structure and control system. Organizational energy is devoted to survival and the production of a single product or service.

Collectivity. This is the organization's youth. Growth is rapid, and employees are excited and committed to the organization's mission. The structure is still mostly informal, although some procedures are emerging. Strong charismatic leaders like Scott McNealy of Sun Microsystems or Steve Jobs of Apple provide direction and goals for the organization. Continued growth is a major goal.

Formalization. At this point, the organization is entering midlife. Bureaucratic characteristics emerge. The organization adds staff support groups, formalizes procedures, and establishes a clear hierarchy and division of labor. Innovation may be achieved by establishing a separate research and development department. Major goals are internal stability and market expansion. Top management has to delegate, but it also implements formal control systems.

EXHIBIT 6.3   *Organization Characteristics During Four Stages of Life Cycle*

Characteristic	1. ENTREPRENEURIAL Nonbureaucratic	2. COLLECTIVITY Prebureaucratic	3. FORMALIZATION Bureaucratic	4. ELABORATION Very Bureaucratic
Structure	Informal, one-person show	Mostly informal, some procedures	Formal procedures, division of labor, new specialties added	Teamwork within bureaucracy, small-company thinking
Products or services	Single product or service	Major product or service, with variations	Line of products or services	Multiple product or service lines
Reward and control systems	Personal, paternalistic	Personal, contribution to success	Impersonal, formalized systems	Extensive, tailored to product and department
Innovation	By owner-manager	By employees and managers	By separate innovation group	By institutionalized R & D department
Goal	Survival	Growth	Internal stability, market expansion	Reputation, complete organization
Top management style	Individualistic, entrepreneurial	Charismatic, direction-giving	Delegation with control	Team approach, attack bureaucracy

Source: Adapted from Larry E. Greiner, "Evolution and Revolution as Organizations Grow," *Harvard Business Review* 50 (July–August 1972): 37–46; G. L. Lippitt and W. H. Schmidt, "Crises in a Developing Organization," *Harvard Business Review* 45 (November–December 1967): 102–12; B. R. Scott, "The Industrial State: Old Myths and New Realities," *Harvard Business Review* 51 (March–April 1973): 133–48; Robert E. Quinn and Kim Cameron, "Organizational Life Cycles and Shifting Criteria of Effectiveness," *Management Science* 29 (1983): 33–51.

At Dell Computer, for example, Michael Dell has hired a cadre of experienced managers to help him develop and implement formal planning, management, and budgeting systems. According to vice chairman Kevin B. Rollins, "Michael realized that he needed professionals to run this company, so that he could continue to be a visionary."[15] At the formalization stage, organizations may also develop complementary products to offer a complete product line.

Elaboration. The mature organization is large and bureaucratic, with extensive control systems, rules, and procedures. Organization managers attempt to develop a team orientation within the bureaucracy to prevent further bureaucratization. Top managers are concerned with establishing a complete organization. Organizational stature and reputation are important. Innovation is institutionalized through an R&D department. Management may attack the bureaucracy and streamline it.

Summary. Growing organizations move through stages of a life cycle, and each stage is associated with specific characteristics of structure, control systems, goals, and innovation. The life cycle phenomenon is a powerful concept used for understanding problems facing organizations and how managers can respond in a positive way to move an organization to the next stage.

ORGANIZATIONAL BUREAUCRACY AND CONTROL

As organizations progress through the life cycle, they usually take on bureaucratic characteristics as they grow larger and more complex. The systematic study of bureaucracy was launched by Max Weber, a sociologist who studied government organizations in Europe and developed a framework of administrative characteristics that would make large organizations rational and efficient.[16] Weber wanted to understand how organizations could be designed to play a positive role in the larger society.

WHAT IS BUREAUCRACY?

Although Weber perceived **bureaucracy** as a threat to basic personal liberties, he also recognized it as the most efficient possible system of organizing. He predicted the triumph of bureaucracy because of its ability to ensure more efficient functioning of organizations in both business and government settings. Weber identified a set of organizational characteristics, listed in Exhibit 6.4, that could be found in successful bureaucratic organizations.

Rules and standard procedures enabled organizational activities to be performed in a predictable, routine manner. Specialized duties meant that each employee had a clear task to perform. Hierarchy of authority provided a sensible mechanism for supervision and control. Technical competence was the basis by which people were hired rather than friendship, family ties, and favoritism that dramatically reduced work performance. The separation of the position from the position holder meant that individuals did not own or have an inherent right to the job, thus promoting efficiency. Written records provided an organizational memory and continuity over time.

Although bureaucratic characteristics carried to an extreme are widely criticized today, the rational control introduced by Weber was a significant idea and a new form of organization. Bureaucracy provided many advantages over organization forms based upon favoritism, social status, family connections, or graft, which are often unfair. For example, in Mexico, a retired American lawyer had to pay a $500 bribe to purchase a telephone, then discovered that a government official had sold his telephone number to another family. In China, the tradition of giving government posts to relatives is widespread even under communism. China's emerging class of educated people doesn't like seeing the best jobs going to children and relatives of officials.[17] By comparison, the logical and rational form of organization described by Weber allows work to be conducted efficiently and according to established rules.

SIZE AND STRUCTURAL CONTROL

In the field of organization theory, organization size has been described as an important variable that influences structural design and methods of control. Should an organization become more bureaucratic as it grows larger? In what size organizations are bureaucratic characteristics most appropriate? More than one hundred studies have attempted to answer these questions.[18] Most of these studies indicate that large organizations are different from small organizations along several dimensions of bureaucratic structure, including formalization, centralization, and personnel ratios.

Formalization and Centralization. Formalization, as described in Chapter 1, refers to rules, procedures, and written documentation, such as policy manuals and job descriptions, that prescribe the rights and duties of employees.[19] The evidence supports the conclusion that large organizations are more formalized. The reason is that large organizations rely on rules, procedures, and paperwork to achieve standardization and control across their large numbers of employees and departments, whereas top managers can use personal observation to control a small organization.[20]

Centralization refers to the level of hierarchy with authority to make decisions. In centralized organizations, decisions tend to be made at the top. In decentralized organizations, similar decisions would be made at a lower level.

EXHIBIT 6.4   *Weber's Dimensions of Bureaucracy and Bases of Organizational Authority*

Bureaucracy	Legitimate Bases of Authority
1. Rules and procedures	1. Rational-legal
2. Specialization and division of labor	2. Traditional
3. Hierarchy of authority	3. Charismatic
4. Technically qualified personnel	
5. Separate position and incumbent	
6. Written communications and records	

Decentralization represents a paradox because, in the perfect bureaucracy, all decisions would be made by the top administrator, who would have perfect control. However, as an organization grows larger and has more people and departments, decisions cannot be passed to the top, or senior managers would be overloaded. Thus, the research on organization size indicates that larger organizations permit greater decentrailization.[21] Hewlett-Packard decentralizes almost every aspect of its business to speed up decision making. In small startup organizations, on the other hand, the founder or top executive is often involved in every decision, large and small.

Personnel Ratios. Another characteristic of bureaucracy is **personnel ratios** for administrative, clerical, and professional support staff. The most frequently studied ratio is the administrative ratio.[22] Two patterns have emerged. The first is that the ratio of top administration to total employees is actually smaller in large organizations,[23] indicating that organizations experience administrative economies as they grow larger. The second pattern concerns clerical and professional support staff ratios.[24] These groups tend to *increase* in proportion to organization size. The clerical ratio increases because of the greater communication and reporting requirements needed as organizations grow larger. The professional staff ratio increases because of the greater need for specialized skills in larger, complex organizations.

Exhibit 6.5 illustrates administrative and support ratios for small and large organizations. As organizations increase in size, the administrative ratio declines and the ratios for other support groups increase.[25] The net effect for direct workers is that they decline as a percentage of total employees. In summary, while top administrators do not make up a disproportionate number of employees in large organizations, the idea that proportionately greater overhead is required in large organizations is supported. Although large organizations

EXHIBIT 6.5   *Percentage of Personnel Allocated to Administrative and Support Activities*

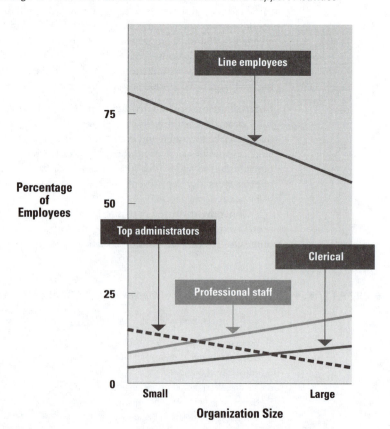

reduced overhead during the difficult economic years of the 1980s, recent studies indicate that overhead costs for many American corporations began creeping back up again as revenues soared during the late 1990s.[26] Keeping costs for administrative, clerical, and professional support staff low represents an ongoing challenge for today's large organizations.[27]

BUREAUCRACY IN A CHANGING WORLD

Weber's prediction of the triumph of bureaucracy proved accurate. Bureaucratic characteristics have many advantages and have worked extremely well for many of the needs of the industrial age.[28] By establishing a hierarchy of authority and specific rules and procedures, bureaucracy provided an effective way to bring order to large groups of people and prevent abuses of power. Impersonal relationships based on roles rather than people reduced the favoritism and nepotism characteristic of many preindustrial organizations. Bureaucracy also provided for systematic and rational ways to organize and manage tasks too complex to be understood and handled by a few individuals, thus greatly improving the efficiency and effectiveness of large organizations.

The world is rapidly changing, however, and the machinelike bureaucratic system of the industrial age no longer works so well as organizations face new challenges. With global competition and uncertain environments, many organizations are fighting against increasing formalization and professional staff ratios. They are cutting layers of the hierarchy, keeping headquarters staff small, and giving lower-level workers greater freedom to make decisions rather than burdening them with excessive rules and regulations. At Nucor Corp., headquarters is staffed by only twenty-three people. Nucor's plant managers handle everything from marketing to personnel to production. Centex Corporation, which has annual revenues of about $3.8 billion, is run from a modest headquarters in Dallas by a staff of fewer than one hundred. Centex decentralizes authority and responsibility to the operating divisions.[29] The point is to not overload headquarters with lawyers, accountants, and financial analysts who will inhibit the flexibility and autonomy of divisions. Of course, many companies must be large to have sufficient resources and complexity to produce products for a global environment; but companies such as Johnson & Johnson, Wal-Mart, 3M, Coca-Cola, Emerson Electric, and Heinz are striving toward greater decentralization and leanness. They are giving front-line workers more authority and responsibility to define and direct their own jobs, often by creating self-directed teams that find ways to coordinate work, improve productivity, and better serve customers.

Another attack on bureaucracy is from the increasing professionalism of employees. Professionalism is defined as the length of formal training and experience of employees. More employees need college degrees, MBAs, and other professional degrees to work as attorneys, researchers, or doctors at General Motors, Kmart, and Bristol-Myers Squibb Company. In addition, Internet-based companies, a rapidly growing segment of the economy, are generally staffed entirely by well-educated knowledge workers. Studies of professionals show that formalization is not needed because professional training regularizes a high standard of behavior for employees that acts as a substitute for bureaucracy.[30] Companies also enhance this trend when they provide ongoing training for *all* employees, from the front office to the shop floor, in a push for continuous individual and organizational learning. Increased training substitutes for bureaucratic rules and procedures that can constrain the creativity of employees to solve problems and increase organizational capability.

A form of organization called the *professional partnership* has emerged that is made up completely of professionals.[31] These organizations include medical practices, law firms, and consulting firms, such as McKinsey & Co. and PricewaterhouseCoopers. The general finding concerning professional partnerships is that branches have substantial autonomy and decentralized authority to make necessary decisions. They work with a consensus orientation rather than top-down direction typical of traditional business and government organizations. Thus, the trend of increasing professionalism combined with rapidly changing environments is leading to less bureaucracy in corporate North America.

DYNAMIC CONTROL SYSTEMS

Even though many organizations are trying to decrease bureaucracy and reduce rules and procedures that constrain employees, every organization needs systems for guiding and controlling the organization. Employees may have more freedom in today's companies, but control is still a major responsibility of management.

Managers at the top and middle levels of an organization can choose among three overall approaches for control. These approaches come from a framework for organizational control proposed by William Ouchi of the University of California at Los Angeles. Ouchi suggested three control strategies that organizations could adopt—bureaucratic, market and clan.[32] Each form of control uses different types of information. However, all three types may appear simultaneously in an organization. The requirements for each control strategy are given in Exhibit 6.6.

BUREAUCRATIC CONTROL

Bureaucratic control is the use of rules, policies, hierarchy of authority, written documentation, standardization, and other bureaucratic mechanisms to standardize behavior and assess performance. Bureaucratic control uses the bureaucratic characteristics defined by Weber. The primary purpose of bureaucratic rules and procedures is to standardize and control employee behavior.

Recall that as organizations progress through the life cycle and grow larger, they become more formalized and standardized. Within a large organization, thousands of work behaviors and information exchanges take place both vertically and horizontally. Rules and policies evolve through a process of trial and error to regulate these behaviors. Some degree of bureaucratic control is used in virtually every organization. Rules, regulations, and directives contain information about a range of behaviors.

Bases of Control. To make bureaucratic control work, managers must have the authority to maintain control over the organization. Weber argued that legitimate, rational authority granted to managers was preferred over other types of control (for example, favoritism or payoffs) as the basis for organizational decisions and activities. Within the larger society, however, Weber identified three types of authority that could explain the creation and control of a large organization.[33]

Rational-legal authority is based on employees' belief in the legality of rules and the right of those elevated to positions of authority to issue commands. Rational-legal authority is the basis for both creation and control of most government organizations and is the most common base of control in organizations worldwide. **Traditional authority** is the belief in traditions and in the legitimacy of the status of people exercising authority through those traditions. Traditional authority is the basis for control for monarchies and churches and for some organizations in Latin America and the Persian Gulf. **Charismatic authority** is based on devotion to the exemplary character or to the heroism of an individual person and the order defined by him or her. Revolutionary military organizations are often based on the leader's charisma, as are North American organizations led by charismatic individuals such as Jack Welch or Herb Kelleher.

EXHIBIT 6.6   *Three Organizational Control Strategies*

Type	Requirements
Bureaucracy	Rules, standards, hierarchy, legitimate authority
Market	Prices, competition, exchange relationship
Clan	Tradition, shared values and beliefs, trust

Source: Based upon William G. Ouchi, "A Conceptual Framework for the Design of Organizational Control Mechanisms," *Management Science* 25 (1979): 833–48.

More than one type of authority—such as long tradition and the leader's special charisma—may exist in today's organizations, but rational–legal authority is the most widely used form to govern internal work activities and decision making, particularly in large organizations.

Management control systems are broadly defined as the formalized routines, reports, and procedures that use information to maintain or alter patterns in organizational activity.[34] Control systems include the formalized information-based activities for planning, budgeting, performance evaluation, resource allocation, and employee rewards. These systems operate as feedback systems, with the targets set in advance, outcomes compared with targets, and variance reported to managers for remedial actions.[35] These systems are valuable tools to help managers monitor and control the organization.

The four control system elements listed in Exhibit 6.7 are often considered the core of management control systems. These four elements include the budget, periodic nonfinancial statistical reports, reward systems, and standard operating procedures.[36] The management control system elements enable middle and upper management to both monitor and influence major departments.

The operating budget is used to set financial targets for the year and then report costs on a monthly or quarterly basis. Periodic statistical reports are used to evaluate and monitor nonfinancial performance. These reports typically are computer-based and may be available daily, weekly, or monthly.

Reward systems offer incentives for managers and employees to improve performance and meet departmental goals. Managers and superiors may sit down and evaluate how well previous goals were met, set new goals for the year, and establish rewards for meeting the new targets. Operating procedures are traditional rules and regulations. Managers use all of these systems to correct variances and bring activities back into line.

One finding from research into management control systems is that each of the four control systems focuses on a different aspect of the production process. These four systems thus form an overall management control system that provides middle managers with control information about resource inputs, process efficiency, and output.[37] Moreover, the use of and reliance on control systems depend on the strategic targets set by top management.

The budget is used primarily to allocate resource inputs. Managers use the budget for planning the future and reducing uncertainty about the availability of human and material resources needed to perform department tasks. Computer-based statistical reports are used to control outputs. These reports contain data about output volume and quality and other indicators that provide feedback to middle management about departmental results. The reward system and the policies and procedures are directed at the production process. Operating procedures give explicit guidelines about appropriate behaviors. Reward systems provide incentives to meet goals and can help guide and correct employee activities. Managers also use direct supervision to keep departmental work activities within desired limits.

EXHIBIT 6.7   *Management Control Systems Used as Part of Bureaucratic Control*

Subsystem	Content and Frequency
Budget	Financial, resource expenditures, monthly
Statistical reports	Nonfinancial outputs, weekly or monthly, often computer-based
Reward systems	Annual evaluation of managers based on department goals and performance
Operating procedures	Rules and regulations, policies that prescribe correct behavior, continuous

Source: Based on Richard L. Daft and Norman B. Macintosh, "The Nature and Use of Formal Control Systems for Management Control and Strategy Implementation," *Journal of Management* 10 (1984): 43–66.

Advances in computer technology have dramatically improved the efficiency and effectiveness of management control systems. The British express delivery and logistics company TNT UK uses computerized management control systems to measure and control every aspect of the company's performance, helping TNT UK win the prestigious 1998 European Quality Award.[38]

MARKET CONTROL

Market control occurs when price competition is used to evaluate the output and productivity of an organization. The idea of market control originated in economics.[39] A dollar price is an efficient form of control because managers can compare prices and profits to evaluate the efficiency of their corporation. Top managers nearly always use the price mechanism to evaluate performance in corporations. Corporate sales and costs are summarized in a profit-and-loss statement that can be compared against performance in previous years or with that of other corporations.

The use of market control requires that outputs be sufficiently explicit for a price to be assigned and that competition exist. Without competition, the price will not accurately reflect internal efficiency. Even some government and traditionally not-for-profit organizations are turning to market control. For example, the U.S. Federal Aviation Administration took bids to operate its payroll computers (the Department of Agriculture beat out IBM and two other private companies to win the bid). Seventy-three percent of local governments now use private janitorial services and 54 percent use private garbage collectors.[40] The city of Indianapolis requires all its departments to bid against private companies. When the transportation department was underbid by a private company on a contract to fill potholes, the city's union workers made a counter-proposal that involved eliminating most of the department's middle managers and reengineering union jobs to save money. Eighteen supervisors were laid off, costs were cut by 25 percent, and the department won the bid.[41]

Market control was once used primarily at the level of the entire organization, but it is increasingly used in product divisions. Profit centers are self-contained product divisions, such as those described in Chapter 3. Each division contains resource inputs needed to produce a product. Each division can be evaluated on the basis of profit or loss compared with other divisions. Asea Brown Boveri (ABB), a multinational electrical contractor and manufacturer of electrical equipment, includes three different types of profit centers, all operating according to their own bottom line and all interacting through buying and selling with one another and with outside customers.[42]

Some firms require that individual departments interact with one another at market prices—buying and selling products or services among themselves at prices equivalent to those quoted outside the firm. To make the market control system work, internal units also have the option to buy and sell with outside companies.

Market control can only be used when the output of a company, division, or department can be assigned a dollar price and when there is competition. Companies are finding that they can apply the market control concept to internal departments such as accounting, data processing, legal departments, and information services.

CLAN CONTROL

Clan control is the use of social characteristics, such as corporate culture, shared values, commitment, traditions, and beliefs, to control behavior. Organizations that use clan control require shared values and trust among employees.[43] Clan control is important when ambiguity and uncertainty are high. High uncertainty means the organization cannot put a price on its services, and things change so fast that rules and regulations are not able to specify every correct behavior. Under clan control, people may be hired because they are committed to the organization's purpose, such as in a religious organization. New employees may be subjected to a long period of socialization to gain acceptance by colleagues. Clan control is most often used in small, informal organizations or in organizations with a strong culture, because of personal involvement in and commitment to the organization's purpose. For example, St. Luke's Communications Ltd., a London advertising firm committed to equal employee ownership, is especially careful to bring in only new employees who believe in the agency's philosophy and mission. The company even turned down a $90 million contract because it would mean rapidly recruiting new employees who might not fit with St. Luke's distinctive culture. Clan control works for St. Luke's; the agency is highly respected and its revenues continue to grow, increasing by 75 percent last year.[44]

The growing use of computer networks and the Internet, which often leads to a democratic spread of information throughout the organization, may force many companies to depend less on bureaucratic control and more on shared values that guide individual actions for the corporate good.[45]

Traditional control mechanisms based on strict rules and close supervision are ineffective for controlling behavior in conditions of high uncertainty and rapid change.[46] Today's companies that are trying to become learning organizations often use clan control or *self-control* rather than relying on rules and regulations. Self-control is similar to clan control, but whereas clan control is a function of being socialized into a group, self-control stems from individual values, goals, and standards. The organization attempts to induce a change such that individual employees' own internal values and work preferences are brought in line with the organization's values and goals.[47] With self-control, employees generally set their own goals and monitor their own performance, yet companies relying on self-control need strong leaders who can clarify boundaries within which employees exercise their own knowledge and discretion.

Clan or self-control may also be used in certain departments, such as strategic planning, where uncertainty is high and performance is difficult to measure. Managers of departments that rely on these informal control mechanisms must not assume that the absence of written, bureaucratic control means no control is present. Clan control is invisible yet very powerful. One recent study found that the actions of employees were controlled even more powerfully and completely with clan control than with a bureaucratic hierarchy.[48] When clan control works, bureaucratic control is not needed.

DISCUSSION QUESTIONS

1. Discuss the key differences between large and small organizations. Why do large organizations tend to be more formalized?
2. If you were managing a department of college professors, how might you structure the department differently than if you were managing a department of bookkeepers? Why?
3. Apply the concept of life cycle to an organization with which you are familiar, such as a university or a local business. What stage is the organization in now? How did the organization handle or pass through its life cycle crises?
4. Describe the three bases of authority identified by Weber. Is it possible for each of these types of authority to function at the same time within an organization?
5. In writing about types of control, William Ouchi said, "The Market is like the trout and the Clan like the salmon, each a beautiful highly specialized species which requires uncommon conditions for its survival. In comparison, the bureaucratic method of control is the catfish—clumsy, ugly, but able to live in the widest range of environments and ultimately, the dominant species." Discuss what Ouchi meant with that analogy.
6. Government organizations often seem more bureaucratic than for-profit organizations. Could this partly be the result of the type of control used in government organizations? Explain.

NOTES

1. James Q. Wilson, *Bureaucracy* (Basic Books: 1989); and Charles Perrow, *Complex Organizations: A Critical Essay* (Glenview, Ill.: Scott, Foresman, 1979), 4.

2. Tom Peters, "Rethinking Scale," *California Management Review* (Fall 1992): 7–29.

3. David Friedman, "Is Big Back? Or Is Small Still Beautiful?" *Inc.* (April 1998): 23–28.

4. James B. Treece, "Sometimes, You've Still Gotta Have Size," *Business Week/Enterprise,* 1993, 200– 01.

5. Friedman, "Is Big Back?

6. Peter F. Drucker, "Toward the New Organization," *Executive Excellence* (February 1997): 7.

7. Thomas Petzinger, Jr., *The New Pioneers: The Men and Women Who Are Transforming the Workplace and Marketplace* (New York: Simon & Schuster, 1999), 21.

8. Glenn R. Carroll, "Organizations . . . The Smaller They Get," *California Management Review* 37, no. 1 (Fall 1994): 28–41.

9. John R. Kimberly, Robert H. Miles, and Associates, *The Organizational Life Cycle* (San Francisco: Jossey-Bass, 1980); Ichak Adices, "Organizational Passages— Diagnosing and Treating Lifecycle Problems of Organizations," *Organizational Dynamics* (Summer 1979): 3–25; Danny Miller and Peter H. Friesen, "A Longitudinal Study of the Corporate Life Cycle," *Management Science* 30 (October 1984): 1161–83; Neil C. Churchill and Virginia L. Lewis, "The Five Stages of Small Business Growth," *Harvard Business Review* 61 (May–June 1983): 30–50.

10. Larry E. Greiner, "Evolution and Revolution as Organizations Grow," *Harvard Business Review* 50 (July–August 1972): 37–46; Robert E. Quinn and Kim Cameron, "Organizational Life Cycles and Shifting Criteria of Effectiveness: Some Preliminary Evidence," *Management Science* 29 (1983): 33–51.

11. George Land and Beth Jarman, "Moving beyond Breakpoint," in Michael Ray and Alan Rinzler, eds., *The New Paradigm* (New York: Jeremy P. Tarcher/Perigee Books, 1993), 250–66; Michael L. Tushman, William H. Newman, and Elaine Romanelli, "Convergence and Upheaval: Managing the Unsteady Pace of Organizational Evolution," *California Management Review* 29 (1987): 1–16.

12. David A. Whetten, "Sources, Responses, and Effects of Organizational Decline," in John R. Kimberly, Robert H. Miles, and Associates, *The Organizational Life Cycle* (San Francisco: Jossey-Bass, 1980), 342–74.

13. David Kirkpatrick, "The Second Coming of Apple," *Fortune*, 9 November 1998, 86–92; Ira Sager and Peter Burrows with Andy Reinhardt, *Business Week*, 25 May 1998, 56–60; and Peter Burrows, "A Peek at Steve Jobs' Plan," *Business Week*, 17 November 1997, 144–46.

14. Land and Jarman, "Moving Beyond Breakpoint."

15. Richard Murphy, "Michael Dell," *Success*, January 1999, 50–53.

16. Max Weber, *The Theory of Social and Economic Organizations*, translated by A. M. Henderson and T. Parsons (New York: Free Press, 1947).

17. John Crewdson, "Corruption Viewed as a Way of Life," *Bryan-College Station Eagle,* 28 November 1982, 13A; Barry Kramer, "Chinese Officials Still Give Preference to Kin, Despite Peking Policies," *The Wall Street Journal,* 29 October 1985, 1, 21.

18. Allen C. Bluedorn, "Pilgrim's Progress: Trends and Convergence in Research on Organizational Size and Environment," *Journal of Management Studies* 19 (Summer 1993): 163–91; John R. Kimberly, "Organizational Size and the Structuralist Perspective: A Review, Critique, and Proposal," *Administrative Science Quarterly* (1976): 571–97; Richard L. Daft and Selwyn W. Becker, "Managerial, Institutional, and Technical Influences on Administration: A Longitudinal Analysis," *Social Forces* 59 (1980): 392–413.

19. James P. Walsh and Robert D. Dewar, "Formalization and the Organizational Life Cycle," *Journal of Management Studies* 24 (May 1987): 215–31.

20. Nancy M. Carter and Thomas L. Keon, "Specialization as a Multidimensional Construct," *Journal of Management Studies* 26 (1989): 11–28; Cheng-Kuang Hsu, Robert M. March, and Hiroshi Mannari, "An Examination of the Determinants of Organizational Structure," *American Journal of Sociology* 88 (1983): 975–96; Guy Geeraerts, "The Effect of Ownership on the Organization Structure in Small Firms," *Administrative Science Quarterly* 29 (1984): 232–37; Bernard Reimann, "On the Dimensions of Bureaucratic Structure: An Empirical Reappraisal," *Administrative Science Quarterly* 18 (1973): 462–76; Richard H. Hall, "The Concept of Bureaucracy: An Empirical Assessment," *American Journal of Sociology* 69 (1963): 32–40; William A. Rushing, "Organizational Rules and Surveillance: A Proposition in Comparative Organizational Analysis," *Administrative Science Quarterly* 10 (1966): 423–43.

21. Jerald Hage and Michael Aiken, "Relationship of Centralization to Other Structural Properties," *Administrative Science Quarterly* 12 (1967): 72–91.

22. Peter Brimelow, "How Do You Cure Injelitance?" *Forbes,* 7 August 1989, 42–44; and Jeffrey D. Ford and John W. Slocum, Jr., "Size, Technology, Environment and the Structure of Organizations," *Academy of Management Review* 2 (1977): 561–75; John D. Kasarda, "The Structural Implications of Social System Size: A Three-Level Analysis," *American Sociological Review* 39 (1974): 19–28.

23. Graham Astley, "Organizational Size and Bureaucratic Structure," *Organization Studies* 6 (1985): 201–28; Spyros K. Lioukas and Demitris A. Xerokostas, "Size and Administrative Intensity in Organizational Divisions," *Management Science* 28 (1982): 854–68; Peter M. Blau, "Interdependence and Hierarchy in Organizations," *Social Science Research* 1 (1972): 1–24; Peter M. Blau and R. A. Schoenherr, *The Structure of Organizations* (New York: Basic Books, 1971); A. Hawley, W. Boland, and M. Boland, "Population Size and Administration in Institutions of Higher Education," *American Sociological Review* 30 (1965): 252–55; Richard L. Daft, "System Influence on Organization Decision-Making: The Case of Resource Allocation," *Academy of Management Journal* 21 (1978): 6–22; B. P. Indik, "The Relationship between Organization Size and the Supervisory Ratio," *Administrative Science Quarterly* 9 (1964): 301–12.

24. T. F. James, "The Administrative Component in Complex Organizations," *Sociological Quarterly* 13 (1972): 533–39; Daft, "System Influence on Organization Decision-Making"; E. A. Holdaway and E. A. Blowers, "Administrative Ratios and Organization Size: A Longitudinal Examination," *American Sociological Review* 36 (1971): 278–86; John Child, "Parkinson's Progress: Accounting for the Number of Specialists in Organizations," *Administrative Science Quarterly* 18 (1973): 328–48.

25. Richard L. Daft and Selwyn Becker, "School District Size and the Development of Personnel Resources," *Alberta Journal of Educational Research* 24 (1978): 173–87.

26. Thomas A. Stewart, "Yikes! Deadwood is Creeping Back," *Fortune,* 18 August 1997, 221–222.

27. Cathy Lazere, "Resisting Temptation: The Fourth Annual SG&A Survey," *CFO* (December 1997): 64–70.

28. Based on Gifford and Elizabeth Pinchot, *The End of Bureaucracy and the Rise of the Intelligent Organization* (San Francisco: Berrett-Koehler Publishers, 1993), 21–29.

29. Lazere, "Resisting Temptation."

30. Philip M. Padsakoff, Larry J. Williams, and William D. Todor, "Effects of Organizational Formalization on Alienation among Professionals and Nonprofessionals," *Academy of Management Journal* 29 (1986): 820–31.

31. Royston Greenwood, C. R. Hinings, and John Brown, "'P2-Form' Strategic Management: Corporate Practices in Professional Partnerships," *Academy of Management Journal* 33 (1990): 725–55; Royston Greenwood and C. R. Hinings, "Understanding Strategic Change: The Contribution of Archtypes," *Academy of Management Journal* 36 (1993): 1052–81.

32. William G. Ouchi, "Markets, Bureaucracies, and Clans," *Administrative Science Quarterly* 25 (1980): 129–41;—idem, "A Conceptual Framework for the Design of Organizational Control Mechanisms," *Management Science* 25 (1979): 833–48.

33. Weber, *Theory of Social and Economic Organizations,* 328–340.

34. Robert Simons, "Strategic Organizations and Top Management Attention to Control Systems," *Strategic Management Journal* 12 (1991): 491-62.

35. Stephen G. Green and M. Ann Welsh, "Cybernetics and Dependents: Reframing the Control Concept," *Academy of Management Review* 13 (1988): 287–301.

36. Richard L. Daft and Norman B. Macintosh, "The Nature and Use of Formal Control Systems for Management Control and Strategy Implementation," *Journal of Management* 10 (1984): 43–66.

37. Ibid.; Scott S. Cowen and J. Kendall Middaugh II, "Matching an Organization's Planning and Control System to Its Environment," *Journal of General Management* 16 (1990): 69–84.

38. Trevor Merriden, "Measured for Success," *Management Review* (April 1999): 27–32.

39. Oliver A. Williamson, *Markets and Hierarchies: Analyses and Antitrust Implications* (New York: Free Press, 1975).

40. David Wessel and John Harwood, "Capitalism is Giddy with Triumph: Is It Possible to Overdo It?" *The Wall Street Journal,* 14 May 1998, A1, A10.

41. Anita Micossi, "Creating Internal Markets," *Enterprise* (April 1994): 43–44.

42. Raymond E. Miles, Henry J. Coleman, Jr., and W. E. Douglas Creed, "Keys to Success in Corporate Redesign," *California Management Review* 37, no. 3 (Spring 1995): 128–45.

43. Ouchi, "Markets, Bureaucracies, and Clans."

44. Anna Muoio, ed., "Growing Smart," *Fast Company,* August 1998, 73-83.

45. Stratford Sherman, "The New Computer Revolution," *Fortune,* 14 June 1993, 56–80.

46. Richard Leifer and Peter K. Mills, "An Information Processing Approach for Deciding Upon Control Strategies and Reducing Control Loss in Emerging Organizations," *Journal of Management* 22, no. 1 (1996): 113–37.

47. Leifer and Mills, "An Information Processing Approach for Deciding Upon Control Strategies"; Laurie J. Kirsch, "The Management of Complex Tasks in Organizations: Controlling the Systems Development Process," *Organization Science* 7, no. 1 (January-February 1996): 1–21.

48. James R. Barker, "Tightening the Iron Cage: Concertive Control in Self-Managing Teams," *Administrative Science Quarterly* 38 (1993): 408–37.

CHAPTER 7

Organizational Culture and Ethical Values

*O*rganizational success or failure is often attributed to culture. In *Fortune* magazine's survey of the most admired companies, the single best predictor of overall excellence was the ability to attract, motivate, and retain talented people, and CEOs say organizational culture is their most important mechanism for enhancing this capability.[1] Southwest Airlines, Johnson & Johnson, and 3M have been praised for their innovative cultures. Culture has also been implicated in problems faced by companies such as Kodak and Kellogg, where changing the culture is considered a key to ultimate success.

PURPOSE OF THIS CHAPTER

This chapter explores ideas about corporate culture and associated ethical values and how these are influenced by organizations. The first section will describe the nature of corporate culture, its origins and purpose, and how to identify and interpret culture through ceremonies, stories, and symbols. We will then examine how culture reinforces the strategy and structural design the organization needs to be effective in its environment. Next, the chapter turns to ethical values in organizations and how managers implement the structures and systems that will influence employee behavior. We will also discuss how leaders shape culture and ethical values in a direction suitable for strategy and performance outcomes.

ORGANIZATIONAL CULTURE

The popularity of the organizational culture topic raises a number of questions. Can we identify cultures? Can culture be aligned with strategy? How can cultures be managed or changed? The best place to start is by defining culture and explaining how it can be identified in organizations.

WHAT IS CULTURE?

Culture is the set of values, guiding beliefs, understandings, and ways of thinking that is shared by members of an organization and taught to new members as correct.[2] It represents the unwritten, feeling part of the organization. Everyone participates in culture, but culture generally goes unnoticed. It is only when organizations try to implement new strategies or programs that go against basic culture norms and values that they come face to face with the power of culture.

Organizational culture exists at two levels, as illustrated in Exhibit 7.1. On the surface are visible artifacts and observable behaviors—the ways people dress and act and the symbols, stories, and ceremonies organization members share. The visible elements of culture, however, reflect deeper values in the minds of organization members. These underlying values, assumptions, beliefs, and thought processes are the true culture.[3] For example, at Southwest Airlines, red "LUV" hearts emblazon the company's training manuals and other materials. The hearts are a visible symbol; the underlying value is that "we are one family of people who truly care about each other." The attributes of culture display themselves in many ways but typically evolve into a patterned set of activities carried out through social interactions.[4] Those patterns can be used to interpret culture.

EMERGENCE AND PURPOSE OF CULTURE

Culture provides members with a sense of organizational identity and generates a commitment to beliefs and values that are larger than themselves. Though ideas that become part of culture can come from anywhere within the organization, an organization's culture generally begins with a founder or early leader who articulates and implements particular ideas and values as a vision, philosophy, or business strategy. When these ideas and values lead to success, they become institutionalized, and an organizational culture emerges that reflects the vision and strategy of the founder or leader.[5]

EXHIBIT 7.1   *Levels of Corporate Culture*

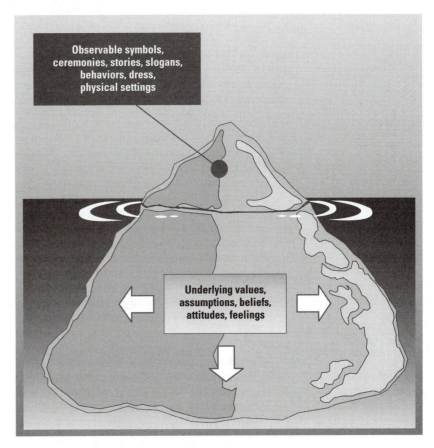

Cultures serve two critical functions in organizations: (1) to integrate members so that they know how to relate to one another, and (2) to help the organization adapt to the external environment. **Internal integration** means that members develop a collective identity and know how to work together effectively. It is culture that guides day-to-day working relationships and determines how people communicate within the organization, what behavior is acceptable or not acceptable, and how power and status are allocated. **External adaptation** refers to how the organization meets goals and deals with outsiders. Culture helps guide the daily activities of workers to meet certain goals. It can help the organization respond rapidly to customer needs or the moves of a competitor. We will discuss culture and adaptation in more detail later in the chapter.

INTERPRETING CULTURE

To identify and interpret the content of culture requires that people make inferences based on observable artifacts. Artifacts can be studied but are hard to decipher accurately. An award ceremony in one company may have a different meaning than in another company. To decipher what is really going on in an organization requires detective work and probably some experience as an insider. Some of the typical and important observable aspects of culture are rites and ceremonies, stories, symbols, and language.

Rites and Ceremonies. Important artifacts for culture are **rites and ceremonies**, the elaborate, planned activities that make up a special event and are often conducted for the benefit of an audience. Managers can hold rites and ceremonies to provide dramatic examples of what a company values. These are special occasions that reinforce specific values, create a bond among people for sharing an important understanding, and anoint and celebrate heroes and heroines who symbolize important beliefs and activities.[6]

Four types of rites that appear in organizations are summarized in Exhibit 7.2. *Rites of passage* facilitate the transition of employees into new social roles. *Rites of enhancement* create stronger social identities and increase the status of employees. *Rites of renewal* reflect training and development activities that improve organization functioning. *Rites of integration* create common bonds and good feelings among employees and increase commitment to the organization. The following examples illustrate how these rites and ceremonies are used by top managers to reinforce important cultural values.

- In a major bank, election as an officer was seen as the key event in a successful career. A series of activities accompanied every promotion to bank officer, including a special method of notification, taking the new officer to the officers' dining room for the first time, and the new officer buying drinks on Friday after his or her notification.[7] This is a rite of passage.
- Mary Kay Cosmetics Company holds elaborate awards ceremonies, presenting gold and diamond pins, furs, and pink Cadillacs to high-achieving sales consultants. The most successful consultants are introduced by film clips, such as the kind used to introduce award nominees in the entertainment industry. This is a rite of enhancement.
- An important annual event at McDonald's is the nationwide contest to determine the best hamburger cooking team in the country. The contest encourages all stores to reexamine the details of how they cook hamburgers. The ceremony is highly visible and communicates to all employees the McDonald's value of hamburger quality.[8] This is a rite of renewal.
- Whenever a Wal-Mart executive visits one of the stores, he or she leads employees in the Wal-Mart cheer: "Give me a W! Give me an A! Give me an L! Give me a squiggly! (all do a version of the twist) Give me an M! Give me an A! Give me an R! Give me a T! What's that spell? Wal-Mart! What's that spell? Wal-Mart! Who's No. 1? THE CUSTOMER!" The cheer strengthens bonds among employees and reinforces their commitment to common goals.[9] This is a rite of integration.

Stories. **Stories** are narratives based on true events that are frequently shared among organizational employees and told to new employees to inform them about an organization. Many stories are about company **heroes** who serve as models or ideals for serving cultural norms and values. Some stories are considered **legends** because the events are historic and may have been embellished with fictional details. Other stories are **myths**, which are consistent with the values and beliefs of the organization but are not supported by facts.[10] Stories keep alive the primary values of the organization and

EXHIBIT 7.2   *A Typology of Organizational Rites and Their Social Consequences*

Type of Rite	Example	Social Consequences
Passage	Induction and basic training, U.S. Army	Facilitate transition of persons into social roles and statuses that are new for them
Enhancement	Annual awards night	Enhance social identities and increase status of employees
Renewal	Organizational development activities	Refurbish social structures and improve organization functioning
Integration	Office Christmas party	Encourage and revive common feelings that bind members together and commit them to the organization

Source: Adapted from Harrison M. Trice and Janice M. Beyer, "Studying Organizational Cultures through Rites and Ceremonials," *Academy of Management Review* 9 (1984): 653–59. Used with permission.

provide a shared understanding among all employees. Examples of how stories shape culture are as follows:

- At 3M Corp., the story is told of a vice-president who was fired early in his career for persisting with a new product even after his boss had told him to stop because he thought it was a stupid idea. After the worker was fired, he stayed in an unused office, working without a salary on the new product idea. Eventually he was rehired, the product was a success, and he was promoted to vice-president. The story symbolizes the 3M value of persisting in what you believe in.[11]
- One FedEx story concerns a delivery person who had misplaced the key to a FedEx drop box. Rather than allow the packages to be late, the employee uprooted the box, put it in his delivery truck, and rushed it back to the sorting station, where they were able to pry it open and get the contents to their destination the following day.[12] By telling this story, FedEx workers communicate the importance of putting the customer first.

Symbols. Another tool for interpreting culture is the symbol. A symbol is something that represents another thing. In one sense, ceremonies, stories, slogans, and rites are all symbols. They symbolize deeper values of an organization. Another symbol is a physical artifact of the organization. Physical symbols are powerful because they focus attention on a specific item. Examples of physical symbols are as follows:

- Nordstrom department store symbolizes the importance of supporting lower-level employees with the organization chart in Exhibit 7.3. Nordstrom's is known for its extraordinary customer service, and the organization chart symbolizes that managers are to support the employees who give the service rather than be managers who control them.[13]
- At St. Luke's, a London advertising agency, the office layout symbolizes the company's commitment to values of openness, equality, flexibility, and creativity. There are no

EXHIBIT 7.3   *Organization Chart for Nordstrom, Inc.*

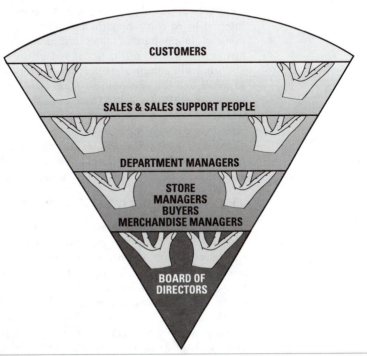

Source: Used with permission of Nordstrom, Inc.

individual desks and personal work spaces: teams gather in large, client-specific brand rooms to generate ideas for new accounts and store work in progress.[14]

Language. The final technique for influencing culture is **language**. Many companies use a specific saying, slogan, metaphor, or other form of language to convey special meaning to employees. Slogans can be readily picked up and repeated by employees as well as customers of the company. Bank One promotes its emphasis on customer service through the slogan, "Whatever it takes." Bank One's culture encourages employees to do whatever it takes to exceed customer expectations. Other significant uses of language to shape culture are as follows:

- At PeopleSoft Inc., which sells enterprise resource planning (ERP) software, employees call themselves PeoplePeople, shop at the company PeopleStore, and munch on company-funded PeopleSnacks. The use of this special lingo reinforces PeopleSoft's close-knit "family" culture.[15]
- T. J. Watson, Jr., son of the founder of International Business Machines, used the metaphor "wild ducks" to describe the type of employees needed by IBM. His point was, "You can make wild ducks tame, but you can never make tame ducks wild again."[16] Wild ducks symbolized the freedom and opportunity that must be available to keep from taming creative employees at IBM.

Recall that culture exists at two levels—the underlying values and assumptions and the visible artifacts and observable behaviors. The slogans, symbols, and ceremonies just described are artifacts that reflect underlying company values. These visible artifacts and behaviors can be used by managers to shape company values and to strengthen organizational culture.

ORGANIZATIONAL DESIGN AND CULTURE

Corporate culture should reinforce the strategy and structural design that the organization needs to be effective within its environment. For example, if the external environment requires flexibility and responsiveness, such as the environment for emerging Internet-based companies, the culture should encourage adaptability. The correct relationship among cultural values, organizational strategy and structure, and the environment can enhance organizational performance.

Studies of culture and effectiveness propose that the fit among culture, strategy and structure, and the environment is associated with four categories of culture, which are illustrated in Exhibit 7.4.[17] These categories are based on two factors: (1) the extent to which the competitive environment requires flexibility or stability, and (2) the extent to which the strategic focus and strength is internal or external. The four categories associated with these differences are adaptability/entrepreneurial, mission, clan, and bureaucratic. Each of the four cultures can be successful, depending on the needs of the external environment and the organization's strategic focus.

THE ADAPTABILITY/ENTREPRENEURIAL CULTURE

The **adaptability/entrepreneurial culture** is characterized by strategic focus on the external environment through flexibility and change to meet customer needs. The culture encourages norms and beliefs that support the capacity of the organization to detect, interpret, and translate signals from the environment into new behavior responses. This type of company, however, doesn't just react quickly to environmental changes—it actively creates change. Innovation, creativity, and risk-taking are valued and rewarded.

An example of the adaptability/entrepreneurial culture is 3M, a company whose values promote individual initiative and entrepreneurship. All new employees attend a class on risk-taking, where they are told to pursue their ideas even if it means defying their supervisors. Acxiom Corp., based in Conway, Arkansas, began changing to an

EXHIBIT 7.4   *Relationship of Environment and Strategy to Corporate Culture*

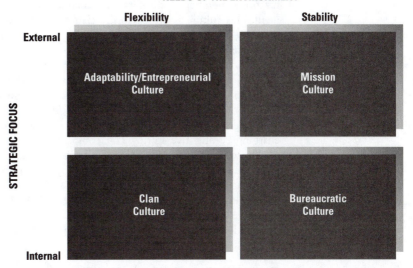

Source: Based on Daniel R. Denison and Aneil K. Mishra, "Toward a Theory of Organizational Culture and Effectiveness," *Organization Science* 6, no. 2 (March–April 1995): 204–23; R. Hooijberg and F. Petrock, "On Cultural Change: Using the Competing Values Framework to Help Leaders Execute a Transformational Strategy," *Human Resource Management* 32 (1993): 29–50; and R. E. Quinn, *Beyond Rational Management: Mastering the Paradoxes and Competing Demands of High Performance* (San Francisco: Jossey-Bass, 1988).

adaptability/entrepreneurial culture in the early 1990s. After years of rapid growth and an explosion of interest in data management products and services, managers discovered that the company's culture, which emphasized internal efficiency, consistency in following established rules and procedures, and top-down decision making, was no longer suitable to meet the demands of the rapidly changing environment. Acxiom shifted to an external focus emphasizing the importance of employee empowerment, flexibility, and initiative.[18] Most e-commerce companies, such as eBay, Drugstore.com and Buy.com, as well as companies in the marketing, electronics, and cosmetics industries, use this type of culture because they must move quickly to satisfy customers.

THE MISSION CULTURE

An organization concerned with serving specific customers in the external environment, but without the need for rapid change, is suited to the mission culture. The **mission culture** is characterized by emphasis on a clear vision of the organization's purpose and on the achievement of goals, such as sales growth, profitability, or market share, to help achieve the purpose. Individual employees may be responsible for a specified level of performance, and the organization promises specified rewards in return. Managers shape behavior by envisioning and communicating a desired future state for the organization. Because the environment is stable, they can translate the vision into measurable goals and evaluate employee performance for meeting them. In some cases, mission cultures reflect a high level of competitiveness and a profit-making orientation.

One example is PepsiCo, where former CEO Wayne Calloway set a vision to be the best consumer products company in the world. Managers who met the high performance standards were generously rewarded—first class air travel, fully loaded company cars, stock options, bonuses, and rapid promotion. Annual performance reviews focus specifically on meeting performance goals, such as sales targets or marketing goals.[19] Another example of a mission culture is Nucor Corp., a steel company with headquarters in Charlotte, North Carolina. Nucor keeps employees focused on bottom-line profits and long-term survival. It asks its managers to produce more steel for less money and rewards them well for doing so.[20]

THE CLAN CULTURE

The **clan culture** has a primary focus on the involvement and participation of the organization's members and on rapidly changing expectations from the external environment. This culture is similar to the clan form of control described in Chapter 6. More than any other, this culture focuses on the needs of employees as the route to high performance. Involvement and participation create a sense of responsibility and ownership and, hence, greater commitment to the organization.

SAS Institute, which produces statistical analysis software, is an example of a clan culture. The most important value is taking care of employees and making sure they have whatever they need to help them be satisfied as well as productive. Employees are encouraged to lead a balanced life rather than to work long hours and display a hard-charging competitive spirit. The company offers two Montessori day care centers, a 36,000 square-foot fitness center, unlimited sick days, an on-site health clinic, and live piano music in the cafeteria, where employees can eat with their families if they like.[21] By taking care of employees, SAS is able to adapt to competition and changing markets. The creativity of employees is highly valued at SAS, where more than 30 percent of revenues are plowed back into research and development. Companies in the fashion and retail industries also use this culture because it releases the creativity of employees to respond to rapidly changing tastes.

THE BUREAUCRATIC CULTURE

The **bureaucratic culture** has an internal focus and a consistency orientation for a stable environment. This organization has a culture that supports a methodical approach to doing business. Symbols, heroes, and ceremonies support cooperation, tradition, and following established policies and practices as a way to achieve goals. Personal involvement is somewhat lower here, but that is outweighed by a high level of consistency, conformity, and collaboration among members. This organization succeeds by being highly integrated and efficient.

One example of a bureaucratic culture is Safeco Insurance Company, considered by some to be stuffy and regimented. Employees take their coffee breaks at an assigned time, and the dress codes specify white shirts and suits for men and no beards. However, employees like this culture. Reliability counts. Extra work is not required. The culture is appropriate for the insurance company, which succeeds because it can be trusted to deliver on insurance policies as agreed.[22]

CULTURE STRENGTH AND ORGANIZATIONAL SUBCULTURES

A strong organizational culture can have a powerful impact on company performance. **Culture strength** refers to the degree of agreement among members of an organization about the importance of specific values. If widespread consensus exists about the importance of those values, the culture is cohesive and strong; if little agreement exists, the culture is weak.[23]

A strong culture is typically associated with the frequent use of ceremonies, symbols, stories, heroes, and slogans. These elements increase employee commitment to the desired values. In addition, managers who want to create and maintain strong corporate cultures often give emphasis to the selection and socialization of employees. For example, at Southwest Airlines, prospective employees are subjected to rigorous interviewing, sometimes even by Southwest's regular customers, so that only those who fit the culture are hired. At Trilogy Software, Inc., one of today's fastest-growing software companies, selection and socialization of new employees is a companywide mission.

However, culture is not always uniform throughout the organization. Even in organizations that have strong cultures, there may be several sets of subcultures, particularly within large organizations. **Subcultures** develop to reflect the common problems, goals, and experiences that members of a team, department, or other unit share. An office, branch, or unit of a company that is physically separated from the company's main operations may also take on a distinctive subculture.

For example, although the dominant culture of an organization may be a mission culture, various departments may also reflect characteristics of adaptability/ entrepreneurial, clan, or bureaucratic cultures. The manufacturing department of a large organization may thrive in an environment that emphasizes order, efficiency, and obedience to rules, whereas the research and development department may be characterized by employee empowerment, flexibility, and customer focus. This is similar to the concept of differentiation described in Chapter 4, where employees in manufacturing, sales, and research departments studied by Paul Lawrence and Jay Lorsch[24] developed different values with respect to time horizon, interpersonal relationships, and formality in order to perform the job of each particular department most effectively.

ETHICAL VALUES IN ORGANIZATIONS

Of the values that make up an organization's culture, ethical values are now considered among the most important. Ethical standards are becoming part of the formal policies and informal cultures of many organizations, and courses in ethics are taught in many business schools. **Ethics** is the code of moral principles and values that governs the behaviors of a person or group with respect to what is right or wrong. Ethical values set standards as to what is good or bad in conduct and decision making.[25]

Ethics is distinct from behaviors governed by law. The **rule of law** arises from a set of codified principles and regulations that describe how people are required to act, are generally accepted in society, and are enforceable in the courts.[26]

The relationship between ethical standards and legal requirements is illustrated in Exhibit 7.5. Ethical standards for the most part apply to behavior not covered by the law, and the rule of law covers behaviors not necessarily covered by ethical standards. Current laws often reflect combined moral judgments, but not all moral judgments are codified into law. The morality of aiding a drowning person, for example, is not specified by law, and driving on the righthand side of the road has no moral basis; but in areas such as robbery or murder, rules and moral standards overlap.

Unethical conduct in organizations is surprisingly widespread. More than 54 percent of human resource professionals polled by the Society for Human Resource Management and the Ethics Resource Center reported observing employees lying to supervisors or

EXHIBIT 7.5   *Relationship Between the Rule of Law and Ethical Standards*

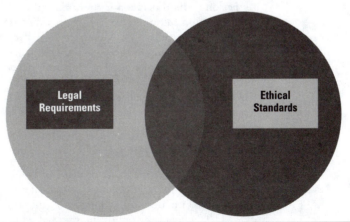

Source: LaRue Tone Hosmer, *The Ethics of Management,* 2d ed. (Homewood, Ill.: Irwin, 1991).

coworkers, falsifying reports or records, or abusing drugs or alcohol while on the job.[27] Many people believe that if you are not breaking the law, then you are behaving in an ethical manner, but ethics often go far beyond the law.[28] Many behaviors have not been codified, and managers must be sensitive to emerging norms and values about those issues. **Managerial ethics** are principles that guide the decisions and behaviors of managers with regard to whether they are right or wrong in a moral sense. The notion of **social responsibility** is an extension of this idea and refers to management's obligation to make choices and take action so that the organization contributes to the welfare and interest of society as well as to itself.[29]

Examples of the need for managerial ethics are as follows:[30]

- The supervisor of a travel agency was aware that her agents and she could receive large bonuses for booking one hundred or more clients each month with an auto rental firm, although clients typically wanted the rental agency selected on the basis of lowest cost.
- The executive in charge of a parts distribution facility told employees to tell phone customers that inventory was in stock even if it was not. Replenishing the item only took one to two days, no one was hurt by the delay, and the business was kept from competitors.
- The project manager for a consulting project wondered whether some facts should be left out of a report because the marketing executives paying for the report would look bad if the facts were reported.
- A North American manufacturer operating abroad was asked to make cash payments (a bribe) to government officials and was told it was consistent with local customs, despite being illegal in North America.

These issues are exceedingly difficult to resolve and often represent dilemmas. An **ethical dilemma** arises when each alternative choice or behavior seems undesirable because of a potentially negative ethical consequence. Right or wrong cannot be clearly identified. These choices can be aided by establishing ethical values within the organization as part of corporate culture. Corporate culture can embrace the ethical values needed for business success.

SOURCES OF ETHICAL VALUES IN ORGANIZATIONS

The standards for ethical or socially responsible conduct are embodied within each employee as well as within the organization itself. In addition, external stakeholders can influence standards of what is ethical and socially responsible. The immediate forces that impinge on ethical decisions are summarized in Exhibit 7.6. Individual beliefs and values, a person's ethical decision framework, and moral development influence personal ethics. Organization culture, as we have already discussed, shapes the overall framework of values within the organization. Moreover, formal organization systems influence values and behaviors according to the organization's policy framework and reward systems.

Companies also respond to numerous stakeholders in determining what is right. They consider how their actions may be viewed by customers, government agencies, shareholders, and the general community, as well as the impact each alternative course of action may have on various stakeholders. All of these factors can be explored to understand ethical decisions in organizations.[31]

PERSONAL ETHICS

Every individual brings a set of personal beliefs and values into the workplace. Personal values and the moral reasoning that translates these values into behavior are an important aspect of ethical decision making in organizations.[32]

The family backgrounds and spiritual values of managers provide principles by which they carry out business. In addition, people go through stages of moral development that

EXHIBIT 7.6   *Forces That Shape Managerial Ethics*

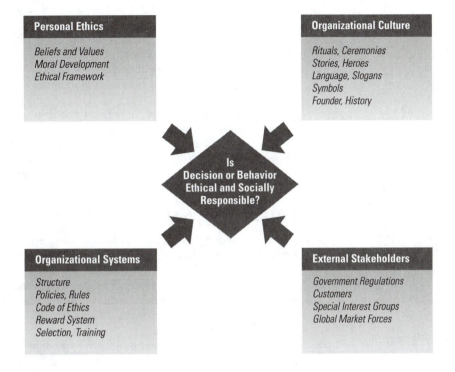

affect their ability to translate values into behavior. For example, children have a low level of moral development, making decisions and behaving to obtain rewards and avoid physical punishment. At an intermediate level of development, people learn to conform to expectations of good behavior as defined by colleagues and society. Most managers are at this level, willingly upholding the law and responding to societal expectations. At the highest level of moral development are people who develop an internal set of standards. These are self-chosen ethical principles that are more important to decisions than external expectations. Only a few people reach this high level, which can mean breaking laws if necessary to sustain higher moral principles.[33]

The other personal factor is whether managers have developed an *ethical framework* that guides their decisions. *Utilitarian theory*, for example, argues that ethical decisions should be made to generate the greatest benefits for the largest number of people. This framework is often consistent with business decisions because costs and benefits can be calculated in dollars. The *personal liberty* framework argues that decisions should be made to ensure the greatest possible freedom of choice and liberty for individuals. Liberties include freedom to act on one's conscience, free speech, due process, and the right to privacy. The *distributive justice* framework holds that moral decisions are those that promote equity, fairness, and impartiality with respect to the distribution of rewards and the administration of rules, which are essential for social cooperation.[34]

ORGANIZATIONAL CULTURE

Rarely can ethical or unethical business practices be attributed entirely to the personal ethics of a single individual. Because business practices reflect the values, attitudes, and behavior patterns of an organization's culture, ethics is as much an organizational issue as a personal one. To promote ethical behavior in the workplace, companies should make ethics an integral part of the organization's culture. At Certified Transmission Rebuilders, a small company based in Omaha, Nebraska, the culture is built on putting the customers' interests first. Employees receive ongoing in-house training to develop "honest communication" skills. Owner Peter Fink doesn't pay diagnosticians on commission because he doesn't want that to influence their decisions. Customers who have had their transmission repaired at Certified are asked to bring the car back in fifteen days for a free re-check to make sure everything is working right, even though the process is expensive and time-consuming. If Certified has to redo any work, it provides the customer with a rental car, plus the additional work, at no charge. Fink has built a highly successful business by giving customers the assurance that they're not paying for repairs they don't really need.[35]

One large company in which ethical standards are embedded in the organizational culture is Johnson & Johnson. Although the company's handling of the Tylenol poisoning incident has sometimes been attributed to the ethical standards of then-CEO James Burke, Burke himself has pointed out that the decisions in connection with that crisis reflected a set of values and principles that has been deeply ingrained throughout the company since its early days.[36]

ORGANIZATIONAL SYSTEMS

The third category of influences that shape managerial ethics is formal organizational systems. This includes the basic architecture of the organization, such as whether ethical values are incorporated in policies and rules; whether an explicit code of ethics is available and issued to members; whether organizational rewards, including praise, attention, and promotions, are linked to ethical behavior; and whether ethics is a consideration in the selection and training of employees. These formal efforts can reinforce ethical values that exist in the informal culture.

Today, more and more companies are establishing formal ethics programs. For example, after being maligned by the national press and pursued by federal officials for questionable billing practices and fraud, Columbia/HCA Healthcare Corp., an $18.8 billion hospital chain based in Nashville, Tennessee, brought in a new management team to clean up the mess and make sure similar ethical and legal problems never happen again. When he was hired as senior vice-president of ethics, compliance, and corporate responsibility, Alan R. Yuspeh found only a rudimentary compliance program and a set of perfunctory ethical guidelines that no one could understand. Yuspeh drafted a clear and concise code of conduct that emphasized the values of compassion, honesty, fairness, loyalty, respect, and kindness, then posted it on the intranet for comment from the company's entire work force. The final version was distributed to all 285,000 Columbia/HCA employees. In addition, Yuspeh developed a massive ethics program that includes comprehensive training for all employees and an ethics hotline that answers about 1,200 employee calls annually.[37]

EXTERNAL STAKEHOLDERS

Managerial ethics and social responsibility are also influenced by a variety of external stakeholders, groups outside the organization that have a stake in the organization's performance. Ethical and socially responsible decision making recognizes that the organization is part of a larger community and considers the impact of a decision or action on all stakeholders.[38] Important external stakeholders are government agencies, customers, special interest groups such as those concerned with the natural environment, and global market forces.

Companies must operate within the limits of certain government regulations, such as safety laws, environmental protection requirements, and many other laws and regulations. At Columbia/HCA, part of the training program is designed to make sure all employees are familiar with health care laws and regulations. Customers are concerned about the quality, safety, and availability of goods and services. For example, even though Dow Corning has an ambitious ethics program, the company's reputation as an ethical company was seriously damaged by the failure to keep customers satisfied with the safety of its silicone breast implants.[39]

Special interest groups continue to be one of the largest stakeholder concerns that companies face. Today, those concerned with corporate responsibility to the natural environment are particularly vocal. Thus, environmentalism is becoming an integral part of organizational planning and decision making for leading companies. The concept of *sustainable development*, a dual concern for economic growth and environmental sustainability, has been gaining ground among many business leaders. The public is no longer comfortable with organizations focusing solely on profit at the expense of the natural environment. Environmental sustainability—meaning that what is taken out of the environmental system for food, shelter, clothing, energy, and other human uses is restored to the system in waste that can be reused—is a part of strategy for companies like Monsanto, Interface, IKEA, Electrolux, Scandic Hotels, and MacMillan-Bloedel. Interface, the $1-billion leader in the floor covering industry, is instituting changes that will allow the company to manufacture without pollution, waste, or fossil fuels. CEO Ray Anderson is so committed to the concept of environmental sustainability that he had the following credo set in bronze at his newest factory: "If we are successful, then we will spend the rest of our days harvesting yesteryear's carpet and other petrochemically derived products, recycling them into new materials, converting sunlight into energy—with zero scrap going into the landfill and zero emissions going into the ecosystem. And we'll be doing well—very well—by doing good."[40]

Another growing pressure on organizations is related to the rapidly changing global market. Companies operating globally face difficult ethical issues. Thousands of U.S. workers have lost jobs or earning power because companies can get the same work done overseas for lower costs. For example, Yakima Products, located in Arcata, California, transferred all production of its cartop carrying systems for bikes, skis and other sporting gear to Mexico. Although the decision was financially sound and clearly served the interests of shareholders, employees and the local community felt angry and betrayed.[41] Levi Strauss contracted for low-cost labor in Burma and China but later felt ethically compelled to pull out of those contracts because of human rights violations in those countries. As the business world becomes increasingly global, issues of ethics and social responsibility will likely become even more difficult.[42]

SHAPING CULTURE AND ETHICS THROUGH STRUCTURE AND SYSTEMS

A report issued by the Business Roundtable—an association of chief executives from 250 large corporations—discussed ethics, policy, and practice in one hundred member companies, including GTE, Xerox, Johnson & Johnson, Boeing, and Hewlett-Packard.[43] In the experience of the surveyed companies, the single most important factor in ethical decision making was the role of top management in providing commitment, leadership, and example for ethical values. The CEO and other top managers must be committed to specific values and must give constant leadership in tending and renewing those values. Values can be communicated in a number of ways—speeches, company publications, policy statements, and, especially, personal actions. Top leaders are responsible for creating and sustaining a culture that emphasizes the importance of ethical behavior for all employees every day. When the CEO engages in unethical practices or fails to take firm and decisive action in response to the unethical practices of others, this attitude filters down through the organization. Formal ethics codes and training programs are worthless if leaders do not set and live up to high standards of ethical conduct.[44]

A set of tools leaders can use to shape cultural and ethical values is the formal structure and systems of the organization. These systems have been especially effective in recent years for influencing managerial ethics.

Structure. Managers can assign responsibility for ethical values to a specific position. This not only allocates organization time and energy to the problem but symbolizes to everyone the importance of ethics. One example is an **ethics committee**, which is a group of executives appointed to oversee company ethics. The committee provides rulings on questionable ethical issues and assumes responsibility for disciplining wrongdoers.

Many companies are setting up ethics offices that go beyond a "police" mentality to act more as counseling centers. Alfred C. Martinez, chairman and CEO of Sears, set up an ethics and business practices office as part of his efforts to revive the company. Martinez recognized that Sears's image had been severely damaged by an early-1990s scandal in the auto centers, where employees allegedly misled customers and charged them for unnecessary repairs in order to make larger commissions. The new ethics department promotes the values in Sears's code of conduct and deals with day-to-day ethical dilemmas, questions, and appeals for advice, focusing more on helping employees make the right choices than on punishing wrongdoers.[45]

Another example is an **ethics ombudsperson**, who is a single manager, perhaps with a staff, who serves as the corporate conscience. As work forces become more diverse and organizations continue to emphasize greater employee involvement, it is likely that more and more companies will assign ombudspersons to listen to grievances, investigate ethical complaints, and point out employee concerns and possible ethical abuses to top management. For the system to work, it is necessary for the person in this position to have direct access to the chairman or CEO, as does the corporate ombudsperson for Pitney Bowes.[46]

Disclosure Mechanisms. The ethics office, committee, or ombudsperson provides mechanisms for employees to voice concerns about ethical practices. One important function is to establish supportive policies and procedures about whistle-blowing. **Whistle-blowing** is employee disclosure of illegal, immoral, or illegitimate practices on the part of the organization.[47] One value of corporate policy is to protect whistle-blowers so they will not be transferred to lower-level positions or fired because of their ethical concerns. A policy can also encourage whistle-blowers to stay within the organization—for instance, to quietly blow the whistle to responsible managers.[48] Whistle-blowers have the option to stop organizational activities by going to newspaper or television reporters, but as a last resort.

Although whistle-blowing has become widespread in recent years, it is still risky for employees, who can lose their jobs or be ostracized by co-workers. Sometimes managers believe a whistle-blower is out of line and think they are acting correctly to fire or sabotage that employee. As ethical problems in the corporate world increase, many companies are looking for ways to protect whistle-blowers. In addition, calls are increasing for legal protection for those who report illegal or unethical business activities.[49]

When there are no protective measures, whistle-blowers suffer, and the company may continue its unethical or illegal practices. When Curtis Overall reported nearly two hundred broken screws at the bottom of a massive ice condenser system at TVA's Watts Bar nuclear plant, he thought he was just doing his job, making sure the primary safety system would work properly once the reactor was fired up. However, Overall lost his job and security clearance and endured an escalating series of threats, which eventually caused him to seek treatment for stress and depression. Although he eventually won his job back, he left again after a fake bomb was planted in his pickup truck. The Nuclear Regulatory Commission is still investigating the situation at Watts Bar.[50]

Code of Ethics. A study by the Center for Business Ethics found that 90 percent of *Fortune* 500 companies and almost half of all other companies have developed a corporate code of ethics.[51] The code clarifies company expectations of employee conduct and makes clear that the company expects its personnel to recognize the ethical dimensions of corporate behavior.

Some companies use broader values statements within which ethics is a part. These statements define ethical values as well as corporate culture and contain language about company responsibility, quality of product, and treatment of employees. A formal statement of values can serve as a fundamental organizational document that defines what the organization stands for and legitimizes value choices for employees.[52] United Technologies Corporation, GTE, and Liz Claiborne, Inc. have all established statements of cultural and ethical values. Northern Telecom's *Code of Business Conduct,* which is provided to all employees in booklet form and is also available on the Internet, is a set of standards and guidelines that illustrates how the company's core values and mission translate into ethical business practices.

A code of ethics states the values or behaviors that are expected as well as those that will not be tolerated or backed up by management's action. A code of ethics or larger values statement is an important tool in the management of organizational values.

Training Programs. To ensure that ethical issues are considered in daily decision making, companies can supplement a written code of ethics with employee training programs.[53] A recent survey showed that 45 percent of responding companies were including ethics training in employee seminars. At Sears, all managers receive literature on ethics, attend ethics training courses at Sears University, and annually re-sign a contract signifying their commitment to the company's code of conduct. Texas Instruments employees go through an eight-hour ethics training course, which includes case examples that give participants a chance to wrestle with ethical dilemmas. In addition, TI incorporates an ethics component into every training course it offers.[54]

In an important step, ethics programs also include frameworks for ethical decision making, such as the utilitarian approach described earlier in this chapter. Learning these frameworks helps managers act autonomously and still think their way through a difficult decision. In a few companies, managers are also taught about the stages of moral development, which helps to bring them to a high stage of ethical decision making. This training has been an important catalyst for establishing ethical behavior and integrity as critical components of strategic competitiveness.[55]

These formal systems and structures can be highly effective. However, they alone are not sufficient to build and sustain an ethical company. Leaders should integrate ethics into the organizational culture and support and renew ethical values through their words and actions.

DISCUSSION QUESTIONS

1. Describe observable symbols, ceremonies, dress, or other aspects of culture and the underlying values they represent for an organization where you have worked.
2. What might be some of the advantages of having several subcultures within an organization? The disadvantages?
3. Do you think a bureaucratic culture would be less employee-oriented than a clan culture? Discuss.
4. Discuss the differences among rites of enhancement, renewal, and integration.
5. Are you aware of a situation where either you or someone you know was confronted by an ethical dilemma, such as being encouraged to inflate an expense account? Do you think the person's decision was affected by individual moral development or by the accepted values within the company? Explain.
6. How do external stakeholders influence ethical decision making in an organization? Discuss why globalization has contributed to more complex ethical issues for today's organizations.
7. Codes of ethics have been criticized for transferring responsibility for ethical behavior from the organization to the individual employee. Do you agree? Do you think a code of ethics is valuable for an organization?

NOTES

1. Jeremy Kahn, "What Makes a Company Great?" *Fortune*, 26 October 1998, 218.
2. W. Jack Duncan, "Organizational Culture: 'Getting a Fix' on an Elusive Concept," *Academy of Management Executive* 3 (1989): 229–36; Linda Smircich, "Concepts of Culture and Organizational Analysis," *Administrative Science Quarterly* 28 (1983): 339–58; Andrew D. Brown and Ken Starkey, "The Effect of Organizational Culture on Communication and Information," *Journal of Management Studies* 31 no. 6 (November 1994): 807–28.
3. Edgar H. Schein, "Organizational Culture," *American Psychologist* 45 (February 1990): 109–19.
4. Harrison M. Trice and Janice M. Beyer, "Studying Organizational Cultures through Rites and Ceremonials," *Academy of Management Review* 9 (1984): 653–69; Janice M. Beyer and Harrison M. Trice, "How an Organization's Rites Reveal Its

Culture," *Organizational Dynamics* 15 (Spring 1987): 5–24; Steven P. Feldman, "Management in Context: An Essay on the Relevance of Culture to the Understanding of Organizational Change," *Journal of Management Studies* 23 (1986): 589–607; Mary Jo Hatch, "The Dynamics of Organizational Culture," *Academy of Management Review* 18 (1993): 657–93.

5. This discussion is based on Edgar H. Schein, *Organizational Culture and Leadership,* 2d ed. (Homewood, Ill.: Richard D. Irwin, 1992); John P. Kotter and James L. Heskett, *Corporate Culture and Performance* (New York: Free Press, 1992).

6. Charlotte B. Sutton, "Richness Hierarchy of the Cultural Network: The Communication of Corporate Values" (Unpublished manuscript, Texas A & M University, 1985); Terrence E. Deal and Allan A. Kennedy, "Culture: A New Look through Old Lenses," *Journal of Applied Behavioral Science* 19 (1983): 498–505.

7. Thomas C. Dandridge, "Symbols at Work" (Working paper, School of Business, State University of New York at Albany, 1978), 1.

8. Thomas J. Peters and Robert H. Waterman, Jr., *In Search of Excellence* (New York: Harper & Row, 1982).

9. Don Hellriegel and John W. Slocum, Jr., *Management,* 7th ed. (Cincinnati, Ohio: South-Western, 1996), 537.

10. Trice and Beyer, "Studying Organizational Cultures through Rites and Ceremonials."

11. Sutton, "Richness Hierarchy of the Cultural Network"; Deal and Kennedy, *Corporate Cultures.*

12. Matt Siegel, "The Perils of Culture Conflict," *Fortune,* 9 November 1998, 257-262; and *Blueprints for Service Quality: The Federal Express Approach, AMA Management Briefing* (New York: American Management Association Membership Publications Division, 1991), 29-30.

13. "FYI," *Inc.,* April 1991, 14.

14. Stevan Alburty, "The Ad Agency to End All Ad Agencies," *Fast Company* (December–January 1997); 116–24.

15. Quentin Hardy, "A Software Star Sees Its 'Family' Culture Turn Dysfunctional," *The Wall Street Journal,* 5 May 1999, A1, A12; and Paul Roberts, "We Are One Company, No Matter Where We Are," *Fast Company* (April–May 1998): 122–28.

16. Richard Ott, "Are Wild Ducks Really Wild: Symbolism and Behavior in the Corporate Environment" (Paper presented at the Northeastern Anthropological Association, March 1979).

17. Based on Daniel R. Denison, *Corporate Culture and Organizational Effectiveness* (New York: Wiley, 1990), 11–15; Daniel R. Denison and Aneil K. Mishra, "Toward a Theory of Organizational Culture and Effectiveness," *Organization Science* 6, no. 2 (March-April 1995): 204–23; R. Hooijberg and F. Petrock, "On Cultural Change: Using the Competing Values Framework to Help Leaders Execute a Transformational Strategy," *Human Resource Management* 32 (1993), 29–50; R. E. Quinn, *Beyond Rational Management: Mastering the Paradoxes and Competing Demands of High Performance* (San Francisco: Jossey-Bass, 1988).

18. Daintry Duffy, "Cultural Evolution," *CIO Enterprise,* Section 2, 15 January 1999, 44–50.

19. Brian Dumaine, "Those High Flying PepsiCo Managers," *Fortune,* 10 April 1989; L. Zinn, J. Berry, and G. Burns, "Will the Pepsi Brass Be Drinking Hemlock?" *Business Week,* 25 July 1994, 31; S. Lubove, "We Have a Big Pond to Play In," *Forbes,* 12 September 1993, 216–24; J. Wolfe, "PepsiCo and the Fast Food Industry," in M. A. Hitt, R. D. Ireland, and R.E. Hoskisson, eds., *Strategic Management: Competitiveness and Globalization* (St. Paul, Minn.: West Publishing, 1995), 856–79.

20. Kenneth F. Iverson with Tom Varian, "Plain Talk," *Inc.,* October 1997, 81-83.

21. Charles Fishman, "Sanity Inc.," *Fast Company* (January 1999): 85-96, and Sharon Overton, "And to All a Goodnight," *Sky* (October 1996): 37-40.

22. Carey Quan Jelernter, "Safeco: Success Depends Partly on Fitting the Mold," *Seattle Times,* 5 June 1986, D8.

23. Bernard Arogyaswamy and Charles M. Byles, "Organizational Culture: Internal and External Fits," *Journal of Management* 13 (1987): 647–59.

24. Paul R. Lawrence and Jay W. Lorsch, *Organization and Environment* (Homewood, Ill.: Irwin, 1969).

25. Gordon F. Shea, *Practical Ethics* (New York: American Management Association, 1988); Linda K. Treviño, "Ethical Decision Making in Organizations: A Person–Situation Interactionist Model," *Academy of Management Review* 11 (1986): 601–17; and Linda Klebe Treviño and Katherine A. Nelson, *Managing Business Ethics: Straight Talk About How to Do It Right,* 2nd ed. (New York: John Wiley & Sons, Inc. 1999).

26. LaRue Tone Hosmer, *The Ethics of Management,* 2d ed., (Homewood, Ill.: Irwin, 1991).

27. Geanne Rosenberg, "Truth and Consequences," *Working Woman,* July–August 1998, 79–80.

28. Dawn-Marie Driscoll, "Don't Confuse Legal and Ethical Standards," *Business Ethics,* July–August 1996, 44.

29. Eugene W. Szwajkowski, "The Myths and Realities of Research on Organizational Misconduct," in James E. Post, ed., *Research and Corporate Social Performance and Policy,* vol. 9 (Greenwich, Conn.: JAI Press, 1986), 103–22.

30. These incidents are from Hosmer, *The Ethics of Management.*

31. Linda Klebe Treviño, "A Cultural Perspective on Changing and Developing Organizational Ethics," in Richard Woodman and William Pasmore, eds., *Research and Organizational Change and Development,*

vol. 4 (Greenwich, Conn.: JAI Press, 1990); Lynn Sharp Paine, "Managing for Organizational Integrity," *Harvard Business Review* (March/April 1994), 106–17.

32. James Weber, "Exploring the Relationship between Personal Values and Moral Reasoning," *Human Relations* 46 (1993): 435–63.

33. L. Kohlberg, "Moral Stages and Moralization: The Cognitive-Developmental Approach," in T. Likona, ed., *Moral Development and Behavior: Theory, Research, and Social Issues* (New York: Holt, Rinehart & Winston, 1976).

34. Hosmer, *The Ethics of Management.*

35. Michael Barrier, "Doing the Right Thing," *Nation's Business,* March 1998, 33–38.

36. "James Burke: The Fine Art of Leadership," an interview with Barbara Ettorre, *Management Review* (October 1996): 13–16; Margaret Kaeter, "The 5th Annual Business Ethics Awards for Excellence in Ethics," *Business Ethics,* November– December 1993, 26–29.

37. Jennifer Bresnahan, "For Goodness Sake," *CIO Enterprise*, Section 2, 15 June 1999, 54–62.

38. David M. Messick and Max H. Bazerman, "Ethical Leadership and the Psychology of Decision Making," *Sloan Management Review* (Winter 1996): 9–22; Dawn-Marie Driscoll, "Don't Confuse Legal and Ethical Standards," *Business Ethics*, July–August 1996, 44.

39. Max B. E. Clarkson, "A Stakeholder Framework for Analyzing and Evaluating Corporate Social Performance," *Academy of Management Review* 20, no. 1 (1995): 92–117; and Linda Klebe Treviño and Katherine A. Nelson, *Managing Business Ethics*, 207.

40. Gwen Kinkead, "In the Future, People Like Me Will Go to Jail," *Fortune*, 24 May 1999, 190–200.

41. Howard Rothman, "A Growing Dilemma," *Business Ethics*, July–August 1996, 18–21.

42. Susan Gaines, "Growing Pains," *Business Ethics,* January–February 1996, 20–23.

43. *Corporate Ethics: A Prime Business Asset* (New York: The Business Round Table, February 1988).

44. Andrew W. Singer, "The Ultimate Ethics Test," *Across the Board*, March 1992, 19–22; Ronald B. Morgan,

"Self and Co-Worker Perceptions of Ethics and Their Relationships to Leadership and Salary," *Academy of Management Journal*, 36, no.1 (February 1993): 200–14; Joseph L. Badaracco, Jr. and Allen P. Webb, "Business Ethics: A View From the Trenches," *California Management Review* 37, no. 2 (Winter 1995): 8–28.

45. Bresnahan, "For Goodness Sake."

46. Justin Martin, "New Tricks for an Old Trade," *Across the Board,* June 1992, 40–44.

47. Janet P. Near and Marcia P. Miceli, "Effective Whistle-Blowing," *Academy of Management Review* 20, no. 3 (1995): 679–708.

48. Richard P. Nielsen, "Changing Unethical Organizational Behavior," *Academy of Management Executive* 3 (1989): 123–30.

49. Jene G. James, "Whistle-Blowing: Its Moral Justification," in Peter Madsen and Jay M. Shafritz, eds., *Essentials of Business Ethics* (New York: Meridian Books, 1990), 160–90; Janet P. Near, Terry Morehead Dworkin, and Marcia P. Miceli, "Explaining the Whistle-Blowing Process: Suggestions from Power Theory and Justice Theory," *Organization Science* 4 (1993): 393–411.

50. "Tiny Screws Cause Woes for TVA Whistle-Blower," *The Tennessean*, 21 December 1998, 3B.

51. Carolyn Wiley, "The ABC's of Business Ethics: Definitions, Philosophies, and Implementation," *IM* (January–February 1995): 22–27.

52. Carl Anderson, "Values-Based Management," *Academy of Management Executive* 11, no. 4 (1997): 25–46.

53. James Weber, "Institutionalizing Ethics into Business Organizations: A Model and Research Agenda," *Business Ethics Quarterly* 3 (1993): 419–36.

54. Mark Henricks, "Ethics in Action," *Management Review* (January 1995): 53–55; Dorothy Marcic, *Management and the Wisdom of Love* (San Francisco: Jossey-Bass, 1997); Beverly Geber, "The Right and Wrong of Ethics Offices," *Training,* October 1995, 102–18.

55. Susan J. Harrington, "What Corporate America Is Teaching about Ethics," *Academy of Management Executive* 5 (1991): 21–30.

CHAPTER 8

Innovation and Change

*T*oday, every organization must change to survive. New discoveries and inventions quickly replace standard ways of doing things. The pace of change is revealed in the fact that the parents of today's college-age students grew up without voice mail, compact discs, video games, debit cards, cellular phones, and laser checkout systems in supermarkets. The idea of communicating instantly with people around the world via the Internet was unimaginable to most people as recently as a decade ago. Managers look for ways to encourage innovation so their organizations can respond to changing circumstances. In addition, they search for techniques to help employees cope with rapid change.

PURPOSE OF THIS CHAPTER

This chapter will explore how organizations change and how managers direct the innovation and change process. The next section describes the difference between incremental and radical change, the four types of change—technology, product, structure, people—occurring in organizations, and how to manage change successfully. The organization structure and management approach for facilitating each type of change is then discussed. Management techniques for influencing both the creation and implementation of change are also covered.

THE STRATEGIC ROLE OF CHANGE

Every organization goes through periods of change. Sometimes, change is brought about because of forces outside the organization. At other times, managers within the company want to initiate major change or spur innovation, but they may not know how. To remain successful, organizations must embrace many types of change. Organizations that invest most of their time and resources in maintaining the status quo are unlikely to prosper in today's uncertain envrionment.[1] Depending on an organization's strategic needs and the demands of the external environment, managers may encourage innovation in one or more parts of the organization. They use a number of techniques to successfully implement change when and where it is needed.

STRATEGIC TYPES OF CHANGE

Managers can focus on four types of change within organizations to achieve strategic advantage. These four types of change are summarized in Exhibit 8.1 as products and services, strategy and structure, culture, and technology. We touched on overall leadership and organizational strategy in Chapter 2 and in the previous chapter on corporate culture. These factors provide an overall context within which the four types of change serve as a competitive wedge to achieve an advantage in the international environment. Each company has a unique configuration of products and services, strategy and structure, culture, and technologies that can be focused for maximum impact upon the company's chosen markets.[2]

Technology changes are changes in an organization's production process, including its knowledge and skill base, that enable distinctive competence. These changes are designed to make production more efficient or to produce greater volume. Changes in technology involve the techniques for making products or services. They include work methods, equipment, and work flow. For example, in a university, technology changes are changes in techniques for teaching courses. As another example, the British water and sewage company Anglia Water came up with an innovative way to use its existing technologies to devise a water efficiency recycling system called Waterwise, which allows households to use one-third less water. Anglia also adopted new information technology for disseminating technical knowledge throughout the organization.[3]

EXHIBIT 8.1   *The Four Types of Change Provide a Strategic Competitive Wedge*

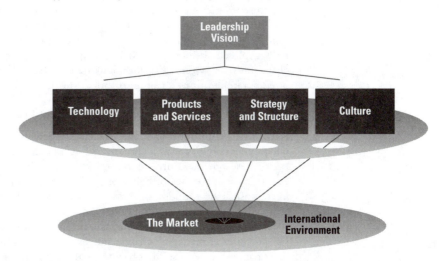

Source: Joseph E. McCann, "Design Principles for an Innovating Company," *Academy of Management Executive* 5 (May 1991): 76–93. Used by permission.

Product and service changes pertain to the product or service outputs of an organization. New products include small adaptations of existing products or entirely new product lines. New products are normally designed to increase the market share or to develop new markets, customers, or clients. When faced with intense foreign competition in the machine-tool business, Cincinnati Milacron transformed itself into a full-service industrial supplier, providing not only tools but all industrial plastics, fluids, and chemicals. Today, machine tools make up only about one-fourth of Milacron's total revenue base. The new products and services expanded the company's market and customer base, helping the 115-year-old organization survive while many of its counterparts in the machine-tool industry failed.[4]

Strategy and structure changes pertain to the administrative domain in an organization. The administrative domain involves the supervision and management of the organization. These changes include changes in organization structure, strategic management, policies, reward systems, labor relations, coordination devices, management information and control systems, and accounting and budgeting systems. Structure and system changes are usually top-down, that is, mandated by top management, whereas product and technology changes may often come from the bottom up. The structure was changed at Cincinnati Milacron when top executives formed "Wolfpack" teams, groups of engineers, managers, outside suppliers, and customers who work together to develop new products. A system change instituted by management in a university might be a new merit pay plan. Corporate downsizing is another example of top-down structure change.

Culture changes refer to changes in the values, attitudes, expectations, beliefs, abilities, and behavior of employees. Culture changes pertain to changes in how employees think; these are changes in mindset rather than technology, structure, or products. At Globe Metallurgical, a top supplier of specialty metals for the chemical and foundry industries, the old culture was marked by suspicion and distrust. Managers often dictated changes without consulting workers and sometimes shifted their approaches and policies abruptly. Globe transformed its culture to one that values employee empowerment and involvement, a new respect for management, and a new commitment to quality.[5]

The four types of changes in Exhibit 8.1 are interdependent—a change in one often means a change in another. A new product may require changes in the production technology, or a change in structure may require new employee skills. For example, when Shenandoah Life Insurance Company acquired new computer technology to process claims, the technology was not fully utilized until clerks were restructured into teams of five to seven members that were compatible with the technology. The structural change was an outgrowth of the technology change. In a manufacturing company, engineers introduced robots and advanced manufacturing technologies, only to find that the technology placed greater demands on employees. Upgrading employee skills required a change in wage systems. Organizations are interdependent systems, and changing one part often has implications for other organization elements.

ELEMENTS FOR SUCCESSFUL CHANGE

Regardless of the type or scope of change, there are identifiable stages of innovation, which generally occur as a sequence of events, though innovation stages may overlap.[6] In the research literature on innovation, **organizational change** is considered the adoption of a new idea or behavior by an organization.[7] **Organizational innovation**, in contrast, is the adoption of an idea or behavior that is new to the organization's industry, market, or general environment.[8] The first organization to introduce a new product is considered the innovator, and organizations that copy are considered to adopt changes. For purposes of managing change, however, the terms *innovation* and *change* will be used interchangeably because the **change process** within organizations tends to be identical whether a change is early or late with respect to other organizations in the environment.

Innovations typically are assimilated into an organization through a series of steps or elements. Organization members first become aware of a possible innovation, evaluate its appropriateness, and then evaluate and choose the idea.[9] The required elements of successful change are summarized in Exhibit 8.2. For a change to be successfully implemented, managers must make sure each element occurs in the organization. If one of the elements is missing, the change process will fail.

1. *Ideas.* Although creativity is a dramatic element of organizational change, creativity within organizations has not been widely and systematically studied. No company can remain competitive without new ideas; change is the outward expression of those

EXHIBIT 8.2   *Sequence of Elements for Successful Change*

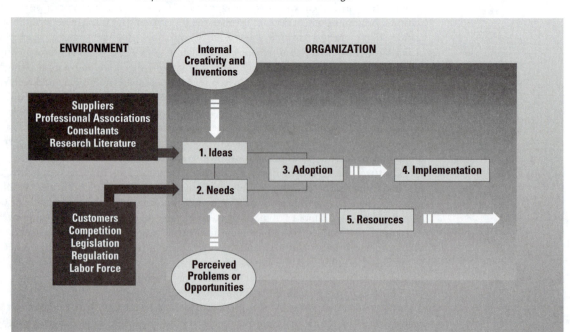

ideas.[10] An idea is a new way of doing things. It may be a new product or service, a new management concept, or a new procedure for working together in the organization. Ideas can come from within or from outside the organization.

2. *Need.* Ideas are generally not seriously considered unless there is a perceived need for change. A perceived need for change occurs when managers see a gap between actual performance and desired performance in the organization. Managers try to establish a sense of urgency so that others will understand the need for change. Sometimes a crisis provides an undoubted sense of urgency. For example, Midwest Contract Furnishings, a small firm that designs and fabricates hotel interiors, faced a crisis when its largest customer, Renaissance Hotels, was sold to Marriott, which did interior designing in-house. Midwest lost 80 percent of its revenues virtually overnight.[11] In many cases, however, there is no crisis, so managers have to recognize a need and communicate it to others.[12] In addition, although many ideas are generated to meet perceived needs, innovative companies encourage the constant development of new ideas that may stimulate consideration of problems or new opportunities.

3. *Adoption.* Adoption occurs when decision makers choose to go ahead with a proposed idea. Key managers and employees need to be in agreement to support the change. For a major organizational change, the decision might require the signing of a legal document by the board of directors. For a small change, adoption might occur with informal approval by a middle manager. When Ray Kroc was CEO of McDonald's, he made the adoption decision about innovations such as the Big Mac and Egg McMuffin.

4. *Implementation.* Implementation occurs when organization members actually use a new idea, technique, or behavior. Materials and equipment may have to be acquired, and workers may have to be trained to use the new idea. Implementation is a very important step because without it, previous steps are to no avail. Implementation of change is often the most difficult part of the change process. Until people use the new idea, no change has actually taken place.

5. *Resources.* Human energy and activity are required to bring about change. Change does not happen on its own; it requires time and resources, for both creating and implementing a new idea. Employees have to provide energy to see both the need and the idea to meet that need. Someone must develop a proposal and provide the time and effort to implement it.

   3M has an unwritten but widely understood rule that its 8,300 researchers can spend up to 15 percent of their time working on any idea of their choosing, without management approval. Most innovations go beyond ordinary budget allocations and require special funding. At 3M, exceptionally promising ideas become "pacing programs" and receive high levels of funding for further development. Some companies use task forces, as described in Chapter 3, to focus resources on a change. Others set up seed funds or venture funds that employees with promising ideas can tap into. Fluke Corporation, which manufactures electronic testing devices, creates teams of workers and gives them a hundred days and $100,000 to generate proposals for new business opportunities.[13]

One point about Exhibit 8.2 is especially important. Needs and ideas are listed simultaneously at the beginning of the change sequence. Either may occur first. Many organizations adopted the computer, for example, because it seemed a promising way to improve efficiency. Today's search for a vaccine against the AIDS virus, on the other hand, was stimulated by a severe need. Whether the need or the idea occurs first, for the change to be accomplished, each of the steps in Exhibit 8.2 must be completed.

TECHNOLOGY CHANGE

In today's business world, any company that isn't constantly developing, acquiring, or adapting new technology will likely be out of business in a few years. However, organizations face a contradiction when it comes to technology change, for the conditions that promote new ideas are not generally the best for implementing those ideas for routine production. An innovative organization is characterized by flexibility, empowered employees, and the absence of rigid work rules.[14] As discussed earlier in this book, an organic, free-flowing organization is typically associated with change and is considered the best organization form for adapting to a chaotic environment.

The flexibility of an organic organization is attributed to people's freedom to create and introduce new ideas. Organic organizations encourage a bottom–up innovation process. Ideas bubble up from middle- and lower-level employees because they have the freedom to propose ideas and to experiment. A mechanistic structure, on the other hand, stifles innovation with its emphasis on rules and regulations, but it is often the best structure for efficiently producing routine products. The challenge for organizations is to create both organic and mechanistic conditions within organizations to achieve both innovation and efficiency. To achieve both aspects of technological change, many organizations use the ambidextrous approach.

THE AMBIDEXTROUS APPROACH

Recent thinking has refined the idea of organic versus mechanistic structures with respect to innovation creation versus innovation utilization. For example, sometimes an organic structure generates innovative ideas but is not the best structure for using those ideas.[15] In other words, the initiation and the utilization of change are two distinct processes. Organic characteristics such as decentralization and employee freedom are excellent for initiating ideas; but these same conditions often make it hard to use a change because employees are less likely to comply. Employees can ignore the innovation because of decentralization and a generally loose structure.

How does an organization solve this dilemma? One approach is for the organization to be **ambidextrous**—to incorporate structures and management processes that are appropriate to both the creation and use of innovation.[16] The organization can behave in an organic way when the situation calls for the initiation of new ideas and in a mechanistic way to implement and use the ideas.

An example of the ambidextrous approach is the Freudenberg-NOK auto-parts factory in Ligonier, Indiana. Shifting teams of twelve, including plant workers, managers, and outsiders, each spend three days creating ideas to cut costs and boost productivity in various sections of the plant. At the end of the three days, team members go back to their regular jobs, and a new team comes in to look for even more improvements. Over a year's time, there are approximately forty of these GROWTTH (Get Rid of Waste Through Team Harmony) teams roaming through the sprawling factory. Management has promised that no one will be laid off as a result of suggestions from GROWTTH teams, which further encourages employees to both create and use innovations.[17]

TECHNIQUES FOR ENCOURAGING TECHNOLOGY CHANGE

Freudenberg–NOK has created both organic and mechanistic conditions in the factory. Some of the techniques used by many companies to maintain an ambidextrous approach are switching structures, separate creative departments, venture teams, and corporate entrepreneurship.

Switching Structures. Switching structures means an organization creates an organic structure when such a structure is needed for the initiation of new ideas.[18] Some of the ways organizations have switched structures to achieve the ambidextrous approach are as follows.

- Philips Corporation, a building materials producer based in Ohio, each year creates up to 150 transient teams—made up of members from various departments—to develop ideas for improving Philips products. After five days of organic brainstorming and problem solving, the company reverts to a more mechanistic basis to implement the changes.[19]

- Gardetto's, a family-run snack-food business, sends small teams of workers to Eureka Ranch, where they may engage in a Nerf gun battle to set the tone for fun and freedom, then participate in brainstorming exercises with the idea of generating as many new ideas as possible by the end of the day. Doug Hall, who runs Eureka Ranch, uses cans of baked beans, bags of cookies, and competitors' snack foods to stimulate ideas. After two and a half days, the group returns to the regular organizational structure to put the best of the ideas into action.[20]
- Xerox Corporation's Palo Alto Research Center (PARC) is purposely isolated from the corporation's bureaucracy and is staffed with mavericks not afraid to break the rules. John Seely Brown, Xerox's director of research, encourages his researchers to make trouble and upset conventional thinking. Xerox, which counts on the free thinkers at PARC for new insights, new solutions, and sometimes even entirely new businesses, knows that it is easy for maverick ideas to get trampled in the traditional organization.[21]
- The NUMMI plant, a Toyota subsidiary located in Fremont, California, creates a separate, organically organized cross-functional subunit, called the Pilot Team, to design production processes for new car and truck models. When the model they are preparing moves into production, workers return to their regular jobs on the shop floor.[22]

Each of these organizations found creative ways to be ambidextrous, establishing organic conditions for developing new ideas in the midst of more mechanistic conditions for implementing and using those ideas.

Creative Departments. In many large organizations the initiation of innovation is assigned to separate **creative departments**.[23] Staff departments, such as research and development, engineering, design, and systems analysis, create changes for adoption in other departments. Departments that initiate change are organically structured to facilitate the generation of new ideas and techniques. Departments that use those innovations tend to have a mechanistic structure more suitable for efficient production. Exhibit 8.3 indicates how one department is responsible for creation and another department implements the innovation.

Raytheon's New Products Center, in operation for thirty years, illustrates how creativity and entrepreneurial spirit can coexist with discipline and controls. The center has been responsible for many technical innovations, including industry-leading combination ovens, which added microwave capabilities to conventional stoves. The New Products Center provides autonomy and freedom for staff to explore new ideas, yet staff must also establish a working relationship with other departments so that innovations meet a genuine need for Raytheon departments.[24]

Venture Teams. Venture teams are a recent technique used to give free rein to creativity within organizations. Venture teams are often given a separate location and facili-

EXHIBIT 8.3   *Division of Labor Between Departments to Achieve Changes in Technology*

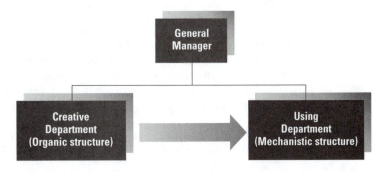

ties so they are not constrained by organizational procedures. Dow Chemical created an innovation department that has virtually total license to establish new venture projects for any department in the company. DataCard Corp, which makes products that are critical to the creation of bank cards, ID cards, and smart cards, provides teams with the autonomy and resources to develop start-up business plans, which are then presented to the board of directors for venture funding. At 3M, venture teams are referred to as *action teams*. An employee with a promising new product idea is allowed to recruit team members from throughout the company. These people may end up running the newly created division if the idea is successful.[25] Action teams and venture teams are kept small so they have autonomy and no bureaucracy emerges.

A venture team is like a small company within a large company. Monsanto, Levi Strauss, and Exxon have all used the venture team concept to free creative people from the bureaucracy of a large corporation. Most large companies that have successfully created e-commerce divisions have set them up like venture firms so they have the freedom to explore and develop emerging technologies. For example, Provident American Life & Health CEO Al Clemens set up a separate online company called Health-Axis.com, which became the Web's first full-service insurance agency. The venture was so successful that Provident American eventually shed its bricks-and-mortar operations and moved its entire business into cyberspace.[26]

A variation of the venture team concept is the **new-venture fund**, which provides financial resources for employees to develop new ideas, products, or businesses. In order to tap into its employees' entrepreneurial urges, Lockheed Martin allows workers to take up to two years' unpaid leave to explore a new idea, using company labs and equipment and paying company rates for health insurance. If the idea is successful, the corporation's venture fund invests around $250,000 in the start-up company. One successful start-up is Genase, which created an enzyme that "stonewashes" denim.[27]

Corporate Entrepreneurship. Corporate entrepreneurship attempts to develop an internal entrepreneurial spirit, philosophy, and structure that will produce a higher than average number of innovations.[28] Corporate entrepreneurship may involve the use of creative departments and new venture teams as described above, but it also attempts to release the creative energy of all employees in the organization. The most important outcome is to facilitate **idea champions** which go by a variety of names, including advocate, intrapreneur, or change agent. Idea champions provide the time and energy to make things happen. They fight to overcome natural resistance to change and to convince others of the merit of a new idea.[29] Peter Drucker suggests that idea champions need not be within the organization, and that fostering potential idea champions among regular customers can be a highly successful approach.[30] At Anglia Water, every innovation project has a sponsor or champion who is a customer seeking a solution to a specific problem.[31] The importance of the idea champion is illustrated by a fascinating fact discovered by Texas Instruments: When TI reviewed fifty successful and unsuccessful technical projects, it discovered that every failure was characterized by the absence of a volunteer champion. There was no one who passionately believed in the idea, who pushed the idea through all the necessary obstacles to make it work. Texas Instruments took this finding so seriously that now its number one criterion for approving new technical projects is the presence of a zealous champion.[32]

Companies encourage idea champions by providing freedom and slack time to creative people. IBM and General Electric allow employees to develop new technologies without company approval. Known as *bootlegging*, the unauthorized research often pays big dividends. As one IBM executive said, "We wink at it. It pays off. It's just amazing what a handful of dedicated people can do when they are really turned on."[33]

Idea champions usually come in two types. The **technical** or **product champion** is the person who generates or adopts and develops an idea for a technological innovation and is devoted to it, even to the extent of risking position or prestige. The **management champion** acts as a supporter and sponsor to shield and promote an idea within the organization.[34] The management champion sees the potential application and has the prestige and authority to get it a fair hearing and to allocate resources to it. Technical and management champions often work together because a technical idea will have a greater chance of success if a manager can be found to sponsor it. At Black & Decker, Peter Chaconas is a technical champion. He invented the Piranha circular saw blade, which is a best-selling tool accessory. Next, he invented the Bullet, which is a bit for home power drills and is the first major innovation in this product in almost one hundred years. Chaconas works full time designing products and promoting their acceptance. Randy Blevins, his boss, acts as management champion for Chaconas's ideas.[35]

NEW PRODUCTS AND SERVICES

Many of the concepts described for technology change are also relevant to the creation of new products and services. However, in many ways, new products and services are a special case of innovation because they are used by customers outside the organization. Since new products are designed for sale in the environment, uncertainty about the suitability and success of an innovation is very high.

NEW PRODUCT SUCCESS RATE

Research has explored the enormous uncertainty associated with the development and sale of new products.[36] To understand what this uncertainty can mean to organizations, just consider such flops as RCA's VideoDisc player, which lost an estimated $500 million, or Time Incorporated's *TV-Cable Week*, which lost $47 million. Producing new products that fail is a part of business in all industries. Organizations take the risk because product innovation is one of the most important ways companies adapt to changes in markets, technologies, and competition.[37]

Experts estimate that about 80 percent of new products fail upon introduction and another 10 percent disappear within five years. Considering that it costs $20 million to $50 million to successfully launch a new product, new product development is a risky, high-stakes game for organizations. Nevertheless, more than 25,000 new products appeared in 1998 alone, including more than 5,000 new toys.[38]

A survey some years ago examined two hundred projects in nineteen chemical, drug, electronics, and petroleum laboratories to learn about success rates. To be successful, the new product had to pass three stages of development: technical completion, commercialization, and market success. The findings about success rates are given in Exhibit 8.4. On the average, only 57 percent of all projects undertaken in the R&D laboratories achieved technical objectives, which means all technical problems were solved and the projects moved on to production. Of all projects that were started, however, less than one-third (31 percent) were fully marketed and commercialized. Several projects failed at this stage because production estimates or test market results were unfavorable.

Finally, only 12 percent of all projects originally undertaken achieved economic success. Most of the commercialized products did not earn sufficient returns to cover the cost of development and production. This means that only about one project in eight returned a profit to the company.

EXHIBIT 8.4   *Probability of New Product Success*

	Probability
Technical completion (technical objectives achieved)	.57
Commercialization (full-scale marketing)	.31
Market success (earns economic returns)	.12

Source: Based on Edwin Mansfield, J. Rapaport, J. Schnee, S. Wagner, and M. Hamburger, *Research and Innovation in Modern Corporations* (New York: Norton, 1971), 57.

REASONS FOR NEW PRODUCT SUCCESS

The next question to be answered by research was, "Why are some products more successful than others?" Why did a product such as Frappuccino succeed in the marketplace while those such as Miller Clear Beer and Frito-Lay's lemonade failed? Further studies indicated that innovation success was related to collaboration between technical and marketing departments. Successful new products and services seemed to be technologically sound and also carefully tailored to customer needs.[39] A study called Project SAPPHO examined seventeen pairs of new product innovations, with one success and one failure in each pair, and concluded the following.

1. Successful innovating companies had a much better understanding of customer needs and paid much more attention to marketing.
2. Successful innovating companies made more effective use of outside technology and outside advice, even though they did more work in-house.
3. Top management support in the successful innovating companies was from people who were more senior and had greater authority.

Thus, there is a distinct pattern of tailoring innovations to customer needs, making effective use of technology, and having influential top managers support the project. These ideas taken together indicate that the effective design for new product innovation is associated with horizontal linkage across departments.

HORIZONTAL LINKAGE MODEL

The organization design for achieving new product innovation involves three components—departmental specialization, boundary spanning, and horizontal linkages. These components are similar to the information linkage mechanisms in Chapter 3 and the differentiation and integration ideas in Chapter 4. Exhibit 8.5 illustrates these components in the **horizontal linkage model**.

Specialization. The key departments in new product development are R&D, marketing, and production. The specialization component means that the personnel in all three of these departments are highly competent at their own tasks. The three departments are differentiated from each other and have skills, goals, and attitudes appropriate for their specialized functions.

EXHIBIT 8.5   *Horizontal Linkage Model for New Product Innovations*

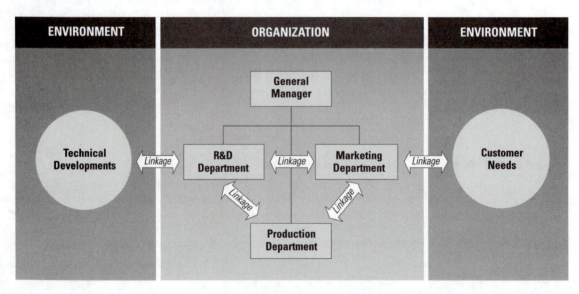

Boundary Spanning. This component means each department involved with new products has excellent linkage with relevant sectors in the external environment. R&D personnel are linked to professional associations and to colleagues in other R&D departments. They are aware of recent scientific developments. Marketing personnel are closely linked to customer needs. They listen to what customers have to say, and they analyze competitor products and suggestions by distributors. For example, Kimberly-Clark had amazing success with Huggies Pull-Ups because marketing researchers worked closely with customers in their own homes and recognized the emotional appeal of pull-on diapers for toddlers. By the time competitors caught on, Kimberly-Clark was selling $400 million worth of Huggies annually.[40]

Horizontal Linkages. This component means that technical, marketing, and production people share ideas and information. Research people inform marketing of new technical developments to learn whether the developments are applicable to customers. Marketing people provide customer complaints and information to R&D to use in the design of new products. People from both R&D and marketing coordinate with production because new products have to fit within production capabilities so costs are not exorbitant. The decision to launch a new product is ultimately a joint decision among all three departments.

At General Electric, members of the R&D department have a great deal of freedom to imagine and invent, and then they have to shop their ideas around other departments and divisions, sometimes finding applications for new technologies that are far from their original intentions. As a result, one study shows that of 250 technology products GE undertook to develop over a four-year period, 150 of them produced major applications, far above the U.S. average.[41] Famous innovation failures—such as McDonald's Arch Deluxe, the Apple Newton, RJR Nabisco's Premier smokeless cigarettes, and Gerber's Singles, a line of meals for adults—usually violate the horizontal linkage model. Employees fail to connect with customer needs, or internal departments fail to adequately share needs and coordinate with one another.

Companies are increasingly using cross-functional teams for product development to ensure a high level of communication and coordination from the beginning. The functional diversity increases both the amount and the variety of information for new product development, enabling the design of products that meet customer needs and circumventing manufacturing and marketing problems.[42] Kellogg has revised its approach to new product development to improve horizontal collaboration. For years, product development at Kellogg was the exclusive province of marketing, which came up with new ideas and then tossed them over the wall to manufacturing. Today, however, employees work in cross-functional teams, with market researchers alongside nutritionists, food scientists, production specialists, and engineers. So far, the approach seems to be working. The company is pumping out twice as many products annually, including some decided hits, such as Raisin Bran Crunch and Rice Krispies Treats, a snack-food version of the crunchy marshmallow squares.[43]

Companies such as Kellogg and General Electric are using the horizontal linkage model to achieve competitive advantage in today's global marketplace.

ACHIEVING COMPETITIVE ADVANTAGE WITH RAPID PRODUCT INNOVATION

For many companies, creating new products is a critical way to adapt and survive in a rapidly changing environment.[44] Getting new products to market fast and developing products that can compete in a competitive international market are key issues for companies like Xerox, 3M, and Levi Strauss. One authority on time-based competition has said that the old paradigm for success—"provide the most value for the least cost"—has been updated to "provide the most value for the least cost in the least elapsed time."[45]

To gain business, companies are learning to develop new products and services incredibly fast. Whether the approach is called the horizontal linkage model, concurrent engineering, companies without walls, the parallel approach, or simultaneous coupling of departments, the point is the same—get people working together simultaneously on a project rather than in sequence. Many companies are learning to sprint to market with new products.

Hewlett-Packard has made speed a top priority, getting products out the door twice as fast and urging employees to rethink every process in terms of speed. A printer that once took fifty-four months to develop is now on the market in twenty-two. Speed is becoming a major competitive issue and requires the use of cross-functional teams and other horizontal linkages.[46]

Another critical issue is designing products that can compete on a global scale and successfully marketing those products internationally. Companies such as Quaker Oats, Häagen Dazs, and Levi's are trying to improve horizontal communication and collaboration across geographical regions, recognizing that they can pick up winning product ideas from customers in other countries. A new Häagen Dazs flavor, *dulce de leche*, developed primarily for sale in Argentina, has quickly become a favorite in the United States, with sales growing by about 27 percent monthly.[47] Ford has boosted its global competitiveness by using its intranet and global teleconferencing to link car design teams around the world into a single unified group. Black & Decker has also been redesigning its product development process to become a stronger international player. To make global product development faster and more effective, new products are developed by cross-functional project delivery teams, which are answerable to a global business unit team.[48]

Failing to pay attention to global horizontal linkages can hurt companies trying to compete internationally. The Dutch giant Philips Electronics NV was certain its compact disk interactive player called The Imagination Machine would be a hit in the crucial U.S. market, and ultimately, the rest of the world. Five years later, the product, which was promoted as an interactive teaching aid and was so complex it required a thirty-minute sales demonstration, had all but disappeared from the shelves. Marketing employees, salespeople, and major customers had crucial information that would have helped Philips understand the U.S. market, but by the time the executives gathered the information and tried to change course, it was too late. "We should have done things differently," said one Philips executive. "The world isn't as easy as it seems."[49] When companies enter the arena of intense international competition, horizontal coordination across countries is essential to new product development.

STRATEGY AND STRUCTURE CHANGE

The preceding discussion focused on new production processes and products, which are based in the technology of an organization. The expertise for such innovation lies within the technical core and professional staff groups, such as research and engineering. This section turns to an examination of structural and strategy changes.

All organizations need to make changes in their strategies and structures from time to time. In the past, when the environment was relatively stable, most organizations focused on small, incremental changes to solve immediate problems or take advantage of new opportunities. However, over the past decade, companies throughout the world have faced the need to make radical changes in strategy, structure, and management processes to adapt to new competitive demands.[50] Many organizations are cutting out layers of management and decentralizing decision making. There is a strong shift toward more horizontal structures, with teams of front-line workers empowered to make decisions and solve problems on their own. Some companies are moving their entire business into cyberspace. Many others are reorganizing and shifting their strategies as the expansion of e-commerce changes the rules. For example, online banking, credit cards, and ATMs are affecting the role of branch banks. Global competition and rapid technological change will likely lead to even greater strategy-structure realignments over the next decade.

These types of changes are the responsibility of the organization's top managers, and the overall process of change is typically different from the process for innovation in technology or new products.

THE DUAL-CORE APPROACH

The dual-core approach compares administrative and technical changes. Administrative changes pertain to the design and structure of the organization itself, including restructuring, downsizing, teams, control systems, information systems, and departmental grouping. Research into administrative change suggests two things. First, administrative changes occur less frequently than do technical changes. Second, administrative changes occur in response to different environmental sectors and follow a different internal process than do technology-based changes.[51] The **dual-core approach** to organizational change identifies the unique processes associated with administrative change.[52]

Organizations—schools, hospitals, city governments, welfare agencies, government bureaucracies, and many business firms—can be conceptualized as having two cores: a technical core and an administrative core. Each core has its own employees, tasks, and environmental domain. Innovation can originate in either core.

The administrative core is above the technical core in the hierarchy. The responsibility of the administrative core includes the structure, control, and co-ordination of the organization itself and concerns the environmental sectors of government, financial resources, economic conditions, human resources, and competitors. The technical core is concerned with the transformation of raw materials into organizational products and services and involves the environmental sectors of customers and technology.[53]

The findings from research comparing administrative and technical change suggest that a mechanistic organization structure is appropriate for frequent administrative changes, including changes in goals, strategy, structure, control systems, and personnel.[54] For example, administrative changes in policy, regulations, or control systems are more critical than technical changes in many government organizations that are bureaucratically structured. Organizations that successfully adopt many administrative changes often have a larger administrative ratio, are larger in size, and are centralized and formalized compared with organizations that adopt many technical changes.[55] The reason is the top-down implementation of changes in response to changes in the government, financial, or legal sectors of the environment. In contrast, if an organization has an organic structure, lower-level employees have more freedom and autonomy and, hence, may resist top-down initiatives. An organic structure is more often used when changes in organizational technology or products are important to the organization.

The innovation approaches associated with administrative versus technical change are summarized in Exhibit 8.6. Technical change, such as changes in production techniques and innovation technology for new products, is facilitated by an organic structure, which allows ideas to bubble upward from lower- and middle-level employees. Organizations that must adopt frequent administrative changes tend to use a top-down process and a mechanistic structure. For example, policy changes, such as the adoption of tough no-smoking policies by companies like Park Nicollet Medical Center in Minnesota, are facilitated by a top-down approach. Downsizing and restructuring are nearly always managed top down, such as when Raymond Lane, president of Oracle Corp., split the sales force into two teams (one focused on selling database software and the other on selling applications), cut out two levels of management, and placed himself directly in charge of U.S. sales.[56]

The point of the dual-core approach is that many organizations—especially not-for-profit and government organizations—must adopt frequent administrative changes, so a mechanistic structure may be appropriate. For example, research into civil service reform found that the implementation of administrative innovation was extremely difficult in organizations that had an organic technical core. The professional employees in a decentralized agency could resist civil service changes. By contrast, organizations that were considered more bureaucratic in the sense of high formalization and centralization adopted administrative changes readily.[57]

What about business organizations that are normally technologically innovative in bottom-up fashion but suddenly face a crisis and need to reorganize? Or consider a technically innovative, high-tech firm that must reorganize frequently or must suddenly cut back to accommodate changes in production technology or the environment. Technically innovative

EXHIBIT 8.6   *Dual-Core Approach to Organization Change*

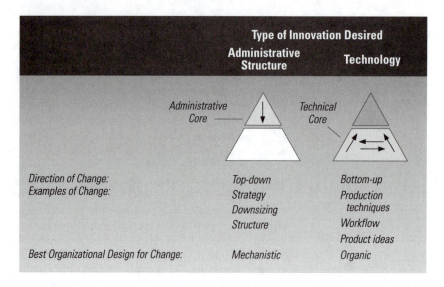

firms may suddenly have to restructure, reduce the number of employees, alter pay systems, disband teams, or form a new division.[58] The answer is to use a top-down change process. The authority for strategy and structure change lies with top management, who should initiate and implement the new strategy and structure to meet environmental circumstances. Employee input may be sought, but top managers have the responsibility to direct the change. *Downsizing, restructuring*, and *reorganizing* are common terms for what happens in times of rapid change and global competition. Often, strong top-down changes follow the installation of new top management. For example, when Carol Bartz first arrived at Autodesk, Inc., a leading software company, she introduced a first for the company: a management hierarchy. Autodesk had always been an organic organization, but Bartz believed a more mechanistic approach was needed to revive profits and get the struggling company back on track. She recognized that a top-down change process was needed to develop new goals and strategies and firmly direct the restructuring needed to help Autodesk survive.[59] Changes such as restructuring and downsizing can often be painful for employees, so top managers should move quickly and authoritatively to make both as humane as possible.[60]

Top managers should also remember that top-down change means initiation of the idea occurs at upper levels and is implemented downward. It does not mean that lower-level employees are not educated about the change or allowed to participate in it.

CULTURE CHANGE

Organizations are made up of people and their relationships with one another. Changes in strategy, structure, technologies, and products do not happen on their own, and changes in any of these areas involve changes in people as well. Employees must learn how to use new technologies, or market new products, or work effectively in a team-based structure.

In a world where any organization can purchase new technology, the motivation, skill, and commitment of employees can provide the competitive edge. Human resource systems can be designed to attract, develop, and maintain an efficient force of employees.

Sometimes achieving a new way of thinking requires a focused change on the underlying corporate culture values and norms. In the last decade, numerous large corporations, including Kodak, IBM, and Ford Motor Company, have undertaken some type of culture change initiative. Changing corporate culture fundamentally shifts how work is done in an organization and generally leads to renewed commitment and empowerment of employees and a stronger bond between the company and its customers.[61]

Two recent trends that generally lead to significant changes in corporate culture are reengineering and the implementation of total quality management programs, which require employees to think in new ways about how work is done.

Organizational development programs also focus on changing old culture values to new ways of thinking, including greater employee participation and empowerment and developing a shared companywide vision.

REENGINEERING

Reengineering is a cross-functional initiative involving the radical redesign of business processes to bring about simultaneous changes in culture, structure, and information technology and produce dramatic performance improvements in areas such as customer service, quality, cost, and speed.[62] Reengineering basically means taking a clean-slate approach, pushing aside all the notions of how work is done now and looking at how work can best be designed for optimal performance. The idea is to squeeze out the dead space and time lags in work flows. Such companies as Hoechst Celanese, Union Carbide, BellSouth Telecommunications, and DuPont are among the dozens of companies involved in major reengineering efforts. After reengineering, Union Carbide cut $400 million out of fixed costs in just three years. Hoechst Celanese identified $70 million in cost savings and productivity improvements over a two-year period, without making massive job cuts.[63] Many more organizations have reengineered one or a few specific processes.

Because the focus is on process rather than function, reengineering generally leads to a shift from a vertical organization structure to greater use of teams and task forces as described in Chapter 3. This, in turn, requires major changes in corporate culture and management philosophy. In his book *The Reengineering Revolution*, Michael Hammer refers to people change as "the most perplexing, annoying, distressing, and confusing part" of reengineering.[64] Managers may confront powerful emotions as employees react to rapid, massive change with fear or anger. Top leaders at Jaguar of North America coped with resistance to reengineering by putting their loudest dissenters in charge of solutions and then getting out of the way. They implemented employee suggestions that corrected so many of Jaguar's shortcomings that even the most skeptical dealers accepted that the company truly cared about its employees and its customers.[65]

Most top managers have little experience dealing with the complexities of human behavior; yet, they should remember that culture changes are crucial to the success of reengineering.

TOTAL QUALITY MANAGEMENT

The approach known as **total quality management** infuses quality values throughout every activity within a company. The concept is simple: workers, not managers, are handed the responsibility for achieving standards of quality. No longer are quality control departments and other formal control systems in charge of checking parts and improving quality. Companies train their workers and then trust them to infuse quality into everything they do. The results of TQM programs can be staggering. After noticing that Ford Motor Company cut $40 billion out of its operating budget by adopting quality principles and changing corporate culture, the Henry Ford Health System also instituted a quality program. CEO Gail Warden says of quality programs at Henry Ford and other U.S. health-care institutions, "We have to change the way we practice medicine" to get health-care costs down and remain competitive in the rapidly changing health-care industry.[66]

By requiring organizationwide participation in quality control, TQM requires a major shift in mind-set for both managers and workers. In TQM, workers must be trained, involved, and empowered in a way that many managers at first find frightening. One way in which workers are involved is through **quality circles**, groups of six to twelve volunteer workers who meet to analyze and solve problems.

Another technique of total quality management is known as **benchmarking**, a process whereby companies find out how others do something better than they do and then try to imitate or improve on it. Through research and field trips by small teams of workers, companies compare their products, services, and business practices with those of their competitors and other companies. AT&T, Xerox, DuPont, Kodak, and Motorola are constantly benchmarking.

While the focus of total quality programs is generally on improving quality and productivity, it always involves a significant culture change. Managers should be prepared for this aspect before undertaking quality programs.

ORGANIZATION DEVELOPMENT

One method for bringing about significant culture change is known as **organization development**, which focuses on the human and social aspects of the organization as a way to improve the organization's ability to adapt and solve problems. Organization development (OD) emphasizes the values of human development, fairness, openness, freedom from coercion, and individual autonomy that allows workers to perform the job as they see fit, within reasonable organizational constraints.[67] In the 1970s, OD evolved as a separate field that applied the behavioral sciences in a process of planned organizationwide change, with the goal of increasing organizational effectiveness. Organization development is not a step-by-step procedure to solve a specific problem but a process of fundamental change in the human and social systems of the organization, including organizational culture.[68]

OD uses knowledge and techniques from the behavioral sciences to improve performance through increased trust, open confrontation of problems, employee empowerment and participation, knowledge and information sharing, the design of meaningful work, cooperation and collaboration between groups, and the full use of human potential.

OD practitioners believe the best performance occurs by breaking down hierarchical and authoritarian approaches to management. However, consistent with the arguments in the environment and technology chapters, research has shown that the OD approach may not enhance performance or satisfaction in stable business environments and for routine tasks.[69] It is best for organizations that are facing environmental and technological discontinuities and rapid change.

Changing organizational culture is not easy, but organization development techniques can smooth the process. For example, OD can help managers and employees think in new ways about human relationships, making the transition to more participative management less stressful. At Hewlett-Packard's direct marketing organization, self-confessed "authoritarian" manager Sharon Jacobs used concepts based in organization development to create a better quality of life and participation for employees as well as improve the organization's performance. Spurred by pleas from new staffers who felt constricted by the excessive top-down control, Jacobs is doing her best to let go, to ask her telemarketers for solutions, to listen to the ideas of even lowest-level staff members. Despite the difficulties in the beginning, the new style has resulted in a 40 percent increase in productivity, a rise in employee morale significant enough to warrant a note from HP's president, and a 44 percent decline in the unit's annual attrition rate.[70]

OD CULTURE CHANGE INTERVENTIONS

OD interventions involve training of specific groups or of everyone in the organization. For OD intervention to be successful, senior management in the organization must see the need for OD and provide enthusiastic support for the change. Techniques used by many organizations for improving people skills through OD include the following.

Large Group Intervention. Most early OD activities involved small groups and focused on incremental change. However, in recent years, there has been growing interest in the application of OD techniques to large group settings, which are more attuned to bringing about radical or transformational change in organizations operating in complex environments.[71] The **large group intervention** approach[72] brings together participants from all parts of the organization—often including key stakeholders from outside the organization as well—in an off-site setting to discuss problems or opportunities and plan for change. A large-group intervention might involve fifty to five hundred people and last for several days. The off-site setting limits interference and distractions, enabling participants to focus on new ways of doing things. General Electric's "Work Out" program, an ongoing process of solving problems, learning, and improving, began with large-scale off-site meetings that grew out of Jack Welch's desire to create a "culture of boundary-lessness" he felt was critical to learning and growth. Hourly and salaried workers from many different parts of the organization join with customers and suppliers to discuss and solve problems.[73]

Team Building. Team building promotes the idea that people who work together can work as a team. A work team can be brought together to discuss conflicts, goals, the decision-making process, communication, creativity, and leadership. The team can then plan to overcome problems and improve results. Team-building activities are also used in many companies to train task forces, committees, and new product development groups. These activities enhance communication and collaboration and strengthen the cohesiveness of organizational groups and teams.

Interdepartmental Activities. Representatives from different departments are brought together in a mutual location to surface conflict, diagnose its causes, and plan improvement in communication and coordination. This type of intervention has been applied to union–management conflict, headquarters–field office conflict, interdepartmental conflict, and mergers.[74]

In today's world, the work force is becoming more and more diverse, and organizations are constantly adapting to environmental uncertainty and increasing international competition. OD interventions can respond to these new realities as organizations strive to create greater capability for change and growth.[75]

STRATEGIES FOR IMPLEMENTING CHANGE

This chapter began by looking at the four types of changes managers can use to gain a competitive edge and the five elements that must be present for any change to succeed—idea, need, adoption, implementation, and resources. In this final section, we are going to briefly discuss resistance to change at the organizational level, and some techniques managers can use to implement change.

BARRIERS TO CHANGE

Managers should expect to encounter resistance as they attempt to implement changes. It is natural for people to resist change, and many barriers to change exist at the individual and organizational level.[76]

1. *Excessive focus on costs.* Management may possess the mind-set that costs are all-important and may fail to appreciate the importance of a change that is not focused on costs—for example, a change to increase employee motivation or customer satisfaction.
2. *Failure to perceive benefits.* Any significant change will produce both positive and negative reactions. Education may be needed to help managers and employees perceive more positive than negative aspects of the change. In addition, if the organization's reward system discourages risk-taking, a change process may falter because employees think that the risk of making the change is too high.
3. *Lack of coordination and cooperation.* Organizational fragmentation and conflict often result from the lack of coordination for change implementation. Moreover, in the case of new technology, the old and new systems must be compatible.

4. *Uncertainty avoidance.* At the individual level, many employees fear the uncertainty associated with change. Constant communication is needed so that employees know what is going on and understand how it impacts their jobs.

5. *Fear of loss.* Managers and employees may fear the loss of power and status or even their jobs. In these cases, implementation should be careful and incremental, and all employees should be involved as closely as possible in the change process.

Implementation can typically be designed to overcome many of the organizational and individual barriers to change.

TECHNIQUES FOR IMPLEMENTATION

Managers and employees throughout the organization are involved in the process of change. There are a number of techniques that can be used to successfully implement change.

1. *Identify a true need for change.* A careful diagnosis of the existing situation is necessary to determine the extent of the problem or opportunity. If the people affected by the change do not agree with a problem, the change process should not proceed without further analysis and communication among all employees. As mentioned early in the chapter, sometimes a sense of urgency is needed to unfreeze people and make them willing to invest the time and energy to adopt new techniques or procedures. For example, ALLTEL, an information services and telecommunications company, faced both productivity and customer service problems as the company coped with rapid growth in the mid-1990s, but managers found it difficult to convince employees of the need for change. When ALLTEL Technology Center's errors began to mount and the Center almost lost its largest client, GTE, managers used the incident to help establish a sense of urgency. Management and employees began meeting in small groups to talk about the need for change and how they could revise their work to improve the organization.[77]

2. *Find an idea that fits the need.* Finding the right idea often involves search procedures—talking with other managers, assigning a task force to investigate the problem, sending out a request to suppliers, or asking creative people within the organization to develop a solution. The creation of a new idea requires organic conditions. This is a good opportunity to encourage employee participation, because they need the freedom to think about and explore new options.[78] ALLTEL set up a program called Team Focus to gather input from all employees. In twenty group meetings over a period of two weeks, managers gathered 2,800 suggestions, which they then narrowed down to 170 critical action items that specifically addressed problems that were affecting employee morale and performance.

3. *Get top management support.* Successful change requires the support of top management. Top managers should articulate clear innovation goals. For a single large change, such as a structural reorganization, the president and vice presidents must give their blessing and support. For smaller changes, the support of influential managers in relevant departments is required. The lack of top management support is one of the most frequent causes of implementation failure.[79]

4. *Design the change for incremental implementation.* Sometimes large changes cannot be implemented all at once or employees may feel overwhelmed and resist the change. When a large bank in South Carolina installed a complete new $6 million system to computerize processing, it was stunned that the system didn't work very well. The prospect for success of such a large change is improved if the change can be broken into subparts and each part adopted sequentially. Then designers can make adjustments to improve the innovation, and hesitant users who see success can throw support behind the rest of the change program.

5. *Develop plans to overcome resistance to change.* Many good ideas are never used because managers failed to anticipate or prepare for resistance to change by consumers, employees, or other managers. No matter how impressive the performance

characteristics of an innovation, its implementation will conflict with some interests and jeopardize some alliances in the organization. To increase the chance of successful implementation, management must acknowledge the conflict, threats, and potential losses perceived by employees. Several strategies can be used by managers to overcome the resistance problem:

- *Alignment with needs and goals of users.* The best strategy for overcoming resistance is to make sure change meets a real need. Employees in R&D often come up with great ideas that solve nonexistent problems. This happens because initiators fail to consult with the people who use a change. Resistance can be frustrating for managers, but moderate resistance to change is good for an organization. Resistance provides a barrier to frivolous changes or to change for the sake of change. The process of overcoming resistance to change normally requires that the change be good for its users.

- *Communication and training.* Communication informs users about the need for change and about the consequences of a proposed change, preventing false rumors, misunderstanding, and resentment. In one study of change efforts, the most commonly cited reason for failure was that employees learned of the change from outsiders. Top managers concentrated on communicating with the public and with shareholders, but failed to communicate with the people who would be most intimately involved and most affected by the changes—their own employees.[80] Open communication often gives management an opportunity to explain what steps will be taken to ensure that the change will have no adverse consequences for employees. Training is also needed to help employees understand and cope with their role in the change process.

- *Participation and involvement.* Early and extensive participation in a change should be part of implementation. Participation gives those involved a sense of control over the change activity. They understand it better, and they become committed to successful implementation. One recent study of the implementation and adoption of computer technology at two companies showed a much smoother implementation process at the company that introduced the new technology using a participatory approach.[81] The team-building and large-group intervention activities described earlier can be effective ways to involve employees in a change process.

- *Forcing and coercion.* As a last resort, managers may overcome resistance by threatening employees with loss of jobs or promotions or by firing or transferring them. In other words, management power is used to overwhelm resistance. In most cases, this approach is not advisable because it leaves people angry at change managers, and the change may be sabotaged. However, this technique may be needed when speed is essential, such as when the organization faces a crisis. It may also be required for needed administrative changes that flow from the top down, such as downsizing the work force.[82]

6. *Create change teams.* Throughout, this chapter has discussed the need for resources and energy to make change happen. Separate creative departments, new venture groups, or an ad hoc team or task force are ways to focus energy on both creation and implementation. A separate department has the freedom to create a new technology that fits a genuine need. A task force can be created to see that implementation is completed. The task force can be responsible for communication, involvement of users, training, and other activities needed for change.

7. *Foster idea champions.* One of the most effective weapons in the battle for change is the idea champion. The most effective champion is a volunteer champion who is deeply committed to a new idea. The idea champion sees that all technical activities are correct and complete. An additional champion, such as a manager sponsor, may also be needed to persuade people about implementation, even using coercion if necessary. For example, John Cunningham was the idea champion at Chesebrough-Ponds who

developed the polishing pen through which nail polish is applied. Management supporters at Chesebrough-Ponds then solved the implementation problems of manufacturing, packaging, and marketing. Both technical and management champions may break the rules and push ahead even when others are nonbelieving, but the enthusiasm pays off.[83]

DISCUSSION QUESTIONS

1. Describe the dual-core approach. How does administrative change normally differ from technology change? Discuss.
2. How might organizations manage the dilemma of needing both stability and change? Discuss.
3. How are organic characteristics related to changes in technology? To administrative changes?
4. Why do organizations experience resistance to change? What steps can managers take to overcome this resistance?
5. "Bureaucracies are not innovative." Discuss.
6. Of the five elements required for successful change, which element do you think managers are most likely to overlook? Discuss.
7. How do the underlying values of organization development compare to the values underlying other types of change?
8. The manager of R&D for a drug company said only 5 percent of the company's new products ever achieve market success. He also said the industry average is 10 percent and wondered how his organization might increase its success rate. If you were acting as a consultant, what advice would you give him concerning organization structure?

NOTES

1. Peter F. Drucker, *Management Challenges for the 21st Century* (New York: Harper Business, 1999).
2. Joseph E. McCann, "Design Principles for an Innovating Company," *Academy of Management Executive* 5 (May 1991): 76–93.
3. Stuart Crainer and Des Dearlove, "Water Works," *Management Review* (May 1999): 39–43.
4. Anita Lienert, "Jedi Masters and Paradigm Busters," *Management Review* (March, 1998): 11–14.
5. Bruce Rayner, "Trial-by-Fire Transformation: An Interview with Globe Metallurgical's Arden C. Sims," *Harvard Business Review* (May–June 1992): 117–29.
6. Richard A. Wolfe, "Organizational Innovation: Review, Critique and Suggested Research Directions," *Journal of Management Studies* 31, no. 3 (May 1994): 405–31.
7. John L. Pierce and Andre L. Delbecq, "Organization Structure, Individual Attitudes and Innovation," *Academy of Management Review* 2 (1977): 27–37; Michael Aiken and Jerald Hage, "The Organic Organization and Innovation," *Sociology* 5 (1971): 63–82.
8. Richard L. Daft, "Bureaucratic versus Nonbureaucratic Structure in the Process of Innovation and Change," in Samuel B. Bacharach, ed., *Perspectives in Organizational Sociology: Theory and Research* (Greenwich, Conn.: JAI Press, 1982), 129–66.

9. Alan D. Meyer and James B. Goes, "Organizational Assimilation of Innovations: A Multilevel Contextual Analysis," *Academy of Management Journal* 31 (1988): 897–923.
10. Richard W. Woodman, John E. Sawyer, and Ricky W. Griffin, "Toward a Theory of Organizational Creativity," *Academy of Management Review* 18 (1993): 293–321; Alan Farnham, "How to Nurture Creative Sparks," *Fortune,* 10 January 1994, 94–100.
11. Michael Barrier, "Managing Workers in Times of Change," *Nation's Business* (May 1998): 31–34.
12. John P. Kotter, *Leading Change* (Boston: Harvard University Press, 1996), 20-25, and "Leading Change," *Harvard Business Review* (March–April 1995): 59–67.
13. Eric Matson, "Here, Innovation is No Fluke," *Fast Company* (August–September 1977): 42–44.
14. D. Bruce Merrifield, "Intrapreneurial Corporate Renewal," *Journal of Business Venturing* 8 (September 1993): 383–89; Linsu Kim, "Organizational Innovation and Structure," *Journal of Business Research* 8 (1980): 225–45; Tom Burns and G. M. Stalker, *The Management of Innovation* (London: Tavistock Publications, 1961).
15. James Q. Wilson, "Innovation in Organization: Notes toward a Theory," in James D. Thompson, ed., *Approaches to Organizational Design* (Pittsburgh: University of Pittsburgh Press, 1966), 193–218.

16. J. C. Spender and Eric H. Kessler, "Managing the Uncertainties of Innovation: Extending Thompson (1967)," *Human Relations* 48, no. 1 (1995): 35–56; Robert B. Duncan, "The Ambidextrous Organization: Designing Dual Structures for Innovation," in Ralph H. Killman, Louis R. Pondy, and Dennis Slevin, eds., *The Management of Organization*, vol. 1 (New York: North-Holland, 1976), 167–88.

17. James B. Treece, "Improving the Soul of an Old Machine," *Business Week*, 25 October 1993, 134–36.

18. Edward F. McDonough III and Richard Leifer, "Using Simultaneous Structures to Cope with Uncertainty," *Academy of Management Journal* 26 (1983): 727–35.

19. John McCormick and Bill Powell, "Management for the 1990s," *Newsweek*, 25 April 1988, 47–48.

20. Todd Datz, "Romper Ranch," *CIO Enterprise*, Section 2, 15 May 1999, 39–52.

21. Perry Glasser, "Revolutionary Soldiers," *CIO Enterprise*, Section 2, 15 May 1999, 54–60; and John Holusha, "The Case of Xerox PARC," *Strategy & Business*, Issue 10 (First Quarter 1998): 76–82.

22. Paul S. Adler, Barbara Goldoftas, and David I. Levine, "Flexibility Versus Efficiency? A Case Study of Model Changeovers in the Toyota Production System" (Working Paper, School of Business Administration, University of Southern California, Los Angeles, 1996).

23. Judith R. Blau and William McKinley, "Ideas, Complexity, and Innovation," *Administrative Science Quarterly* 24 (1979): 200–19.

24. Rosabeth Moss Kanter, Jeffrey North, Lisa Richardson, Cynthia Ingols, and Joseph Zolner, "Engines of Progress: Designing and Running Entrepreneurial Vehicles in Established Companies: Raytheon's New Product Center, 1969–1989," Journal of Business Venturing 6 (March 1991): 145–63.

25. Russell Mitchell, "Masters of Innovation: How 3M Keeps Its New Products Coming," *Business Week*, 10 April 1989, 58–63.

26. Marcia Stepanek, "Closed, Gone to the Net," *Business Week*, 7 June 1999, 113–116.

27. Phaedra Hise, "New Recruitment Strategy: Ask Your Best Employees to Leave," *Inc.*, July 1997, 2.

28. Daniel F. Jennings and James R. Lumpkin, "Functioning Modeling Corporate Entrepreneurship: An Empirical Integrative Analysis," *Journal of Management* 15 (1989): 485–502.

29. Jane M. Howell and Christopher A. Higgins, "Champions of Technology Innovation," *Administrative Science Quarterly* 35 (1990): 317–41; Jane M. Howell and Christopher A. Higgins, "Champions of Change: Identifying, Understanding, and Supporting Champions of Technology Innovations," *Organizational Dynamics* (Summer 1990): 40–55.

30. Peter F. Drucker, "Change Leaders," *Inc.*, June 1999, 65–72, and Peter F. Drucker, *Management Challenges for the 21st Century* (New York: Harper Business, 1999).

31. Crainer and Dearlove, "Water Works."

32. Thomas J. Peters and Robert H. Waterman, Jr., *In Search of Excellence* (New York: Harper & Row, 1982).

33. Ibid., p. 205.

34. Peter J. Frost and Carolyn P. Egri, "The Political Process of Innovation," in L. L. Cummings and Barry M. Staw, eds., *Research in Organizational Behavior*, vol. 13 (New York: JAI Press, 1991), 229–95; Jay R. Galbraith, "Designing the Innovating Organization," *Organizational Dynamics* (Winter 1982): 5–25; Marsha Sinatar, "Entrepreneurs, Chaos, and Creativity—Can Creative People Really Survive Large Company Structure?" *Sloan Management Review* (Winter 1985): 57–62.

35 "Black & Decker Inventory Makes Money for Firm by Just Not 'Doing the Neat Stuff,'" *Houston Chronicle*, 25 December 1987, sec. 3, p. 2.

36. Christopher Power with Kathleen Kerwyn, Ronald Grover, Keith Alexander, and Robert D. Hof, "Flops," *Business Week*, 16 August 1993, 76–82; Modesto A. Maidique and Billie Jo Zirger, "A Study of Success and Failure in Product Innovation: The Case of the U.S. Electronics Industry," *IEEE Transactions in Engineering Management* 31 (November 1984): 192–203.

37. Deborah Dougherty and Cynthia Hardy, "Sustained Product Innovation in Large, Mature Organizations: Overcoming Innovation-to-Organization Problems," *Academy of Management Journal* 39, No. 5 (1996): 1120–1153

38. Cliff Edwards, "Many Products Have Gone Way of the Edsel," *Johnson City Press*, 23 May 1999, 28, 30; Paul Lukas, "The Ghastliest Product Launches," *Fortune*, 16 March 1998, 44; and Robert McMath, *What Were They Thinking? Marketing Lessons I've Learned from Over 80,000 New-Product Innovations and Idiocies* (New York: Times Business, 1998); Edwin Mansfield, J. Rapaport, J. Schnee, S. Wagner, and M. Hamburger, *Research and Innovation in Modern Corporations* (New York: Norton, 1971); Antonio J. Bailetti and Paul F. Litva, "Integrating Customer Requirements into Product Designs," *Journal of Product Innovation Management* (1995): 12: 3–15.

39. Shona L. Brown and Kathleen M. Eisenhardt, "Product Development: Past Research, Present Findings, and Future Directions," *Academy of Management Review* 20, no. 2 (1995): 343–78; F. Axel Johne and Patricia A. Snelson, "Success Factors in Product Innovation: A Selective Review of the Literature," *Journal of Product Innovation Management* 5 (1988): 114–28; Science Policy Research Unit,

University of Sussex, *Success and Failure in Industrial Innovation* (London: Centre for the Study of Industrial Innovation, 1972).

40. Dorothy Leonard and Jeffrey F. Rayport, "Spark Innovation through Empathic Design," *Harvard Business Review* (November–December 1997): 102–13.

41. Amal Kumar Naj, "GE's Latest Invention: A Way to Move Ideas from Lab to Market," *The Wall Street Journal*, 14 June 1990, A1, A99.

42. Shona L. Brown and Kathleen M. Eisenhardt, "Product Development: Past Research, Present Findings, and Future Directions," *Academy of Management Review* 20, no. 2 (1995): 343–78; Dan Dimancescu and Kemp Dwenger, "Smoothing the Product Development Path," *Management Review* (January 1996): 36–41.

43. Alex Taylor III, "Kellogg Cranks Up Its Idea Machine," *Fortune*, 5 July 1999, 181–182.

44. Kathleen M. Eisenhardt and Behnam N. Tabrizi, "Accelerating Adaptive Processes: Product Innovation in the Global Computer Industry," *Administrative Science Quarterly* 40 (1995): 84–110; and Dougherty and Hardy, "Sustained Product Innovation in Large, Mature Organizations."

45. George Stalk, Jr., "Time and Innovation," *Canadian Business Review*, Autumn 1993, 15–18.

46. Robert D. Hof, "From Dinosaur to Gazelle: HP's Evolution Was Painful but Necessary," *Business Week/Reinventing America*, 1992, 65; Karne Bronikowski, "Speeding New Products to Market," *Journal of Business Strategy* (September–October 1990): 34–37; Brian Dumaine, "How Managers Can Succeed through Speed," *Fortune*, 13 February 1989, 54–59; Otis Port, Zachary Schiller, and Resa W. King, "A Smarter Way to Manufacture," *Business Week*, 30 April 1990, 110–17; Tom Peters, "Time-Obsessed Competition," *Management Review* (September 1990): 16–20.

47. David Leonhardt, "It Was a Hit in Buenos Aires—So Why Not Boise?" *Business Week*, 7 September 1998, 56, 58.

48. Dan Dimancescu and Kemp Dwenger, "Smoothing the Product Development Path," *Management Review*, January 1996, 36–41.

49. Jeffrey A. Trachtenberg, "How Philips Flubbed Its U.S. Introduction of Electronic Product," *The Wall Street Journal*, 28 June 1996, A1.

50. Raymond E. Miles, Henry J. Coleman, Jr., and W. E. Douglas Creed, "Keys to Success in Corporate Redesign," *California Management Review* 37, no. 3 (Spring 1995): 128–45.

51. Fariborz Damanpour and William M. Evan, "Organizational Innovation and Performance: The Problem of 'Organizational Lag,'" *Administrative Science Quarterly*, 29 (1984): 392–409; David J. Teece, "The Diffusion of an Administrative Innovation," *Management Science* 26 (1980): 464–70; John R. Kimberly and Michael J. Evaniski, "Organizational Innovation: The Influence of Individual, Organizational and Contextual Factors on Hospital Adoption of Technological and Administrative Innovation," *Academy of Management Journal* 24 (1981): 689–713; Michael K. Moch and Edward V. Morse, "Size, Centralization, and Organizational Adoption of Innovations," *American Sociological Review* 42 (1977): 716–25; Mary L. Fennell, "Synergy, Influence, and Information in the Adoption of Administrative Innovation," *Academy of Management Journal* 27 (1984): 113–29.

52. Richard L. Daft, "A Dual-Core Model of Organizational Innovation," *Academy of Management Journal* 21 (1978): 193–210.

53. Daft, "Bureaucratic versus Nonbureaucratic Structure"; Robert W. Zmud, "Diffusion of Modern Software Practices: Influence of Centralization and Formalization," *Management Science* 28 (1982): 1421–31.

54. Daft, "A Dual-Core Model of Organizational Innovation"; Zmud, "Diffusion of Modern Software Practices."

55. Fariborz Damanpour, "The Adoption of Technological, Administrative, and Ancillary Innovations: Impact of Organizational Factors," *Journal of Management* 13 (1987): 675–88.

56. Steve Hamm, "Is Oracle Finally Seeing Clearly?" *Business Week*, 3 August 1998, 86–88.

57. Gregory H. Gaertner, Karen N. Gaertner, and David M. Akinnusi, "Environment, Strategy, and the Implementation of Administrative Change: The Case of Civil Service Reform," *Academy of Management Journal* 27 (1984): 525–43.

58. Claudia Bird Schoonhoven and Mariann Jelinek, "Dynamic Tension in Innovative, High Technology Firms: Managing Rapid Technology Change through Organization Structure," in Mary Ann Von Glinow and Susan Albers Mohrman, eds., *Managing Complexity in High Technology Organizations* (New York: Oxford University Press, 1990), 90–118.

59. Lawrence M. Fisher, "Imposing a Hierarchy on a Gaggle of Techies," *New York Times*, 29 November 1992, F4.

60. David Ulm and James K. Hickel, "What Happens after Restructuring?" *Journal of Business Strategy* (July–August 1990): 37–41; John L. Sprague, "Restructuring and Corporate Renewal: A Manager's Guide," *Management Review* (March 1989): 34–36.

61. Benson L. Porter and Warrington S. Parker, Jr., "Culture Change," *Human Resource Management* 31 (Spring–Summer 1992): 45–67.

62. Donna B. Stoddard, Sirkka L. Jarvenpaa, and Michael Littlejohn, "The Reality of Business Reengineering: Pacific Bell's Centrex Provisioning Process," *California Management Review* 38, No. 3 (Spring 1996): 57–76; and Michael Hammer with Steven Stanton, "The Art of Change," *Success* (April 1995): 44A–44H.

63. Thomas A. Stewart, "Reengineering: The Hot New Managing Tool," *Fortune*, 23 August 1993, 41–48; and Brian S. Moskal, "Reengineering without Downsizing," *IW*, 19 February 1996, 23–28.

64. Anne B. Fisher, "Making Change Stick," *Fortune*, 17 April 1995, 122.

65. Ibid.

66. Ron Winslow, "Healthcare Providers Try Industrial Tactics to Reduce Their Costs," *The Wall Street Journal*, 3 November 1993, A1, A16.

67. W. Warner Burke, "The New Agenda for Organization Development," in Wendell L. French, Cecil H. Bell, Jr., and Robert A. Zawacki, *Organization Development and Transformation: Managing Effective Change* (Burr Ridge, Ill.: Irwin McGraw-Hill, 2000), 523–35.

68. W. Warner Burke, *Organization Development: A Process of Learning and Changing*, 2nd ed. (Reading, Mass.: Addison-Wesley, 1994); Wendell L. French and Cecil H. Bell, Jr., "A History of Organizational Development," in French, Bell, and Zawacki, *Organization Development and Transformation*, 20–42.

69. Michael Beer and Elisa Walton, "Developing the Competitive Organization: Interventions and Strategies," *American Psychologist* 45 (February 1990): 154–61.

70. Joseph Weber, "Letting Go Is Hard to Do," *Business Week/Enterprise*, 1993, 218–19.

71. French and Bell, "A History of Organization Development."

72. The information on large-group intervention is based on Kathleen D. Dannemiller and Robert W. Jacobs, "Changing the Way Organizations Change: A Revolution of Common Sense," *The Journal of Applied Behavioral Science* 28, No. 4 (December 1992): 48–498; Barbara B. Bunker and Billie T. Alban, "Conclusion: What Makes Large Group Interventions Effective?" *The Journal of Applied Behavioral Science* 28, No. 4 (December 1992): 570–91; and Marvin R. Weisbord, "Inventing the Future: Search Strategies for Whole System Improvements," in French, Bell, and Zawacki, *Organization Development and Transformation*, 242–50.

73. J. Quinn, "What a Workout!" *Performance* (November 1994): 58–63; and Bunker and Alban, "Conclusion: What Makes Large Group Interventions Effective?"

74. Paul F. Buller, "For Successful Strategic Change: Blend OD Practices with Strategic Management," *Organizational Dynamics* (Winter 1988): 42–55.

75. Jyotsna Sanzgiri and Jonathan Z. Gottlieb, "Philosophic and Pragmatic Influences on the Practice of Organization Development, 1950–2000," *Organizational Dynamics* (Autumn 1992): 57–69.

76. Based on Carol A. Beatty and John R. M. Gordon, "Barriers to the Implementation of CAD/CAM Systems," *Sloan Management Review* (Summer 1988): 25–33.

77. Jim Cross, "Back to the Future," *Management Review* (February 1999): 50–54.

78. Richard L. Daft and Selwyn W. Becker, *Innovation in Organizations* (New York: Elsevier, 1978); John P. Kotter and Leonard A. Schlesinger, "Choosing Strategies for Change," *Harvard Business Review* 57 (1979): 106–14.

79. Everett M. Rogers and Floyd Shoemaker, *Communication of Innovations: A Cross Cultural Approach*, 2d ed. (New York: Free Press, 1971); Stratford P. Sherman, "Eight Big Masters of Innovation," *Fortune*, 15 October 1984, 66–84.

80. Peter Richardson and D. Keith Denton, "Communicating Change," *Human Resource Management* 35, no. 2 (Summer 1996): 203–16.

81. Philip H. Mirvis, Amy L. Sales, and Edward J. Hackett, "The Implementation and Adoption of New Technology in Organizations: The Impact on Work, People, and Culture," *Human Resource Management* 30 (Spring 1991): 113–39; Arthur E. Wallach, "System Changes Begin in the Training Department," *Personnel Journal* 58 (1979): 846–48, 872; Paul R. Lawrence, "How to Deal with Resistance to Change," *Harvard Business Review* 47 (January–February 1969): 4–12, 166–76.

82. Dexter C. Dunphy and Doug A. Stace, "Transformational and Coercive Strategies for Planned Organizational Change: Beyond the O. D. Model," *Organizational Studies* 9 (1988): 317–34; Kotter and Schlesinger, "Choosing Strategies for Change."

83. "How Chesebrough-Ponds Put Nail Polish in a Pen," *Business Week*, 8 October 1984: 196–200; Richard L. Daft and Patricia J. Bradshaw, "The Process of Horizontal Differentiation: Two Models," *Administrative Science Quarterly* 25 (1980): 441–56; Alok K. Chakrabarti, "The Role of Champion in Product Innovation," *California Management Review* 17 (1974): 58–62.

PART 5

Managing Dynamic Processes

CHAPTER *9*

Decision–Making Processes

Definitions

Individual Decision Making
Rational Approach • *Bounded Rationality Perspective*

Organizational Decision Making
Management Science Approach • *Carnegie Model* • *Incremental Decision Process Model* • *Garbage Can Model*

Special Decision Circumstances
High-Velocity Environments • *Decision Mistakes and Learning* • *Escalating Commitment*

*E*very organization grows, prospers, or fails as a result of decisions by its managers, and decisions can be risky and uncertain, without any guarantee of success. Decision making must be done amid constantly changing factors, unclear information, and conflicting points of view. Intel Corporation, the leading supplier of microprocessors in the computer industry, was propelled to its current dominance by a decision its then-CEO Andrew Grove made in the 1980s. Over the strong objections of other executives, Grove decided to take Intel out of the DRAM memory-chip business—a technology Intel had invented—and focus relentlessly on micrprocessors. The decision proved to be a boon to the company, but the outcome was certainly not clear in 1985.[1]

Many organizational decisions are complete failures. For example, McDonald's Arch Deluxe sandwich, introduced at a cost of $100 million, was axed from the menu after only a few years. Toy makers Mattel and Hasbro both passed on the Ninja Turtles idea in the late 1980s, and the action figures went on to make billions. The decision by previous Toys "R" Us executives to cling to their 1970s-format stores enabled Wal-Mart to overtake the company as the biggest U.S. toy retailer and gave online rivals such as eToys a head start in selling toys over the Internet.[2]

Managers also make many successful decisions every day. Mickey Drexler decided to launch Old Navy, a new kind of discount store, when sales and profits slowed at his Gap stores, and it was an instant success. In less than three years, Gap opened 282 Old Navy stores and sales hit $1 billion. Nokia became a $10 billion leader in the cellular phone and electronics industry because managers at the Finnish company decided to sell off unrelated businesses such as paper, tires, and aluminum and concentrate the company's energy and resources on electronics. Richard Branson, founder of Virgin Airlines, created a whole new retail category when he opened Virgin Bride, a bridal superstore that handles every aspect of wedding planning, from the invitations to the dress and wedding cake.[3]

PURPOSE OF THIS CHAPTER

At any time, an organization may be identifying problems and implementing alternatives for hundreds of decisions. Managers and organizations somehow muddle through these processes.[4] The purpose here is to analyze these processes to learn what decision making is actually like in organizational settings. Decision-making processes can be thought of as the brain and nervous system of an organization. Decisions are made about organization strategy, structure, innovation, and acquisitions. This chapter explores how organizations can and should make decisions about these issues.

The first section defines decision making. The next section examines how individual managers make decisions. Then several models of organizational decision making are explored. Each model is used in a different organizational situation.

DEFINITIONS

Organizational decision making is formally defined as the process of identifying and solving problems. The process contains two major stages. In the **problem identification stage**, information about environmental and organizational conditions is monitored to determine if performance is satisfactory and to diagnose the cause of shortcomings. The **problem solution** stage is when alternative courses of action are considered and one alternative is selected and implemented.

Organizational decisions vary in complexity and can be categorized as programmed or nonprogrammed.[5] **Programmed decisions** are repetitive and well defined, and procedures exist for resolving the problem. They are well structured because criteria of performance are normally clear, good information is available about current performance, alternatives are easily specified, and there is relative certainty that the chosen alternative will be successful. Examples of programmed decisions include decision rules, such as when to replace an office copy machine, when to reimburse managers for travel expenses, or whether an applicant has sufficient qualifications for an assembly-line job. Many companies adopt rules based on experience with programmed decisions. For example, general pricing rules in the restaurant industry are that food is marked up three times direct cost, beer four times, and liquor six times. A rule for large hotels staffing banquets is to allow one server per thirty guests for a sit-down function and one server per forty guests for a buffet.[6]

Nonprogrammed decisions are novel and poorly defined, and no procedure exists for solving the problem. They are used when an organization has not seen a problem before and may not know how to respond. Clear-cut decision criteria do not exist. Alternatives are fuzzy. There is uncertainty about whether a proposed solution will solve the problem. Typically, few alternatives can be developed for a nonprogrammed decision, so a single solution is custom-tailored to the problem.

Many nonprogrammed decisions involve strategic planning, because uncertainty is great and decisions are complex. For example, when he first began his job as CEO of Continental Airlines, Gordon M. Bethune decided to ground forty-one planes, cut more than 4,200 jobs, and abolish cut-rate fares as part of his strategy to make the ailing airline profitable again. Bethune and other top managers had to analyze complex problems, evaluate alternatives, and make a choice about how to pull Continental out of its slump.[7] These and other decisions have proved to be right on target, as Continental has enjoyed renewed profitability and a vastly improved service record.

Particularly complex nonprogrammed decisions have been referred to as "wicked" decisions, because simply defining the problem can turn into a major task. Wicked problems are associated with manager conflicts over objectives and alternatives, rapidly changing circumstances, and unclear linkages among decision elements. Managers dealing with a wicked decision may hit on a solution that merely proves they failed to correctly define the problem to begin with.[8]

INDIVIDUAL DECISION MAKING

Individual decision making by managers can be described in two ways. First is the **rational approach**, which suggests how managers should try to make decisions. Second is the **bounded rationality perspective**, which describes how decisions actually have to be made under severe time and resource constraints. The rational approach is an ideal managers may work toward but never reach.

RATIONAL APPROACH

The rational approach to individual decision making stresses the need for systematic analysis of a problem followed by choice and implementation in a logical step-by-step sequence. The rational approach was developed to guide individual decision making because many managers were observed to be unsystematic and arbitrary in their approach to organizational decisions. Although the rational model is an "ideal" not fully achievable in the real world of uncertainty, complexity, and rapid change, the model does help managers think about decisions more clearly and rationally. Managers should use systematic procedures to make decisions whenever possible. When managers have a deep understanding of the rational decision-making process, it can help them make better decisions even when there is a lack of clear information. The authors of a recent book on decision making use the example of the U.S. Marines, who have a reputation for handling complex problems quickly and decisively. However, the Marines are trained to quickly go through a series of mental routines that help them analyze the situation and take action.[9]

According to the rational approach, decision making can be broken down into eight steps.[10]

1. *Monitor the decision environment.* In the first step, a manager monitors internal and external information that will indicate deviations from planned or acceptable behavior. He or she talks to colleagues and reviews financial statements, performance evaluations, industry indices, competitors' activities, and so forth. For example, during the pressure-packed five-week Christmas season, Linda Koslow, general manager of Marshall Fields's Oakbrook, Illinois, store, checks out competitors around the mall, eyeing whether they are marking down merchandise. She also scans printouts of her store's previous day's sales to learn what is or is not moving.[11]

2. *Define the decision problem.* The manager responds to deviations by identifying essential details of the problem: where, when, who was involved, who was affected, and how current activities are influenced. For Koslow, this means defining whether store profits are low because overall sales are less than expected or because certain lines of merchandise are not moving as expected.

3. *Specify decision objectives.* The manager determines what performance outcomes should be achieved by a decision.

4. *L gnose the problem.* In this step, the manager digs below the surface to analyze the cause of the problem. Additional data may be gathered to facilitate this diagnosis. Understanding the cause enables appropriate treatment. For Koslow at Marshall Fields, the cause of slow sales may be competitors' marking down of merchandise or Marshall Fields's failure to display hot-selling items in a visible location.

5. *Develop alternative solutions.* Before a manager can move ahead with a decisive action plan, he or she must have a clear understanding of the various options available to achieve desired objectives. The manager may seek ideas and suggestions from other people. Koslow's alternatives for increasing profits could include buying fresh merchandise, running a sale, or reducing the number of employees.

6. *Evaluate alternatives.* This step may involve the use of statistical techniques or personal experience to assess the probability of success. The merits of each alternative are assessed as well as the probability that it will reach the desired objectives.

7. *Choose the best alternative.* This step is the core of the decision process. The manager uses his or her analysis of the problem, objectives, and alternatives to select a single alternative that has the best chance for success. At Marshall Fields, Koslow may choose to reduce the number of staff as a way to meet the profit goals rather than increase advertising or markdowns.

8. *Implement the chosen alternative.* Finally, the manager uses managerial, administrative, and persuasive abilities and gives directions to ensure that the decision is carried out. The monitoring activity (step 1) begins again as soon as the solution is implemented. For Linda Koslow, the decision cycle is a continuous process, with new decisions made daily based on monitoring her environment for problems and opportunities.

The first four steps in this sequence are the problem identification stage, and the next four steps are the problem solution stage of decision making. All eight steps normally appear in a manager's decision, although each step may not be a distinct element. Managers may know from experience exactly what to do in a situation, so one or more steps will be minimized.

The rational approach works best for programmed decisions, when problems, objectives, and alternatives are clearly defined and the decision maker has time for an orderly, thoughtful process. When decisions are nonprogrammed, ill defined, and piling on top of one another, the individual manager should still try to use the steps in the rational approach, but he or she often will have to take shortcuts by relying on intuition and experience. Deviations from the rational approach are explained by the bounded rationality perspective.

BOUNDED RATIONALITY PERSPECTIVE

The point of the rational approach is that managers should try to use systematic procedures to arrive at good decisions. When organizations are facing little competition and are dealing with well-understood issues, managers generally use rational procedures to make decisions.[12] Yet research into managerial decision making shows managers often are unable to follow an ideal procedure. In today's competitive environment, decisions often must be made very quickly. Time pressure, a large number of internal and external factors affecting a decision, and the ill-defined nature of many problems make systematic analysis virtually impossible. Managers have only so much time and mental capacity and, hence, cannot evaluate every goal, problem, and alternative. The attempt to be rational is bounded (limited) by the enormous complexity of many problems. There is a limit to how rational managers can be. For example, an executive in a hurry may have a choice of fifty ties on a rack but will take the first or second one that matches his suit. The executive doesn't carefully weigh all fifty alternatives because the short amount of time and the large number of plausible alternatives would be overwhelming. The manager simply selects the first tie that solves the problem and moves on to the next task.

Large organizational decisions are not only too complex to fully comprehend, but many other constraints impinge on the decision maker, as illustrated in Exhibit 9.1. The circumstances are ambiguous, requiring social support, a shared perspective on what happens, and acceptance and agreement. For example, in a study of the decision making surrounding the Cuban missile crisis, the executive committee in the White House knew a problem existed but was unable to specify exact goals and objectives. The act of discussing the decision led to personal objections and finally to the discovery of desired objectives that helped clarify the desired course of action and possible consequences.[13] In addition, personal constraints—such as decision style, work pressure, desire for prestige, or simple feelings of insecurity—may constrain either the search for alternatives or the acceptability of an alternative. All of these factors constrain a perfectly rational approach that should lead to an obviously ideal choice.[14] Even seemingly simple decisions, such as selecting a job on graduation from college, can quickly become so complex that a bounded rationality

EXHIBIT 9.1   *Constraints and Trade-offs During Nonprogrammed Decision Making*

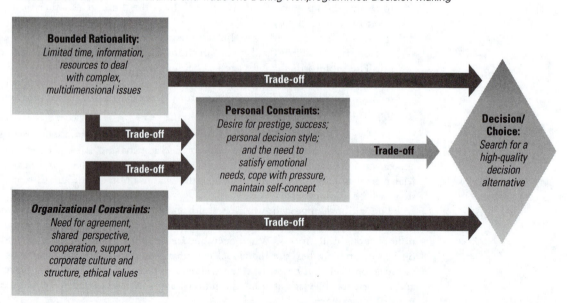

Source: Adapted from Irving L. Janis, *Crucial Decisions* (New York: Free Press, 1989); and A. L. George, *Presidential Decision Making in Foreign Policy: The Effective Use of Information and Advice* (Boulder, Colo.: Westview Press, 1980).

approach is used. Graduating students have been known to search for a job until they have two or three acceptable job offers, at which point their search activity rapidly diminishes. Hundreds of firms may be available for interviews, and two or three job offers are far short of the maximum number that would be possible if students made the decision based on perfect rationality.

The bounded rationality perspective is often associated with intuitive decision processes. In **intuitive decision making**, experience and judgment rather than sequential logic or explicit reasoning are used to make decisions.[15] Intuition is not arbitrary or irrational because it is based on years of practice and hands-on experience, often stored in the subconscious. When managers use their intuition based on long experience with organizational issues, they more rapidly perceive and understand problems, and they develop a gut feeling or hunch about which alternative will solve a problem, speeding the decision-making process.[16] Indeed, many universities are offering courses in creativity and intuition so business students can learn to understand and rely on these processes.

In a situation of great complexity or ambiguity, previous experience and judgment are needed to incorporate intangible elements at both the problem identification and problem solution stages.[17] A study of manager problem finding showed that thirty of thirty-three problems were ambiguous and ill defined.[18] Bits and scraps of unrelated information from informal sources resulted in a pattern in the manager's mind. The manager could not "prove" a problem existed but knew intuitively that a certain area needed attention. A too simple view of a complex problem is often associated with decision failure,[19] and research shows managers are more likely to respond intuitively to a perceived threat to the organization than to an opportunity.[20]

Intuitive processes are also used in the problem solution stage. A survey found that executives frequently made decisions without explicit reference to the impact on profits or to other measurable outcomes.[21] As we saw in Exhibit 9.1, many intangible factors—such as a person's concern about the support of other executives, fear of failure, and social attitudes—influence selection of the best alternative. These factors cannot be quantified in a systematic way, so intuition guided the choice of a solution. Managers may make a decision based on what they sense to be right rather than on what they can document with hard data.

Patrizio Bertelli, CEO of Prada, has transformed the family business into a European fashion powerhouse by making good intuitive decisions—some of which seem inexplicable to his industry colleagues. Even though Bertelli's decisions often seem to come from "out of the blue," they are actually based on a depth of experience, knowledge, and understanding developed over many years in the fashion business. Another example is Jodie Foster, who is known for making good decisions based on intuition at her production company, Egg Pictures. Foster made her movie debut at the age of eight, and her manager–mother involved her in almost all decision making regarding roles, script changes, and so forth. "She understands Hollywood almost mathematically," said one producer.[22] Thus, intuition may be thought of as "recognition" because when managers develop a depth of experience and knowledge in a particular area, problem recognition and problem solution often come almost effortlessly as a recognition of information that has largely been forgotten by the conscious mind.[23]

However, managers may walk a fine line between two extremes: on the one hand, making arbitrary decisions without careful study and on the other, relying obsessively on numbers and rational analysis.[24] Remember that the bounded rationality perspective and the use of intuition applies mostly to nonprogrammed decisions. The novel, unclear, complex aspects of nonprogrammed decisions mean hard data and logical procedures are not available. A study of executive decision making found that managers simply could not use the rational approach for nonprogrammed decisions, such as when to buy a CT scanner for an osteopathic hospital or whether a city had a need for and could reasonably adopt an enterprise resource planning system.[25] In those cases, managers had limited time and resources, and some factors simply couldn't be measured and analyzed. Trying to quantify such information could cause mistakes because it may oversimplify decision criteria.

ORGANIZATIONAL DECISION MAKING

Organizations are composed of managers who make decisions using both rational and intuitive processes; but organization-level decisions are not usually made by a single manager. Many organizational decisions involve several managers. Problem identification and problem solution involve many departments, multiple viewpoints, and even other organizations, which are beyond the scope of an individual manager.

The processes by which decisions are made in organizations are influenced by a number of factors, particularly the organization's own internal structures as well as the degree of stability or instability of the external environment.[26] Research into organization-level decision making has identified four types of organizational decision-making processes: the management science approach, the Carnegie model, the incremental decision process model, and the garbage can model.

MANAGEMENT SCIENCE APPROACH

The **management science approach** to organizational decision making is the analog to the rational approach by individual managers. Management science came into being during World War II.[27] At that time, mathematical and statistical techniques were applied to urgent, large-scale military problems that were beyond the ability of individual decision makers. Mathematicians, physicists, and operations researchers used systems analysis to develop artillery trajectories, antisubmarine strategies, and bombing strategies such as salvoing (discharging multiple shells simultaneously). Consider the problem of a battleship trying to sink an enemy ship several miles away. The calculation for aiming the battleship's guns should consider distance, wind speed, shell size, speed and direction of both ships, pitch and roll of the firing ship, and curvature of the earth. Methods for performing such calculations using trial and error and intuition are not accurate, take far too long, and may never achieve success.

This is where management science came in. Analysts were able to identify the relevant variables involved in aiming a ship's guns and could model them with the use of mathematical equations. Distance, speed, pitch, roll, shell size, and so on could be calculated and entered into the equations. The answer was immediate, and the guns could begin firing. Factors such as pitch and roll were soon measured mechanically and fed directly into the targeting mechanism. Today, the human element is completely removed from the targeting process. Radar picks up the target, and the entire sequence is computed automatically.

Management science yielded astonishing success for many military problems. This approach to decision making diffused into corporations and business schools, where techniques were studied and elaborated. Today, many corporations have assigned departments to use these techniques. The computer department develops quantitative data for analysis. Operations research departments use mathematical models to quantify relevant variables and develop a quantitative representation of alternative solutions and the probability of each one solving the problem. These departments also use such devices as linear programming, Bayesian statistics, PERT charts, and computer simulations.

Management science is an excellent device for organizational decision making when problems are analyzable and when the variables can be identified and measured. Mathematical models can contain a thousand or more variables, each one relevant in some way to the ultimate outcome. Management science techniques have been used to correctly solve problems as diverse as finding the right spot for a church camp, test marketing the first of a new family of products, drilling for oil, and radically altering the distribution of telecommunications services.[28] Other problems amenable to management science techniques are the scheduling of airline employees, ambulance technicians, telephone operators, and turnpike toll collectors.[29]

Management science can accurately and quickly solve problems that have too many explicit variables for human processing. This system is at its best when applied to problems that are analyzable, are measurable, and can be structured in a logical way. Increasingly sophisticated computer technology and software programs are allowing the expansion of management science to cover a broader range of problems than ever before. For example, GE Capital Mortgage Insurance Company used management science techniques to improve the decision making of loss management representatives, who have to decide whether the company can "cure" loans for customers who have stopped making payments or whether it will have to recommend foreclosure on the loan. By creating a sophisticated decision-making software program called Loss Mitigation Optimizer that analyzes and measures relevant variables, GE Capital Mortgage Insurance improved its cure rates from 30 percent of cases to more than 50 percent, while representatives were taking 30 to 50 percent less time per deal. Savings jumped dramatically, to about $8,000 per case, resulting in a savings of $115 million in net income over an eighteen-month period.[30]

Management science has also produced many failures.[31] In recent years, many banks have begun using computerized scoring systems to rate those applying for credit, but some argue that human judgment is needed to account for extenuating circumstances. In one case, a member of the Federal Reserve Board, the agency that sets interest rates and regulates banks, was denied a Toys "R" Us credit card based on his computerized score.[32] One problem with the management science approach is that quantitative data are not rich. Informal cues that indicate the existence of problems have to be sensed on a more personal basis by managers.[33] The most sophisticated mathematical analyses are of no value if the important factors cannot be quantified and included in the model. Such things as competitor reactions, consumer "tastes," and product "warmth" are qualitative dimensions. In these situations, the role of management science is to supplement manager decision making. Quantitative results can be given to managers for discussion and interpretation along with their informal opinions, judgment, and intuition. The final decision can include qualitative factors as well as quantitative calculations.

CARNEGIE MODEL

The **Carnegie model** of organizational decision making is based on the work of Richard Cyert, James March, and Herbert Simon, who were all associated with Carnegie-Mellon University.[34] Their research helped formulate the bounded rationality approach to individual decision making as well as provide new insights about organization decisions. Until their work, research in economics assumed that business firms made decisions as a single entity, as if all relevant information were funneled to the top decision maker for a choice. Research by the Carnegie group indicated that organization-level decisions involved many managers and that a final choice was based on a coalition among those managers. A **coalition** is an alliance among several managers who agree about organizational goals and problem priorities.[35] It could include managers from line departments, staff specialists, and even external groups, such as powerful customers, bankers, or union representatives.

Management coalitions are needed during decision making for two reasons. First, organizational goals are often ambiguous, and operative goals of departments are often inconsistent. When goals are ambiguous and inconsistent, managers disagree about problem priorities. They must bargain about problems and build a coalition around the question of which problems to solve.

The second reason for coalitions is that individual managers intend to be rational but function with human cognitive limitations and other constraints, as described earlier. Managers do not have the time, resources, or mental capacity to identify all dimensions and to process all information relevant to a decision. These limitations lead to coalition-building behavior. Managers talk to each other and exchange points of view to gather information and reduce ambiguity. People who have relevant information or a stake in a decision outcome are consulted. Building a coalition will lead to a decision that is supported by interested parties.

The process of coalition formation has several implications for organizational decision behavior. First, decisions are made to satisfice rather than to optimize problem solutions. **Satisficing** means organizations accept a "satisfactory" rather than a maximum level of performance, enabling them to achieve several goals simultaneously. In decision making, the coalition will accept a solution that is perceived as satisfactory to all coalition members. Second, managers are concerned with immediate problems and short-run solutions. They engage in what Cyert and March called problemistic search.[36] **Problemistic search** means managers look around in the immediate environment for a solution to quickly resolve a problem. Managers don't expect a perfect solution when the situation is ill defined and conflict-laden. This contrasts with the management science approach, which assumes that analysis can uncover every reasonable alternative. The Carnegie model says search behavior is just sufficient to produce a satisfactory solution and that managers typically adopt the first satisfactory solution that emerges. Third, discussion and bargaining are especially important in the problem identification stage of decision making. Unless coalition members perceive a problem, action will not be taken. The decision process described in the Carnegie model is summarized in Exhibit 9.2.

The Carnegie model points out that building agreement through a managerial coalition is a major part of organizational decision making. This is especially true at upper management levels. Discussion and bargaining are time consuming, so search procedures are usually simple and the selected alternative satisfices rather than optimizes problem solution. When problems are programmed—are clear and have been seen before—the organization will rely on previous procedures and routines. Rules and procedures prevent the need for renewed coalition formation and political bargaining. Nonprogrammed decisions, however, require bargaining and conflict resolution.

One of the best and most visible coalition builders of recent years was former President George Bush, who would seek a broad-based coalition at the start of an important decision process. During the decision process regarding the Persian Gulf War, President Bush kept up a barrage of personal calls and visits to world leaders to gain agreement for his vision of forcing Saddam Hussein from Kuwait and for shaping a "new world order."[37]

INCREMENTAL DECISION PROCESS MODEL

Henry Mintzberg and his associates at McGill University in Montreal approached organizational decision making from a different perspective. They identified twenty-five decisions made in organizations and traced the events associated with these decisions from beginning to end.[38] Their research identified each step in the decision sequence. This approach to decision making, called the **incremental decision process model**,

EXHIBIT 9.2 *Choice Processes in the Carnegie Model*

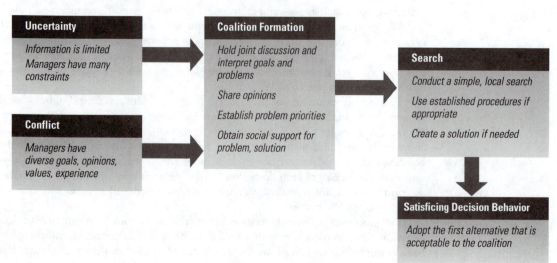

places less emphasis on the political and social factors described in the Carnegie model, but tells more about the structured sequence of activities undertaken from the discovery of a problem to its solution.[39]

Sample decisions in Mintzberg's research included choosing which jet aircraft to acquire for a regional airline, developing a new supper club, developing a new container terminal in a harbor, identifying a new market for a deodorant, installing a controversial new medical treatment in a hospital, and firing a star announcer.[40] The scope and importance of these decisions are revealed in the length of time taken to complete them. Most of these decisions took more than a year, and one-third of them took more than two years. Most of these decisions were nonprogrammed and required custom-designed solutions.

One discovery from this research is that major organization choices are usually a series of small choices that combine to produce the major decision. Thus, many organizational decisions are a series of nibbles rather than a big bite. Organizations move through several decision points and may hit barriers along the way. Mintzberg called these barriers *decision interrupts*. An interrupt may mean an organization has to cycle back through a previous decision and try something new. Decision loops or cycles are one way the organization learns which alternatives will work. The ultimate solution may be very different from what was initially anticipated.

The pattern of decision stages discovered by Mintzberg and his associates is shown in Exhibit 9.3. Each box indicates a possible step in the decision sequence. The steps take place in three major decision phases: identification, development, and selection.

Identification Phase. The identification phase begins with *recognition*. Recognition means one or more managers become aware of a problem and the need to make a decision. Recognition is usually stimulated by a problem or an opportunity. A problem exists when elements in the external environment change or when internal performance is perceived to be below standard. In the case of firing a radio announcer, comments about the announcer came from listeners, other announcers, and advertisers. Managers interpreted these cues until a pattern emerged that indicated a problem had to be dealt with.

The second step is *diagnosis*, which is where more information is gathered if needed to define the problem situation. Diagnosis may be systematic or informal, depending upon the severity of the problem. Severe problems do not have time for extensive diagnosis; the response must be immediate. Mild problems are usually diagnosed in a more systematic manner.

Development Phase. The development phase is when a solution is shaped to solve the problem defined in the identification phase. The development of a solution takes one of two directions. First, *search* procedures may be used to seek out alternatives within the organization's repertoire of solutions. For example, in the case of firing a star announcer, managers asked what the radio station had done the last time an announcer had to be let go. To conduct the search, organization participants may look into their own memories, talk to other managers, or examine the formal procedures of the organization.

The second direction of development is to *design* a custom solution. This happens when the problem is novel so that previous experience has no value. Mintzberg found that in these cases, key decision makers have only a vague idea of the ideal solution. Gradually, through a trial-and-error process, a custom-designed alternative will emerge. Development of the solution is a groping, incremental procedure, building a solution brick by brick.

Selection Phase. The selection phase is when the solution is chosen. This phase is not always a matter of making a clear choice among alternatives. In the case of custom-made solutions, selection is more an evaluation of the single alternative that seems feasible.

Evaluation and choice may be accomplished in three ways. The *judgment* form of selection is used when a final choice falls upon a single decision maker, and the choice involves judgment based upon experience. In analysis, alternatives are evaluated on a more systematic basis, such as with management science techniques. Mintzberg found that most

EXHIBIT 9.3   *The Incremental Decision Process Model*

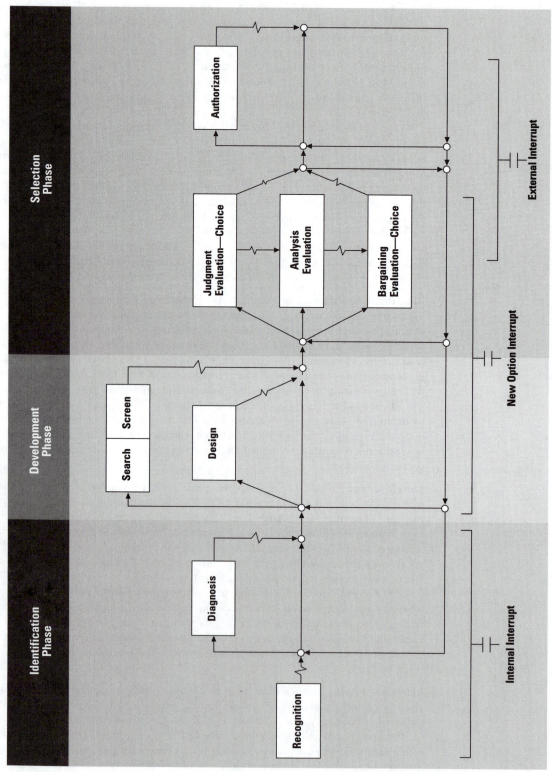

Source: Adapted and reprinted from "The Structure of Unstructured Decision Processes" by Henry Mintzberg, Duru Raisinghani, and André Théorêt, published in *Administrative Science Quarterly* 21, no. 2 (1976): 266, by permission of *The Administrative Science Quarterly.* Copyright © 1976 Cornell University.

decisions did not involve systematic analysis and evaluation of alternatives. *Bargaining* occurs when selection involves a group of decision makers. Each decision maker may have a different stake in the outcome, so conflict emerges. Discussion and bargaining occur until a coalition is formed, as in the Carnegie model described earlier.

When a decision is formally accepted by the organization, *authorization* takes place. The decision may be passed up the hierarchy to the responsible hierarchical level. Authorization is often routine because the expertise and knowledge rest with the lower decision makers who identified the problem and developed the solution. A few decisions are rejected because of implications not anticipated by lower-level managers.

Dynamic Factors. The lower part of the chart in Exhibit 9.3 shows lines running back toward the beginning of the decision process. These lines represent loops or cycles that take place in the decision process. Organizational decisions do not follow an orderly progression from recognition through authorization. Minor problems arise that force a loop back to an earlier stage. These are decision interrupts. If a custom-designed solution is perceived as unsatisfactory, the organization may have to go back to the very beginning and reconsider whether the problem is truly worth solving. Feedback loops can be caused by problems of timing, politics, disagreement among managers, inability to identify a feasible solution, turnover of managers, or the sudden appearance of a new alternative. For example, when a small Canadian airline made the decision to acquire jet aircraft, the board authorized the decision, but shortly after, a new chief executive was brought in who canceled the contract, recycling the decision back to the identification phase. He accepted the diagnosis of the problem but insisted upon a new search for alternatives. Then a foreign airline went out of business and two used aircraft became available at a bargain price. This presented an unexpected option, and the chief executive used his own judgment to authorize the purchase of the aircraft.[41]

Because most decisions take place over an extended period of time, circumstances change. Decision making is a dynamic process that may require a number of cycles before a problem is solved.

GARBAGE CAN MODEL

The **garbage can model** is one of the most recent and interesting descriptions of organizational decision processes. It is not directly comparable to the earlier models, because the garbage can model deals with the pattern or flow of multiple decisions within organizations, whereas the incremental and Carnegie models focus on how a single decision is made. The garbage can model helps you think of the whole organization and the frequent decisions being made by managers throughout.

Organized Anarchy. The garbage can model was developed to explain the pattern of decision making in organizations that experience extremely high uncertainty. Michael Cohen, James March, and Johan Olsen, the originators of the model, called the highly uncertain conditions an **organized anarchy**, which is an extremely organic organization.[42] Organized anarchies do not rely on the normal vertical hierarchy of authority and bureaucratic decision rules. They are caused by three characteristics:

1. *Problematic preferences.* Goals, problems, alternatives, and solutions are ill defined. Ambiguity characterizes each step of a decision process.
2. *Unclear, poorly understood technology.* Cause-and-effect relationships within the organization are difficult to identify. An explicit database that applies to decisions is not available.
3. *Turnover.* Organizational positions experience turnover of participants. In addition, employees are busy and have only limited time to allocate to any one problem or decision. Participation in any given decision will be fluid and limited.

The organized anarchy describes organizations characterized by rapid change and a collegial, nonbureaucratic environment. No organization fits this extremely organic circumstance all the time, although contemporary learning organizations and today's

Internet-based companies may experience it much of the time. Many organizations will occasionally find themselves in positions of making decisions under unclear, problematic circumstances. The garbage can model is useful for understanding the pattern of these decisions.

Streams of Events. The unique characteristic of the garbage can model is that the decision process is not seen as a sequence of steps that begins with a problem and ends with a solution. Indeed, problem identification and problem solution may not be connected to each other. An idea may be proposed as a solution when no problem is specified. A problem may exist and never generate a solution. Decisions are the outcome of independent streams of events within the organization. The four streams relevant to organizational decision making are as follows:

1. *Problems.* Problems are points of dissatisfaction with current activities and performance. They represent a gap between desired performance and current activities. Problems are perceived to require attention. However, they are distinct from solutions and choices. A problem may lead to a proposed solution or it may not. Problems may not be solved when solutions are adopted.

2. *Potential solutions.* A solution is an idea somebody proposes for adoption. Such ideas form a flow of alternative solutions through the organization. Ideas may be brought into the organization by new personnel or may be invented by existing personnel. Participants may simply be attracted to certain ideas and push them as logical choices regardless of problems. Attraction to an idea may cause an employee to look for a problem to which the idea can be attached and, hence, justified. The point is that solutions exist independent of problems.

3. *Participants.* Organization participants are employees who come and go throughout the organization. People are hired, reassigned, and fired. Participants vary widely in their ideas, perception of problems, experience, values, and training. The problems and solutions recognized by one manager will differ from those recognized by another manager.

4. *Choice opportunities.* Choice opportunities are occasions when an organization usually makes a decision. They occur when contracts are signed, people are hired, or a new product is authorized. They also occur when the right mix of participants, solutions, and problems exists. Thus, a manager who happened to learn of a good idea may suddenly become aware of a problem to which it applies and, hence, can provide the organization with a choice opportunity. Match-ups of problems and solutions often result in decisions.

With the concept of four streams, the overall pattern of organizational decision making takes on a random quality. Problems, solutions, participants, and choices all flow through the organization. In one sense, the organization is a large garbage can in which these streams are being stirred, as illustrated in Exhibit 9.4. When a problem, solution, and participant happen to connect at one point, a decision may be made and the problem may be solved; but if the solution does not fit the problem, the problem may not be solved. Thus, when viewing the organization as a whole and considering its high level of uncertainty, one sees problems arise that are not solved and solutions tried that do not work. Organization decisions are disorderly and not the result of a logical, step-by-step sequence. Events may be so ill defined and complex that decisions, problems, and solutions act as independent events. When they connect, some problems are solved, but many are not.[43]

Consequences. Four consequences of the garbage can decision process for organizational decision making are as follows:

1. *Solutions may be proposed even when problems do not exist.* An employee may be sold on an idea and may try to sell it to the rest of the organization. An example was the adoption of computers by many organizations during the 1970s. The computer was an exciting solution and was pushed by both computer manufacturers and systems

EXHIBIT 9.4   *Illustration of Independent Streams of Events in the Garbage Can Model of Decision Making*

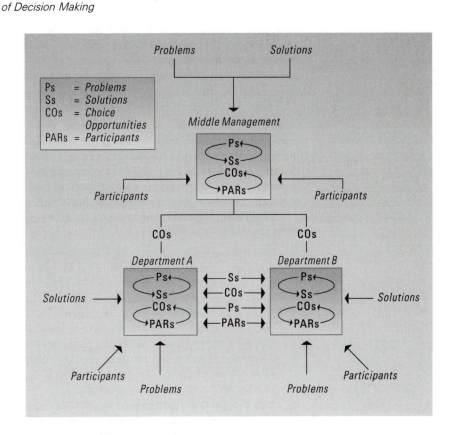

analysts within organizations. The computer did not solve any problems in those initial applications. Indeed, some computers caused more problems than they solved.

2. *Choices are made without solving problems.* A choice such as creating a new department may be made with the intention of solving a problem; but, under conditions of high uncertainty, the choice may be incorrect. Moreover, many choices just seem to happen. People decide to quit, the organization's budget is cut, or a new policy bulletin is issued. These choices may be oriented toward problems but do not necessarily solve them.

3. *Problems may persist without being solved.* Organization participants get used to certain problems and give up trying to solve them; or participants may not know how to solve certain problems because the technology is unclear. A university in Canada was placed on probation by the American Association of University Professors because a professor had been denied tenure without due process. The probation was a nagging annoyance that the administrators wanted to remove. Fifteen years later, the nontenured professor died. The probation continues because the university did not acquiesce to the demands of the heirs of the association to reevaluate the case. The university would like to solve the problem, but administrators are not sure how, and they do not have the resources to allocate to it. The probation problem persists without a solution.

4. *A few problems are solved.* The decision process does work in the aggregate. In computer simulation models of the garbage can model, important problems were often resolved. Solutions do connect with appropriate problems and participants so that a good choice is made. Of course, not all problems are resolved when choices are made, but the organization does move in the direction of problem reduction.

SPECIAL DECISION CIRCUMSTANCES

In a highly competitive world beset by global competition and rapid change, decision making seldom fits the traditional rational, analytical model. To cope in today's world, managers must learn to make decisions fast, especially in high-velocity environments, to learn from decision mistakes, and to avoid escalating commitment to an unsatisfactory course of action.

HIGH-VELOCITY ENVIRONMENTS

In some industries today, the rate of competitive and technological change is so extreme that market data is either unavailable or obsolete, strategic windows open and shut quickly, perhaps within a few months, and the cost of a decision error is company failure. Recent research has examined how successful companies make decisions in these **high-velocity environments**, especially to understand whether organizations abandon rational approaches or have time for incremental implementation.[44]

Comparing successful with unsuccessful decisions in high-velocity environments suggests the following guidelines.

- Successful decision makers track information in real time to develop a deep and intuitive grasp of the business. Two to three intense meetings per week with all key players are usual. Decision makers track operating statistics about cash, scrap, backlog, work in process, and shipments to constantly feel the pulse of what is happening. Unsuccessful firms were more concerned with future planning and forward-looking information, with only a loose grip on immediate happenings.
- During a major decision, successful companies began immediately to build multiple alternatives. Implementation may run in parallel before finally settling on a final choice. Slow-decision companies developed only a single alternative, moving to another only after the first one failed.
- Fast, successful decision makers sought advice from everyone and depended heavily on one or two savvy, trusted colleagues as counselors. Slow companies were unable to build trust and agreement among the best people.
- Fast companies involved everyone in the decision and tried for consensus; but if consensus did not emerge, the top manager made the choice and moved ahead. Waiting for everyone to be on board created more delays than warranted. Slow companies delayed decisions to achieve a uniform consensus.
- Fast, successful choices were well integrated with other decisions and the overall strategic direction of the company. Less successful choices considered the decision in isolation from other decisions; the decision was made in the abstract.[45]

When speed matters, a slow decision is as ineffective as the wrong decision. As we discussed in Chapter 8, speed is a crucial competitive weapon in a growing number of industries, and companies can learn to make decisions fast. Managers must be plugged into the pulse of the company, must seek consensus and advice, and then be ready to take the risk and move ahead. When Deborah Triant, CEO and president of Check Point Software Technologies, has to make a fast decision about a complex problem, she asks everyone she knows for an opinion, but then she trusts her intuition and experience to make the decision and move forward.[46]

DECISION MISTAKES AND LEARNING

Organizational decisions produce many errors, especially when made under high uncertainty. Managers simply cannot determine or predict which alternative will solve a problem. In these cases, the organization must make the decision—and take the risk—often in the spirit of trial and error. If an alternative fails, the organization can learn from it and try another alternative that better fits the situation. Each failure provides new information and learning. The point for managers is to move ahead with the decision process despite the potential for mistakes. "Chaotic action is preferable to orderly inaction."[47]

In many cases, managers have been encouraged to instill a climate of experimentation, even foolishness, to facilitate creative decision making. If one idea fails, another idea should be tried. Failure often lays the groundwork for success, as when technicians at 3M developed Post-it Notes based on a failed product—a not-very-sticky glue. Companies such as PepsiCo believe that if all their new products succeed, they're doing something wrong, not taking the necessary risks to develop new markets.[48]

Only by making mistakes can managers and organizations go through the process of **decision learning** and acquire sufficient experience and knowledge to perform more effectively in the future. Robert Townsend, who was president at Avis Corporation, gives the following advice:

> Admit your mistakes openly, maybe even joyfully. Encourage your associates to do likewise by commiserating with them. Never castigate. Babies learn to walk by falling down. If you beat a baby every time he falls down, he'll never care much for walking.
>
> My batting average on decisions at Avis was no better than a .333. Two out of every three decisions I made were wrong. But my mistakes were discussed openly and most of them corrected with a little help from my friends.[49]

ESCALATING COMMITMENT

A much more dangerous mistake is to persist in a course of action when it is failing. Research suggests that organizations often continue to invest time and money in a solution despite strong evidence that it is not working. Two explanations are given for why managers **escalate commitment** to a failing decision. The first is that managers block or distort negative information when they are personally responsible for a negative decision. They simply don't know when to pull the plug. In some cases, they continue to throw good money after bad even when a strategy seems incorrect and goals are not being met.[50] An example of this distortion is the reaction at Borden when the company began losing customers following its refusal to lower prices on dairy products. When the cost of raw milk dropped, Borden hoped to boost the profit margins of its dairy products, convinced that customers would pay a premium for the brand name. Borden's sales plummeted as low-priced competitors mopped up, but top executives stuck with their premium pricing policy for almost a year. By then, the company's dairy division was operating at a severe loss.[51]

A second explanation for escalating commitment to a failing decision is that consistency and persistence are valued in contemporary society. Consistent managers are considered better leaders than those who switch around from one course of action to another. Even though organizations learn through trial and error, organizational norms value consistency. These norms may result in a course of action being maintained, resources being squandered, and learning being inhibited. Emphasis on consistent leadership was partly responsible for the Long Island Lighting Company's refusal to change course in the construction of the Shoreham Nuclear Power Plant, which was eventually abandoned—after an investment of more than $5 billion—without ever having begun operation. Shoreham's cost was estimated at $75 million when the project was announced in 1966, but by the time a construction permit was granted, LILCO had already spent $77 million. Opposition to nuclear power was growing. Critics continued to decry the huge sums of money being pumped into Shoreham. Customers complained that LILCO was cutting back on customer service and maintenance of current operations. Shoreham officials, however, seemed convinced that they would triumph in the end; their response to criticism was, "If people will just wait until the end, they are going to realize that this is a hell of an investment."

The end came in 1989, when a negotiated agreement with New York led LILCO to abandon the $5.5 billion plant in return for rate increases and a $2.5 billion tax write-off. By the time Governor Mario Cuomo signed an agreement with the company, LILCO had remained firmly committed to a losing course of action for more than twenty-three years.[52]

Failure to admit a mistake and adopt a new course of action is far worse than an attitude that encourages mistakes and learning. Based on what has been said about decision making in this chapter, one can expect companies to be ultimately successful in their decision making by adopting a learning approach toward solutions. They will make mistakes along the way, but they will resolve uncertainty through the trial-and-error process.

DISCUSSION QUESTIONS

1. A professional economist once told his class, "An individual decision maker should process all relevant information and select the economically rational alternative." Do you agree? Why or why not?
2. Why is intuition used in decision making?
3. The Carnegie model emphasizes the need for a political coalition in the decision-making process. When and why are coalitions necessary?
4. What are the three major phases in Mintzberg's incremental decision process model? Why might an organization recycle through one or more phases of the model?
5. An organization theorist once told her class, "Organizations never make big decisions. They make small decisions that eventually add up to a big decision." Explain the logic behind this statement.
6. Why would managers in high-velocity environments worry more about the present than the future? Discuss.
7. Describe the four streams of events in the garbage can model of decision making. Why are they considered to be independent?
8. Are there decision-making situations in which managers should be expected to make the "correct" decision? Are there situations in which decision makers should be expected to make mistakes? Discuss.

NOTES

1. Robert D. Hof, "The Education of Andrew Grove," *Business Week*, 16 January 1995, 60–62.
2. Bruce Horovitz and Gary Strauss, "Fast-Food Icon Wants Shine Restored to Golden Arches," *USA Today*, 1 May 1998, 1B, 2B; "Tickling a Child's Fancy," *The Tennessean*, 6 February 1997, 1E, 4E; and Katrina Brooker, "Toys Were Us," *Fortune*, 27 September 1999, 145–148.
3. Nina Munk, "Gap Gets It," *Fortune*, 3 August 1998, 68–82; and Linda Yates and Peter Skarzynski, "How Do Companies Get to the Future First?" *Management Review*, January 1999, 16–22.
4. Charles Lindblom, "The Science of 'Muddling Through,'" *Public Administration Review* 29 (1954): 79–88.
5. Herbert A. Simon, *The New Science of Management Decision* (Englewood Cliffs, N.J.: Prentice-Hall, 1960), 1–8.
6. Paul J. H. Schoemaker and J. Edward Russo, "A Pyramid of Decision Approaches," *California Management Review* (Fall 1993): 9–31.
7. Wendy Zellner, "Back to Coffee, Tea, or Milk?" *Business Week*, 3 July 1995, 52–56.
8. Michael Pacanowsky, "Team Tools for Wicked Problems," *Organizational Dynamics* 23, no. 3 (Winter 1995): 36–51.
9. Karen Dillon, "The Perfect Decision," (an interview with John S. Hammond and Ralph L. Keeney), *Inc.* October 1998, 74–78; and John S. Hammond and

Ralph L. Keeney, *Smart Choices: A Practical Guide to Making Better Decisions* (Boston, Mass.: Harvard Business School Press, 1998).
10. Earnest R. Archer, "How to Make a Business Decision: An Analysis of Theory and Practice," *Management Review* 69 (February 1980): 54–61; Boris Blai, "Eight Steps to Successful Problem Solving," *Supervisory Management* (January 1986): 7–9.
11. Francine Schwadel, "Christmas Sales' Lack of Momentum Test Store Managers' Mettle," *The Wall Street Journal*, 16 December 1987, 1.
12. James W. Dean, Jr., and Mark P. Sharfman, "Procedural Rationality in the Strategic Decision-Making Process," *Journal of Management Studies* 30 (1993): 587–610.
13. Paul A. Anderson, "Decision Making by Objection and the Cuban Missile Crisis," *Administrative Science Quarterly* 28 (1983): 201–22.
14. Irving L. Janis, *Crucial Decisions: Leadership in Policymaking and Crisis Management* (New York: The Free Press, 1989); Paul C. Nutt, "Flexible Decision Styles and the Choices of Top Executives," *Journal of Management Studies* 30 (1993): 695–721.
15. Herbert A. Simon, "Making Management Decisions: The Role of Intuition and Emotion," *Academy of Management Executive* 1 (February 1987): 57–64; Daniel J. Eisenberg, "How Senior Managers Think," *Harvard Business Review* 62 (November–December 1984): 80–90.

16. Sefan Wally and J. Robert Baum, "Personal and Structural Determinants of the Pace of Strategic Decision Making," *Academy of Management Journal* 37, no. 4 (1994): 932–56; Orlando Behling and Norman L. Eckel, "Making Sense Out of Intuition," *Academy of Management Executive* 5, no. 1 (1991): 46–54.

17. Thomas F. Issack, "Intuition: An Ignored Dimension of Management," *Academy of Management Review* 3 (1978): 917–22.

18. Marjorie A. Lyles, "Defining Strategic Problems: Subjective Criteria of Executives," *Organizational Studies* 8 (1987): 263–80; Marjorie A. Lyles and Ian I. Mitroff, "Organizational Problem Formulation: An Empirical Study," *Administrative Science Quarterly* 25 (1980): 102–19.

19. Marjorie A. Lyles and Howard Thomas, "Strategic Problem Formulation: Biases and Assumptions Embedded in Alternative Decision-Making Models," *Journal of Management Studies* 25 (1988): 131–45.

20. Susan E. Jackson and Jane E. Dutton, "Discerning Threats and Opportunities," *Administrative Science Quarterly* 33 (1988): 370–87.

21. Ross Stagner, "Corporate Decision-Making: An Empirical Study," *Journal of Applied Psychology* 53 (1969): 1–13.

22. Lauren Goldstein, "Prada Goes Shopping," *Fortune*, 27 September 1999, 207–10; and Suzanna Andrews, "Calling the Shots," *Working Woman*, November 1995, 30–35, 90.

23. Michael L. Ray and Rochelle Myers, *Creativity in Business* (Garden City, New Jersey: Doubleday, 1986).

24. Ann Langley, "Between 'Paralysis By Analysis' and 'Extinction By Instinct,'" *Sloan Management Review* (Spring 1995): 63–76.

25. Paul C. Nutt, "Types of Organizational Decision Processes," *Administrative Science Quarterly* 29 (1984): 414–50.

26. Nandini Rajagopalan, Abdul M. A. Rasheed, and Deepak K. Datta, "Strategic Decision Processes: Critical Review and Future Decisions," *Journal of Management* 19 (1993): 349–84; Paul J. H. Schoemaker, "Strategic Decisions in Organizations: Rational and Behavioral Views," *Journal of Management Studies* 30 (1993): 107–29; Charles J. McMillan, "Qualitative Models of Organizational Decision Making," *Journal of Management Studies* 5 (1980): 22–39; Paul C. Nutt, "Models for Decision Making in Organizations and Some Contextual Variables Which Stimulate Optimal Use," *Academy of Management Review* 1 (1976): 84–98.

27. Hugh J. Miser, "Operations Analysis in the Army Air Forces in World War II: Some Reminiscences," *Interfaces* 23 (September–October 1993): 47–49; Harold J. Leavitt, William R. Dill, and Henry B. Eyring, *The Organizational World* (New York: Harcourt Brace Jovanovich, 1973), chap. 6.

28. Stephen J. Huxley, "Finding the Right Spot for a Church Camp in Spain," *Interfaces* 12 (October 1982): 108–14; James E. Hodder and Henry E. Riggs, "Pitfalls in Evaluating Risky Projects," *Harvard Business Review* (January–February 1985): 128–35.

29. Edward Baker and Michael Fisher, "Computational Results for Very Large Air Crew Scheduling Problems," *Omega* 9 (1981): 613–18; Jean Aubin, "Scheduling Ambulances," *Interfaces* 22 (March–April, 1992): 1–10.

30. Anna Muoio, "Decisions, Decisions," (Unit of One column), *Fast Company*, October 1998, 93-101; also see Brian Palmer, "Click Here for Decisions," *Fortune*, 10 May 1999, 153–56, for information on decision making software.

31. Harold J. Leavitt, "Beyond the Analytic Manager," *California Management Review* 17 (1975): 5–12; C. Jackson Grayson, Jr., "Management Science and Business Practice," *Harvard Business Review* 51 (July–August 1973): 41–48.

32. David Wessel, "A Man Who Governs Credit Is Denied a Toys 'R' Us Card," *The Wall Street Journal*, 14 December 1995, B1.

33. Richard L. Daft and John C. Wiginton, "Language and Organization," *Academy of Management Review* (1979): 179–91.

34. Based on Richard M. Cyert and James G. March, *A Behavioral Theory of the Firm* (Englewood Cliffs, N.J.: Prentice-Hall, 1963); and James G. March and Herbert A. Simon, *Organizations* (New York: Wiley, 1958).

35. William B. Stevenson, Joan L. Pearce, and Lyman W. Porter, "The Concept of 'Coalition' in Organization Theory and Research," *Academy of Management Review* 10 (1985): 256–68.

36. Cyert and March, *Behavioral Theory of the Firm*, 120–22.

37. Ann Reilly Dowd, "How Bush Decided," *Fortune*, 11 February 1991, 45–46.

38. Based on Henry Mintzberg, Duru Raisinghani, and André Théorêt, "The Structure of 'Unstructured' Decision Processes," *Administrative Science Quarterly* 21 (1976): 246–75.

39. Lawrence T. Pinfield, "A Field Evaluation of Perspectives on Organizational Decision Making," *Administrative Science Quarterly* 31 (1986): 365–88.

40. Mintzberg, et al., "The Structure of 'Unstructured' Decision Processes."

41. Ibid., 270.

42. Michael D. Cohen, James G. March, and Johan P. Olsen, "A Garbage Can Model of Organizational Choice," *Administrative Science Quarterly* 17 (March 1972): 1–25; Michael D. Cohen and James G. March, *Leadership and Ambiguity: The American College President* (New York: McGraw-Hill, 1974).

43. Michael Masuch and Perry LaPotin, "Beyond Garbage Cans: An AI Model of Organizational Choice," *Administrative Science Quarterly* 34 (1989): 38–67.

44. L. J. Bourgeois III and Kathleen M. Eisenhardt, "Strategic Decision Processes in High Velocity Environments: Four Cases in the Microcomputer Industry," *Management Science* 34 (1988): 816–35.

45. Kathleen M. Eisenhardt, "Speed and Strategic Course: How Managers Accelerate Decision Making," *California Management Review* (Spring 1990): 39–54.

46. Anna Muoio, "Decisions, Decisions."

47. Karl Weick, *The Social Psychology of Organizing,* 2d ed. (Reading, Mass.: Addison-Wesley, 1979), 243.

48. Christopher Power with Kathleen Kerwin, Ronald Grover, Keith Alexander, and Robert D. Hof, "Flops," *Business Week*, 16 August 1993, 76-82.

49. Robert Townsend, *Up the Organization* (New York: Knopf, 1974), 115.

50. Helga Drummond, "Too Little Too Late: A Case Study of Escalation in Decision Making," *Organization Studies* 15, no. 4 (1994): 591–607; Joel Brockner, "The Escalation of Commitment to a Failing Course of Action: Toward Theoretical Progress," *Academy of Management Review* 17 (1992): 39–61; Barry M. Staw and Jerry Ross, "Knowing When to Pull the Plug," *Harvard Business Review* 65 (March–April 1987): 68–74; Barry M. Staw, "The Escalation of Commitment to a Course of Action," *Academy of Management Review* 6 (1981): 577–87.

51. Elizabeth Lesly, "Why Things Are So Sour at Borden," *Business Week*, 22 November 1993, 78–85.

52. Jerry Ross and Barry M. Staw, "Organizational Escalation and Exit: Lessons from the Shoreham Nuclear Power Plant," *Academy of Management Journal* 36 (1993): 701–32.

CHAPTER **10**

Conflict, Power, and Politics

All organizations are a complex mix of individuals and groups pursuing various goals and interests. Conflict is a natural and inevitable outcome of the close interaction of people who may have diverse opinions and values, pursue different objectives, and have differential access to information and resources within the organization. Individuals and groups will use power and political activity to handle their differences and manage conflict.[1]

Too much conflict can be harmful to an organization. However, conflict can also be a positive force because it challenges the status quo, encourages new ideas and approaches, and leads to change.[2] Some degree of conflict occurs in all human relationships—between friends, romantic partners, and teammates as well as between parents and children, teachers and students, and bosses and employees. Conflict is not necessarily a negative force; it results from the normal interaction of varying human interests. Within organizations, individuals and groups frequently have different interests and goals they wish to achieve through the organization. Managers in all organizations regularly deal with conflict and struggle with decisions about how to get the most out of employees, enhance job satisfaction and team identification, and realize high organizational performance.

PURPOSE OF THIS CHAPTER

This chapter will discuss the nature of conflict and the use of power and political tactics to manage and reduce conflict among individuals and groups. The notion of conflict has appeared in previous chapters. In Chapter 3, we talked about horizontal linkages such as task forces and teams that encourage collaboration among functional departments. Chapter 4 introduced the concept of differentiation, which means that different departments pursue different goals and may have different attitudes and values. Chapter 7 discussed the emergence of subcultures, and in Chapter 9, coalition building was proposed as one way to resolve disagreements among departments.

The first sections of this chapter explore the nature of intergroup conflict, characteristics of organizations that contribute to conflict, and the use of a political versus a rational model of organization to manage conflicting interests. Subsequent sections examine individual and organizational power, the vertical and horizontal sources of power for managers and other employees, and how power is used to attain organizational goals. The latter part of the chapter looks at politics, which is the application of power and authority to achieve desired outcomes. We will also discuss some tactics managers can use to enhance collaboration among people and departments.

WHAT IS INTERGROUP CONFLICT?

Intergroup conflict requires three ingredients: group identification, observable group differences, and frustration. First, employees have to perceive themselves as part of an identifiable group or department.[3] Second, there has to be an observable group difference of some form. Groups may be located on different floors of the building, members may have gone to different schools, or members may work in different departments. The ability to identify oneself as a part of one group and to observe differences in comparison with other groups is necessary for conflict.[4]

The third ingredient is frustration. Frustration means that if one group achieves its goal, the other will not; it will be blocked. Frustration need not be severe and only needs to be anticipated to set off intergroup conflict. Intergroup conflict will appear when one group tries to advance its position in relation to other groups. **Intergroup conflict** can be defined as the behavior that occurs among organizational groups when participants identify with one group and perceive that other groups may block their group's goal achievement or expectations.[5] Conflict means that groups clash directly, that they are in fundamental opposition. Conflict is similar to competition but more severe. **Competition** means rivalry among groups in the pursuit of a common prize, while conflict presumes direct interference with goal achievement.

Intergroup conflict within organizations can occur horizontally—across departments—or vertically—between different levels of the organization.[6] For example, the production department of a manufacturing company may have a dispute with quality control because new quality procedures reduce production efficiency. Teammates may argue about the best way to accomplish tasks and achieve goals. Workers may clash with bosses about new work methods, reward systems, or job assignments. Another typical source of conflict is between groups such as unions and management or franchise owners and headquarters. Franchise owners for McDonald's, Taco Bell, Burger King, and KFC have clashed with headquarters because of the increase of company-owned stores in neighborhoods that compete directly with franchisees. The FedEx pilots' union has fought with the company over wage increases, working hours, and control over scheduling. Conflict can also occur between different divisions or business units. For example, a conflict emerged between the two sides of Andersen Worldwide—Andersen Consulting (management consulting) and Arthur Andersen (accounting services)—because the two groups found themselves going after the same business.[7]

WHY CONFLICT EXISTS

Some specific organizational characteristics can generate conflict. These **sources of intergroup conflict** are goal incompatibility, differentiation, task interdependence, and limited resources, as illustrated in Exhibit 10.1. These characteristics of organizational relationships are determined by the contextual factors of environment, size, technology, strategy and goals, and organizational structure, which have been discussed in previous chapters. These characteristics, in turn, help shape the extent to which a rational model of behavior versus a political model of behavior is used to accomplish objectives.

Goal Incompatibility. Goal incompatibility is probably the greatest cause of intergroup conflict in organizations.[8] The goals of each department reflect the specific objectives members are trying to achieve. The achievement of one department's goals often interferes with another department's goals. University police, for example, have a goal of providing a safe and secure campus. They can achieve their goal by locking all buildings on evenings and weekends and not distributing keys. Without easy access to buildings, however, progress toward the science department's research goals will proceed slowly. On the

EXHIBIT 10.1   *Sources of Conflict and Use of Rational Versus Political Model*

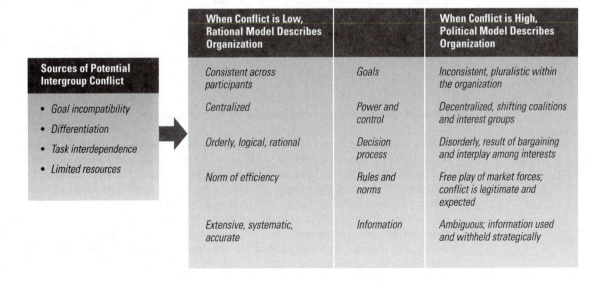

Sources of Potential Intergroup Conflict	When Conflict is Low, Rational Model Describes Organization		When Conflict is High, Political Model Describes Organization
• Goal incompatibility • Differentiation • Task interdependence • Limited resources	Consistent across participants	Goals	Inconsistent, pluralistic within the organization
	Centralized	Power and control	Decentralized, shifting coalitions and interest groups
	Orderly, logical, rational	Decision process	Disorderly, result of bargaining and interplay among interests
	Norm of efficiency	Rules and norms	Free play of market forces; conflict is legitimate and expected
	Extensive, systematic, accurate	Information	Ambiguous; information used and withheld strategically

other hand, if scientists come and go at all hours and security is ignored, police goals for security will not be met. Goal incompatibility throws the departments into conflict with each other.

Differentiation. Differentiation was defined in Chapter 4 as "the differences in cognitive and emotional orientations among managers in different functional departments." Functional specialization requires people with specific education, skills, attitudes, and time horizons. For example, people may join a sales department because they have ability and aptitude consistent with sales work. After becoming members of the sales department, they are influenced by departmental norms and values.

Departments or divisions within an organization often differ in values, attitudes, and standards of behavior, and these cultural differences lead to conflicts.[9] Consider an encounter between a sales manager and an R&D scientist about a new product:

> The sales manager may be outgoing and concerned with maintaining a warm, friendly relationship with the scientist. He may be put off because the scientist seems withdrawn and disinclined to talk about anything other than the problems in which he is interested. He may also be annoyed that the scientist seems to have such freedom in choosing what he will work on. Furthermore, the scientist is probably often late for appointments, which, from the salesman's point of view, is no way to run a business. Our scientist, for his part, may feel uncomfortable because the salesman seems to be pressing for immediate answers to technical questions that will take a long time to investigate. All the discomforts are concrete manifestations of the relatively wide differences between these two men in respect to their working and thinking styles. . . .[10]

Cultural differences can be particularly acute in the case of mergers or acquisitions. Employees in the acquired company may have completely different work styles and attitudes, and a "we against them" attitude can develop. One reason for the failure of many mergers is that although managers can integrate financial and production technologies, they have difficulty integrating the unwritten norms and values that have an even greater impact on company success.[11]

Task Interdependence. Task interdependence refers to the dependence of one unit on another for materials, resources, or information. As described in Chapter 5 on technology, pooled interdependence means little interaction; sequential interdependence means the output of one department goes to the next department; and reciprocal interdependence means departments mutually exchange materials and information.[12]

Generally, as interdependence increases, the potential for conflict increases.[13] In the case of pooled interdependence, units have little need to interact. Conflict is at a minimum. Sequential and reciprocal interdependence require employees to spend time coordinating and sharing information. Employees must communicate frequently, and differences in goals or attitudes will surface. Conflict is especially likely to occur when agreement is not reached about the coordination of services to each other. Greater interdependence means departments often exert pressure for a fast response because departmental work has to wait on other departments.[14]

Limited Resources. Another major source of conflict involves competition between groups for what members perceive as limited resources.[15] Organizations have limited money, physical facilities, staff resources, and human resources to share among departments. In their desire to achieve goals, groups want to increase their resources. This throws them into conflict. Managers may develop strategies, such as inflating budget requirements or working behind the scenes, to obtain a desired level of resources. Resources also symbolize power and influence within an organization. The ability to obtain resources enhances prestige. Departments typically believe they have a legitimate claim on additional resources. However, exercising that claim results in conflict. For example, in almost every organization, conflict occurs during the annual budget exercise, often creating political activity.

Rational Versus Political Model. The degree of goal incompatibility, differentiation, interdependence, and conflict over limited resources determines whether a rational or political model of behavior is used within the organization to accomplish goals. When goals are in alignment, there is little differentiation, departments are characterized by pooled interdependence, and resources seem abundant, managers can use a **rational model** of organization, as outlined in Exhibit 10.1. As with the rational approach to decision making described in Chapter 9, the rational model of organization is an "ideal" that is not fully achievable in the real world, though managers strive to use rational processes whenever possible. In the rational organization, behavior is not random or accidental. Goals are clear and choices are made in a logical way. When a decision is needed, the goal is defined, alternatives are identified, and the choice with the highest probability of success is selected. The rational model is also characterized by centralized power and control, extensive information systems, and an efficiency orientation.[16] The opposite view of organizational processes is the **political model**, also described in Exhibit 10.1. When differences are great, organization groups have separate interests, goals, and values. Disagreement and conflict are normal, so power and influence are needed to reach decisions. Groups will engage in the push and pull of debate to decide goals and reach decisions. Information is ambiguous and incomplete. The political model particularly describes organizations that strive for democracy and participation in decision making by empowering workers. Purely rational procedures do not work in democratic organizations, such as learning organizations.

Both rational and political processes are normally used in organizations. In most organizations, neither the rational model nor the political model characterizes things fully, but each will be used some of the time. Managers may strive to adopt rational procedures but will find that politics is needed to accomplish objectives. The political model means managers learn to acquire, develop, and use power to accomplish objectives.

INDIVIDUAL VERSUS ORGANIZATIONAL POWER

In popular literature, power is often described as a personal characteristic, and a frequent topic is how one person can influence or dominate another person. You probably recall from an earlier management or organizational behavior course that managers have five sources of personal power.[17] *Legitimate power* is the authority granted by the organization to the formal management position a manager holds. *Reward power* stems from the ability to bestow rewards—promotion, raise, pat on the back—to other people. The authority to punish or recommend punishment is called *coercive power*. *Expert power* derives from a person's higher skill or knowledge about the tasks being performed. The last one, *referent power*, derives from personal characteristics such that people admire the manager and want to be like or identify with the manager out of respect and admiration. Each of these sources may be used by individuals within organizations.

Power in organizations, however, is often the result of structural characteristics.[18] Organizations are large, complex systems that contain hundreds, even thousands, of people. These systems have a formal hierarchy in which some tasks are more important regardless of who performs them. In addition, some positions have access to greater resources, or their contribution to the organization is more critical. Thus, the important power processes in organizations reflect larger organizational relationships, both horizontal and vertical, and organizational power usually is vested in the position, not in the person.

POWER VERSUS AUTHORITY

Power is an intangible force in organizations. It cannot be seen, but its effect can be felt. Power is often defined as the potential ability of one person (or department) to influence other persons (or departments) to carry out orders[19] or to do something they would not otherwise have done.[20] Other definitions stress that power is the ability to achieve goals or outcomes that power holders desire.[21] The achievement of desired outcomes is the basis of the definition used here: **Power** is the ability of one person or department in an organization to influence other people to bring about desired outcomes. It is the potential to influence others within the organization but with the goal of attaining desired outcomes for power holders.

Power exists only in a relationship between two or more people, and it can be exercised in either vertical or horizontal directions. The source of power often derives from an exchange relationship in which one position or department provides scarce or valued resources to other departments. When one person is dependent on another person, a power relationship emerges in which the person with the resources has greater power.[22] When power exists in a relationship, the power holders can achieve compliance with their requests. For example, the following outcomes are indicators of power in an organization:

- Obtain a larger increase in budget than other departments.
- Obtain above-average salary increases for subordinates.
- Obtain production schedules that are favorable to your department.
- Get items on the agenda at policy meetings.[23]

The concept of formal authority is related to power but is narrower in scope. **Authority** is also a force for achieving desired outcomes, but only as prescribed by the formal hierarchy and reporting relationships. Three properties identify authority:

1. *Authority is vested in organizational positions.* People have authority because of the positions they hold, not because of personal characteristics or resources.
2. *Authority is accepted by subordinates.* Subordinates comply because they believe position holders have a legitimate right to exercise authority.[24] Even though Jim Heard and Gregg Trueman founded Buoyant Company and served as CEO and president respectively, they learned that employees did not accept their authority to make critical decisions. Staff members were aligned with three top managers who had been hired to handle the day-to-day hands-on work of the company. Staffers accepted the authority of these managers because they worked with them on a daily basis; therefore, they supported the managers' decisions over those of the two co-owners.[25].
3. *Authority flows down the vertical hierarchy.*[26] Authority exists along the formal chain of command, and positions at the top of the hierarchy are vested with more formal authority than are positions at the bottom.

Organizational power can be exercised upward, downward, and horizontally in organizations. Formal authority is exercised downward along the hierarchy and is the same as vertical power and legitimate power. In the following sections, we will examine vertical and horizontal sources of power for employees throughout the organization.

VERTICAL SOURCES OF POWER

All employees along the vertical hierarchy have access to some sources of power. Although a large amount of power is typically allocated to top managers by the organization structure, employees throughout the organization often obtain power disproportionate to their formal positions and can exert influence in an upward direction. Three sources of vertical power are formal position, resources, and network centrality.[27]

Formal Position. Certain rights, responsibilities, and prerogatives accrue to top positions. People throughout the organization accept the legitimate right of top managers to set goals, make decisions, and direct activities. Thus, the power from formal position is sometimes called legitimate power.[28] Senior managers often use symbols and language to perpetuate their legitimate power. Reserving the top floor for senior executives, for example, is a way to communicate legitimate authority to others in the organization.

The amount of power provided to middle managers and lower-level participants can be built into the organization's structural design. The allocation of power to middle managers and staff is important because power enables employees to be productive. When job tasks are nonroutine, and when employees participate in self-directed teams and problem-solving task forces, this encourages employees to be flexible and creative and to use their own discretion. Allowing people to make their own decisions increases their power. Power is also increased when a position encourages contact with high-level people. Access to powerful people and the development of a relationship with them provide a strong base of influence.[29] For example, in some organizations a secretary to the vice-president has more power than a department head because the secretary has access to the senior executive on a daily basis.

The logic of designing positions for more power assumes that an organization does not have a limited amount of power to be allocated among high-level and low-level employees. The total amount of power in an organization can be increased by designing tasks and interactions along the hierarchy so everyone has more influence. If the distribution of power is skewed too heavily toward the top, research suggests the organization will be less effective.[30]

Resources. Organizations allocate huge amounts of resources. Buildings are constructed, salaries are paid, and equipment and supplies are purchased. Each year, new resources are allocated in the form of budgets. These resources are allocated downward from top managers. Top managers often own stock, which gives them property rights over resource allocation. However, in many of today's organizations, employees throughout the organization also share in ownership, which increases their power. At St. Luke's, a London advertising agency, the company is owned entirely by its employees, from the CEO down to the janitors.

In most cases, top managers control the resources and, hence, can determine their distribution. Resources can be used as rewards and punishments, which are also sources of power. Resource allocation also creates a dependency relationship. Lower-level participants depend on top managers for the financial and physical resources needed to perform their tasks. Top management can exchange resources in the form of salaries, personnel, promotion, and physical facilities for compliance with the outcomes they desire.

Network Centrality. **Network centrality** means being centrally located in the organization and having access to information and people that are critical to the company's success. Top executives often increase their power by surrounding themselves with a network of loyal subordinates and using the network to learn about events throughout the organization.[31] They can use their central positions to build alliances and wield substantial power in the organization.

Middle managers and lower-level employees have more power when their jobs are related to current areas of concern or opportunity. When a job pertains to pressing organizational problems, power is more easily accumulated. David Shoenfeld, who is now senior vice-president for worldwide marketing, customer service, and corporate communications at FedEx, increased his power by being central to solving an organizational problem. When pilots threatened to go on strike, Shoenfeld believed the best approach was to warn customers up front on the company's Web site. The strike that had crippled archrival UPS had warned FedEx managers about the dangers of letting customers be caught by surprise. Shoenfeld's idea of openly sharing information with customers on a regular basis through a daily "Pilot Negotiation Update" helped FedEx maintain the trust of its customers.[32] Lower-level employees may also increase their network centrality by becoming knowledgeable and expert about certain activities or by taking on difficult tasks and acquiring specialized knowledge that makes them indispensable to managers above them. People who show initiative, work beyond what is expected, take on undesirable but important projects, and show interest in learning about the company and industry often find themselves with influence. Physical location also helps because some locations are in the center of things. Central location lets a person be visible to key people and become part of important interaction networks.

HORIZONTAL SOURCES OF POWER

Horizontal power pertains to relationships across departments. All vice-presidents are usually at the same level on the organization chart. Does this mean each department has the same amount of power? No. Horizontal power is not defined by the formal hierarchy or the organization chart. Each department makes a unique contribution to organizational success. Some departments will have greater say and will achieve their desired outcomes, whereas others will not. For example, Charles Perrow surveyed managers in several industrial firms.[33] He bluntly asked, "Which department has the most power?" among four major departments: production, sales and marketing, research and development, and finance and accounting. Partial survey results are given in Exhibit 10.2. In most firms, sales had the greatest power. In a few firms, production was also quite powerful. On average, the sales and production departments were more powerful than R&D and finance, although substantial variation existed. Differences in the amount of horizontal power clearly occurred in those firms. Today, e-commerce departments and information services departments have growing power in many organizations.

Horizontal power is difficult to measure because power differences are not defined on the organization chart. However, some initial explanations for departmental power differences, such as those shown in Exhibit 10.2, have been found. The theoretical concept that explains relative power is called strategic contingencies.[34]

STRATEGIC CONTINGENCIES

Strategic contingencies are events and activities both inside and outside an organization that are essential for attaining organizational goals. Departments involved with strategic contingencies for the organization tend to have greater power. Departmental activities are important when they provide strategic value by solving problems or crises for the

EXHIBIT 10.2   *Ratings of Power Among Departments in Industrial Firms*

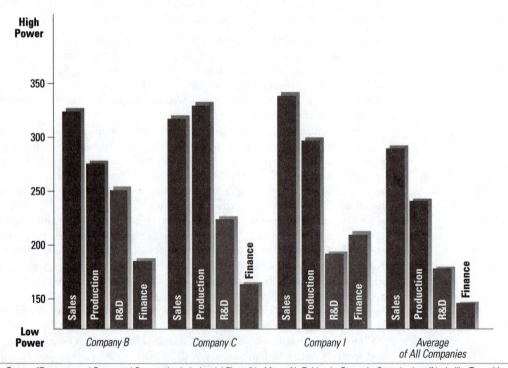

Source: Charles Perrow, "Departmental Power and Perspective in Industrial Firms," in Mayer N. Zald, ed., *Power in Organizations* (Nashville, Tenn.: Vanderbilt University Press, 1970), 64.

organization. For example, if an organization faces an intense threat from lawsuits and regulations, the legal department will gain power and influence over organizational decisions because it copes with such a threat. If product innovation is the key strategic issue, the power of R&D can be expected to be high.

The strategic contingency approach to power is similar to the resource dependence model described in Chapter 4. Recall that organizations try to reduce dependency on the external environment. The strategic contingency approach to power suggests that the departments most responsible for dealing with key resource issues and dependencies in the environment will become most powerful.

POWER SOURCES

Jeffrey Pfeffer and Gerald Salancik, among others, have been instrumental in conducting research on the strategic contingency theory.[35] Their findings indicate that a department rated as powerful may possess one or more of the characteristics illustrated in Exhibit 10.3.[36] In some organizations these five **power sources** overlap, but each provides a useful way to evaluate sources of horizontal power.

Dependency. Interdepartmental dependency is a key element underlying relative power. Power is derived from having something someone else wants. The power of department A over department B is greater when department B depends on A.[37]

Many dependencies exist in organizations. Materials, information, and resources may flow between departments in one direction, such as in the case of sequential task interdependence (Chapter 5). In such cases, the department receiving resources is in a lower power position than the department providing them. The number and strength of dependencies are also important. When seven or eight departments must come for help to the engineering department, for example, engineering is in a strong power position. In contrast, a department that depends on many other departments is in a low power position.

EXHIBIT 10.3   *Strategic Contingencies That Influence Horizontal Power Among Departments*

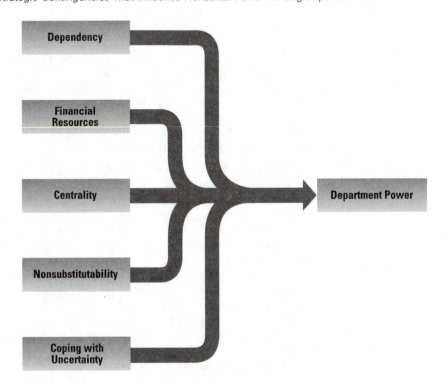

In a cigarette factory, one might expect that the production department would be more powerful than the maintenance department, but this was not the case in a cigarette plant near Paris.[38] The production of cigarettes was a routine process. The machinery was automated and production jobs were small in scope. Production workers were not highly skilled and were paid on a piece-rate basis to encourage high production. On the other hand, the maintenance department required skilled workers. These workers were responsible for repair of the automated machinery, which was a complex task. They had many years of experience. Maintenance was a craft because vital knowledge to fix machines was stored in the minds of maintenance personnel.

Dependency between the two groups was caused by unpredictable assembly line breakdowns. Managers could not remove the breakdown problem; consequently, maintenance was the vital cog in the production process. Maintenance workers had the knowledge and ability to fix the machines, so production managers became dependent on them. The reason for this dependence was that maintenance managers had control over a strategic contingency—they had the knowledge and ability to prevent or resolve work stoppages.

Financial Resources. Control over various kinds of resources, and particularly financial resources, is an important source of power in organizations. Money can be converted into other kinds of resources that are needed by other departments. Money generates dependency; departments that provide financial resources have something other departments want. Departments that generate income for an organization have greater power. The survey of industrial firms reported in Exhibit 10.2 showed sales as the most powerful unit in most of those firms. Sales had power because salespeople find customers and sell the product, thereby removing an important problem for the organization. The sales department ensures the inflow of money.

Power accrues to departments that bring in or provide resources that are highly valued by an organization. Power enables those departments to obtain more of the scarce resources allocated within the organization. "Power derived from acquiring resources is used to obtain more resources, which in turn can be employed to produce more power—the rich get richer."[39]

Centrality. **Centrality** reflects a department's role in the primary activity of an organization.[40] One measure of centrality is the extent to which the work of the department affects the final output of the organization. For example, the production department is more central and usually has more power than staff groups (assuming no other critical contingencies). Centrality is associated with power because it reflects the contribution made to the organization. The corporate finance department of an investment bank generally has more power than the stock research department. By contrast, in the manufacturing firms described in Exhibit 10.2, finance tends to be low in power. When the finance department has the limited task of recording money and expenditures, it is not responsible for obtaining critical resources or for producing the products of the organization.

Nonsubstitutability. Power is also determined by **nonsubstitutability**, which means that a department's function cannot be performed by other readily available resources. Nonsubstitutability increases power. If an employee cannot be easily replaced, his or her power is greater. If an organization has no alternative sources of skill and information, a department's power will be greater. This can be the case when management uses outside consultants. Consultants might be used as substitutes for staff people to reduce the power of staff groups.

The impact of substitutability on power was studied for programmers in computer departments.[41] When computers were first introduced, programming was a rare and specialized occupation. People had to be highly qualified to enter the profession. Programmers controlled the use of organizational computers because they alone possessed the knowledge to program them. Over a period of about ten years, computer programming became a more common activity. People could be substituted easily, and the power of programming departments dropped.

Coping with Uncertainty. The chapters on environment and decision making described how elements in the environment can change swiftly and can be unpredictable and complex. In the face of uncertainty, little information is available to managers on appropriate courses of action. Departments that cope with this uncertainty will increase their power.[42] Just the presence of uncertainty does not provide power; reducing the uncertainty on behalf of other departments will. When market research personnel accurately predict changes in demand for new products, they gain power and prestige because they have reduced a critical uncertainty. Forecasting is only one technique for **coping with uncertainty**. Sometimes uncertainty can be reduced by taking quick and appropriate action after an unpredictable event occurs.

Three techniques that departments can use to cope with critical uncertainties are (1) obtaining prior information, (2) prevention, and (3) absorption.[43] *Obtaining prior information* means a department can reduce an organization's uncertainty by forecasting an event. Departments increase their power through *prevention* by predicting and forestalling negative events. *Absorption* occurs when a department takes action after an event to reduce its negative consequences.

Horizontal power relationships in organizations change as strategic contingencies change. For example, in recent years, giant retailers such as Wal-Mart and Winn-Dixie have increased their power over magazine publishers by refusing to sell issues that contain cover photos or stories that might be objectionable to some customers. Some magazine publishers have agreed to provide advance copies so retailers can spot controversial material ahead of time and decline the issue. "If you don't let them know in advance," one circulation director said, "they will delist the title and never carry it again." These demands from powerful retailers are creating new uncertainties and strategic issues for magazine publishers such as Hearst Corp., Miller Publishing Group, and Time Warner.[44]

POLITICAL PROCESSES IN ORGANIZATIONS

Politics, like power, is intangible and difficult to measure. It is hidden from view and is hard to observe in a systematic way. Two surveys uncovered the following reactions of managers toward political behavior.[45]

1. Most managers have a negative view toward politics and believe that politics will more often hurt than help an organization in achieving its goals.
2. Managers believe political behavior is common to practically all organizations.
3. Most managers think political behavior occurs more often at upper rather than lower levels in organizations.
4. Political behavior arises in certain decision domains, such as structural change, but is absent from other decisions, such as handling employee grievances.

Based on these surveys, politics seems more likely to occur at the top levels of an organization and around certain issues and decisions. Moreover, managers do not approve of political behavior. The remainder of this chapter explores more fully what is political behavior, when it should be used, the type of issues and decisions most likely to be associated with politics, and some political tactics that may be effective.

DEFINITION

Power has been described as the available force or potential for achieving desired outcomes. *Politics* is the use of power to influence decisions in order to achieve those outcomes. The exercise of power and influence has led to two ways to define politics—as self-serving behavior or as a natural organizational decision process. The first definition emphasizes that politics is self-serving and involves activities that are not sanctioned by the organization.[46]

In this view, politics involves deception and dishonesty for purposes of individual self-interest and leads to conflict and disharmony within the work environment. This dark view of politics is widely held by laypeople. Recent studies have shown that workers who perceive this kind of political activity at work within their companies often have related feelings of anxiety and job dissatisfaction. Studies also support the belief that inappropriate use of politics is related to low employee morale, inferior organizational performance, and poor decision making.[47] This view of politics explains why managers in the surveys described above did not approve of political behavior.

Although politics can be used in a negative, self-serving way, the appropriate use of political behavior can serve organizational goals.[48] The second view sees politics as a natural organizational process for resolving differences among organizational interest groups.[49] Politics is the process of bargaining and negotiation that is used to overcome conflicts and differences of opinion. In this view, politics is very similar to the coalition-building decision processes defined in Chapter 9 on decision making.

The organization theory perspective views politics as described in the second definition—as a normal decision-making process. Politics is simply the activity through which power is exercised in the resolution of conflicts and uncertainty. Politics is neutral and is not necessarily harmful to the organization. The formal definition of organizational politics is as follows: **organizational politics** involves activities to acquire, develop, and use power and other resources to obtain the preferred outcome when there is uncertainty or disagreement about choices.[50]

Political behavior can be either a positive or a negative force. Politics is the use of power to get things accomplished—good things as well as bad. Uncertainty and conflict are natural and inevitable, and politics is the mechanism for reaching agreement. Politics includes informal discussions that enable participants to arrive at consensus and make decisions that otherwise might be stalemated or unsolvable.

WHEN IS POLITICAL ACTIVITY USED?

Politics is a mechanism for arriving at consensus when uncertainty is high and there is disagreement over goals or problem priorities. Recall the rational versus political models described in Exhibit 10.1. The political model is associated with conflict over goals, shifting coalitions and interest groups, ambiguous information, and uncertainty. Thus, political activity tends to be most visible when managers confront nonprogrammed decisions, as discussed in Chapter 9, and is related to the Carnegie model of decision making. Because managers at the top of an organization generally deal with more nonprogrammed decisions than do managers at lower levels, more political activity will appear. Moreover, some issues are associated with inherent disagreement. Resources, for example, are critical for the survival and effectiveness of departments, so resource allocation often becomes a political issue. "Rational" methods of allocation do not satisfy participants. Three **domains of political activity** (areas in which politics plays a role) in most organizations are structural change, management succession, and resource allocation.

Structural reorganizations strike at the heart of power and authority relationships. Reorganizations such as those discussed in Chapter 3 change responsibilities and tasks, which also affects the underlying power base from strategic contingencies. For these reasons, a major reorganization can lead to an explosion of political activity.[51] Managers may actively bargain and negotiate to maintain the responsibilities and power bases they have.

Organizational changes such as hiring new executives, promotions, and transfers have great political significance, particularly at top organizational levels where uncertainty is high and networks of trust, cooperation, and communication among executives are important.[52] Hiring decisions can generate uncertainty, discussion, and disagreement. Managers can use hiring and promotion to strengthen network alliances and coalitions by putting their own people in prominent positions.

The third area of political activity is resource allocation. Resource allocation decisions encompass all resources required for organizational performance, including salaries, operating budgets, employees, office facilities, equipment, use of the company airplane, and so forth. Resources are so vital that disagreement about priorities exists, and political processes help resolve the dilemmas.

USING POWER, POLITICS, AND COLLABORATION

One theme in this chapter has been that power in organizations is not primarily a phenomenon of the individual. It is related to the resources departments command, the role departments play in an organization, and the environmental contingencies with which departments cope. Position and responsibility more than personality and style determine a manager's influence on outcomes in the organization.

Power is used through individual political behavior, however. Individual managers seek agreement about a strategy to achieve their departments' desired outcomes. Individual managers negotiate decisions and adopt tactics that enable them to acquire and use power. In addition, managers develop ways to increase cooperation and collaboration within the organization to reduce damaging conflicts.

To fully understand the use of power within organizations, it is important to look at both structural components and individual behavior.[53] Although power comes from larger organizational forms and processes, the political use of power involves individual-level activities. This section briefly summarizes tactics that managers can use to increase the power base of their departments, political tactics they can use to achieve desired outcomes, and tactics for increasing collaboration. These tactics are summarized in Exhibit 10.4.

TACTICS FOR INCREASING POWER

Four **tactics for increasing power** are as follows:

1. *Enter areas of high uncertainty.* One source of departmental power is to cope with critical uncertainties.[54] If department managers can identify key uncertainties and take steps to remove those uncertainties, the department's power base will be enhanced. Uncertainties could arise from stoppages on an assembly line, from the needed quality of a new product, or from the inability to predict a demand for new services. Once an uncertainty is identified, the department can take action to cope with it. By their very nature, uncertain tasks will not be solved immediately. Trial and error will be needed, which is to the advantage of the department. The trial-and-error process provides experience and expertise that cannot easily be duplicated by other departments.

2. *Create dependencies.* Dependencies are another source of power.[55] When the organization depends on a department for information, materials, knowledge, or skills, that department will hold power over the others. This power can be increased by incurring obligations. Doing additional work that helps out other departments will obligate the other departments to respond at a future date. The power accumulated by creating a dependency can be used to resolve future disagreements in the department's favor. An equally effective and related strategy is to reduce dependency on other departments by acquiring necessary information or skills. For example, information technology departments have created dependencies in many organizations because of the rapid changes in this area. Employees in other departments depend on the information technology unit to master complex software programs, changing use of the Internet, and other advances so that they will have the information they need to perform effectively.

EXHIBIT 10.4   *Power and Political Tactics in Organizations*

Tactics for Increasing the Power Base	Political Tactics for Using Power	Tactics for Enhancing Collaboration
1. Enter areas of high uncertainty.	1. Build coalitions.	1. Create integration devices.
2. Create dependencies.	2. Expand networks.	2. Use confrontation and negotiation.
3. Provide resources.	3. Control decision premises.	3. Schedule intergroup consultation.
4. Satisfy strategic contingencies.	4. Enhance legitimacy and expertise.	4. Practice member rotation.
	5. Make preferences explicit, but keep power implicit.	5. Create superordinate goals.

3. *Provide resources.* Resources are always important to organizational survival. Departments that accumulate resources and provide them to an organization in the form of money, information, or facilities will be powerful. For example, university departments with the greatest power are those that obtain external research funds for contributions to university overhead. Likewise, sales departments are powerful in industrial firms because they bring in financial resources.

4. *Satisfy strategic contingencies.* The theory of strategic contingencies says that some elements in the external environment and within the organization are especially important for organizational success. A contingency could be a critical event, a task for which there are no substitutes, or a central task that is interdependent with many others in the organization. An analysis of the organization and its changing environment will reveal strategic contingencies. To the extent that contingencies are new or are not being satisfied, there is room for a department to move into those critical areas and increase its importance and power.

In summary, the allocation of power in an organization is not random. Power is the result of organizational processes that can be understood and predicted. The abilities to reduce uncertainty, increase dependency on one's own department, obtain resources, and cope with strategic contingencies will all enhance a department's power. Once power is available, the next challenge is to use it to attain helpful outcomes.

POLITICAL TACTICS FOR USING POWER

The use of power in organizations requires both skill and willingness. Many decisions are made through political processes because rational decision processes do not fit. Uncertainty or disagreement is too high. **Political tactics for using power** to influence decision outcomes include the following:

1. *Build coalitions.* Coalition building means taking the time to talk with other managers to persuade them to your point of view.[56] Most important decisions are made outside formal meetings. Managers discuss issues with each other and reach agreements on a one-to-one basis. Effective managers are those who huddle, meeting in groups of twos and threes to resolve key issues.[57] An important aspect of coalition building is to build good relationships. Good interpersonal relationships are built on liking, trust, and respect. Reliability and the motivation to work with others rather than exploit others are part of coalition building.[58]

2. *Expand networks.* Networks can be expanded (1) by reaching out to establish contact with additional managers and (2) by co-opting dissenters. The first approach is to build new alliances through the hiring, transfer, and promotion process. Placing in key positions people who are sympathetic to the outcomes of the department can help achieve departmental goals.[59] On the other hand, the second approach, co-optation, is the act of bringing a dissenter into one's network. One example of co-optation involved a university committee whose membership was based on promotion and tenure. Several female professors who were critical of the tenure and promotion process were appointed to the committee. Once a part of the administrative process, they could see the administrative point of view and learned that administrators were not as evil as suspected. Co-optation effectively brought them into the administrative network.[60]

3. *Control decision premises.* To control decision premises means to constrain the boundaries of a decision. One technique is to choose or limit information provided to other managers. A common method is simply to put your department's best foot forward, such as selectively presenting favorable criteria. A variety of statistics can be assembled to support the departmental point of view. A university department that is growing rapidly and has a large number of students can make claims for additional resources by emphasizing its growth and large size. Such objective criteria do not always work, but they are a valuable step.

   Decision premises can be further influenced by limiting the decision process. Decisions can be influenced by the items put on an agenda for an important meeting or even by the sequence in which items are discussed.[61] Items discussed last, when time is short and people want to leave, will receive less attention than those discussed early. Calling attention to specific problems and suggesting alternatives also will affect outcomes. Stressing a specific problem to get it—rather than problems not relevant to your department—on the agenda is an example of agenda setting.

4. *Enhance legitimacy and expertise.* Managers can exert the greatest influence in areas in which they have recognized legitimacy and expertise. If a request is within the task domain of a department and is consistent with the department's vested interest, other departments will tend to comply. Members can also identify external consultants or other experts within the organization to support their cause.[62] For example, a financial vice-president in a large retail firm wanted to fire the director of human resource management. She hired a consultant to evaluate the human resource management projects undertaken to date. A negative report from the consultant provided sufficient legitimacy to fire the director, who was replaced with a director loyal to the financial vice-president.

5. *Make preferences explicit, but keep power implicit.* If managers do not ask, they seldom receive. Political activity is effective only when goals and needs are made explicit so the organization can respond. Managers should bargain aggressively and be persuasive. An assertive proposal may be accepted because other managers have no better alternatives. Moreover, an explicit proposal will often receive favorable treatment because other alternatives are ambiguous and less well defined. Effective political behavior requires sufficient forcefulness and risk taking to at least try to achieve desired outcomes.

   The use of power, however, should not be obvious.[63] If one formally draws upon his or her power base in a meeting by saying, "My department has more power, so the rest of you have to do it my way," the power will be diminished. Power works best when it is used quietly. To call attention to power is to lose it. Explicit claims for power are made by the powerless, not by the powerful. People know who has power. There is substantial agreement on which departments are more powerful. Explicit claims to power are not necessary and can even harm the department's cause.

When using any of the preceding tactics, recall that most people feel self-serving behavior hurts rather than helps an organization. If managers are perceived to be throwing their weight around or are perceived to be after things that are self-serving rather than beneficial to the organization, they will lose respect. On the other hand, managers must recognize the relational and political aspect of their work. It is not sufficient to be rational and technically competent. Politics is a way to reach agreement. When managers ignore political tactics, they may find themselves failing without understanding why.

TACTICS FOR ENHANCING COLLABORATION

Power and political tactics are important means for getting things done within organizations. Most organizations today have at least moderate interunit conflict. An additional approach in many organizations is to overcome conflict by stimulating cooperation and collaboration among departments to support the attainment of organizational goals. **Tactics for enhancing collaboration** include the following:

1. *Create integration devices.* As described in Chapter 3, teams, task forces, and project managers who span the boundaries between departments can be used as integration devices. Bringing together representatives from conflicting departments in joint problem-solving teams is an effective way to enhance collaboration because representatives learn to understand each other's point of view.[64] Sometimes a full-time integrator is assigned to achieve cooperation and collaboration by meeting with members of the respective departments and exchanging information. The integrator has to understand each group's problems and must be able to move both groups toward a solution that is mutually acceptable.[65]

2. *Use confrontation and negotiation.* **Confrontation** occurs when parties in conflict directly engage one another and try to work out their differences. **Negotiation** is the

bargaining process that often occurs during confrontation and that enables the parties to systematically reach a solution. These techniques bring appointed representatives from the departments together to work out a serious dispute.

Confrontation and negotiation involve some risk. There is no guarantee that discussions will focus on a conflict or that emotions will not get out of hand. However, if members are able to resolve the conflict on the basis of face-to-face discussions, they will find new respect for each other, and future collaboration becomes easier. The beginnings of relatively permanent attitude change are possible through direct negotiation.

Confrontation is successful when managers engage in a "win-win" strategy. Win-win means both departments adopt a positive attitude and strive to resolve the conflict in a way that will benefit each other.[66] If the negotiations deteriorate into a strictly win-lose strategy (each group wants to defeat the other), the confrontation will be ineffective. Top management can urge group members to work toward mutually acceptable outcomes. The differences between win-win and win-lose strategies of negotiation are shown in Exhibit 10.5. With a win-win strategy—which includes defining the problem as mutual, communicating openly, and avoiding threats—understanding can be changed while the dispute is resolved.

One type of negotiation, used to resolve a disagreement between workers and management, is referred to as **collective bargaining**. The bargaining process is usually accomplished through a union and results in an agreement that specifies each party's responsibilities for the next two to three years. Union–management negotiations are currently underway at several major U.S. airlines, including US Airways, TWA, Northwest, Delta, and United.[67]

3. *Schedule intergroup consultation.* When conflict is intense and enduring, and department members are suspicious and uncooperative, managers can bring in a third-party consultant to work with the groups. This process, sometimes called *workplace mediation*, is a strong intervention to reduce conflict because it involves bringing the disputing parties together and allowing each side to present its version of "reality." The technique has been developed by such psychologists as Robert Blake, Jane Mouton, and Richard Walton.[68]

Department members attend a workshop, which may last for several days, away from day-to-day work problems. This approach is similar to the OD approach described in Chapter 8 on innovation and change. The steps typically associated with an intergroup training session are as follows:

EXHIBIT 10.5   *Negotiating Strategies*

Win-Win Strategy	Win-Lose Strategy
1. Define the conflict as a mutual problem.	1. Define the problem as a win-lose situation.
2. Pursue joint outcomes.	2. Pursue own group's outcomes.
3. Find creative agreements that satisfy both groups.	3. Force the other group into submission.
4. Use open, honest, and accurate communication of group's needs, goals, and proposals.	4. Use deceitful, inaccurate and misleading communication of group's needs, goals, and proposals.
5. Avoid threats (to reduce the other's defensiveness).	5. Use threats (to force submission).
6. Communicate flexibility of position.	6. Communicate high commitment (rigidity) regarding one's position.

Source: Adapted from David W. Johnson and Frank P. Johnson, *Joining Together: Group Theory and Group Skills* (Englewood Cliffs, N.J.: Prentice-Hall, 1975), 182–83.

a. The conflicting groups are brought into a training setting with the stated goal of exploring mutual perceptions and relationships.

b. The conflicting groups are then separated, and each group is invited to discuss and make a list of its perceptions of itself and the other group.

c. In the presence of both groups, group representatives publicly share the perceptions of self and other that the groups have generated, and the groups are obligated to remain silent. The objective is simply to report to the other group as accurately as possible the images that each group has developed in private.

d. Before any exchange takes place, the groups return to private sessions to digest and analyze what they have heard; there is great likelihood that the representatives' reports have revealed to each group discrepancies between its self-image and the image the other group holds of it.

e. In public session, again working through representatives, each group shares with the other what discrepancies it has uncovered and the possible reasons for them, focusing on actual, observable behavior.

f. Following this mutual exposure, a more open exploration is permitted between the two groups on the now-shared goal of identifying further reasons for perceptual distortions.

g. A joint exploration is then conducted of how to manage future relations in such a way as to encourage cooperation among groups.[69]

Intergroup consultation can be quite demanding for everyone involved. It is fairly easy to have conflicting groups list perceptions and identify discrepancies. However, exploring their differences face-to-face and agreeing to change is more difficult. If handled correctly, these sessions can help department employees understand each other much better and lead to improved attitudes and better working relationships for years to come.

4. *Practice member rotation.* Rotation means individuals from one department can be asked to work in another department on a temporary or permanent basis. The advantage is that individuals become submerged in the values, attitudes, problems, and goals of the other department. In addition, individuals can explain the problems and goals of their original departments to their new colleagues. This enables a frank, accurate exchange of views and information.

Rotation works slowly to reduce conflict but is very effective for changing the underlying attitudes and perceptions that promote conflict.[70]

5. *Develop shared mission and superordinate goals.* Another strategy is for top management to create a shared mission and establish superordinate goals that require cooperation among departments.[71] As discussed in Chapter 7, organizations with strong, adaptive cultures, where employees share a larger vision for their company, are more likely to have a united, cooperative workforce. Recent studies have shown that when employees from different departments see that their goals are linked together, they will openly share resources and information.[72] To be effective, superordinate goals must be substantial, and employees must be granted the time to work cooperatively toward those goals. The reward system can also be redesigned to encourage the pursuit of the superordinate goals rather than departmental subgoals.

DISCUSSION QUESTIONS

1. Briefly describe how differences in tasks, personal background, and training lead to conflict among groups. How does task interdependence lead to conflict among groups?

2. Discuss why some conflict is considered beneficial to organizations.

3. What is the difference between power and authority? Is it possible for a person to have formal authority but no real power? Discuss.

4. State University X receives 90 percent of its financial resources from the state and is overcrowded with students. It is trying to pass regulations to limit student enrollment. Private University Y receives 90 percent of its income from student tuition and has

barely enough students to make ends meet. It is actively recruiting students for next year. In which university will students have greater power? What implications will this have for professors and administrators? Discuss.

5. In Exhibit 10.2, research and development has greater power in Company B than in the other firms. Discuss possible strategic contingencies that give R&D greater power in this firm.

6. The engineering college at a major university brings in three times as many government research dollars as does the rest of the university combined. Engineering appears wealthy and has many professors on full-time research status. Yet, when internal research funds are allocated, engineering gets a larger share of the money, even though it already has substantial external research funds. Why would this happen?

7. Which do you believe would have a greater long-term impact on changing employee attitudes toward increased collaboration—intergroup consultation or confrontation and negotiation? Discuss.

NOTES

1. Lee G. Bolman and Terrence E. Deal, *Reframing Organizations: Artistry, Choice, and Leadership* (San Francisco: Jossey-Bass, 1991).

2. Paul M. Terry, "Conflict Management," *The Journal of Leadership Studies* 3, No. 2 (1996), 3–21; and Kathleen M. Eisenhardt, Jean L. Kahwajy, and L. J. Bourgeois III, "How Management Teams Can Have a Good Fight," *Harvard Business Review* (July–August 1997): 77–85.

3. Clayton T. Alderfer and Ken K. Smith, "Studying Intergroup Relations Imbedded in Organizations," *Administrative Science Quarterly* 27 (1982): 35–65.

4. Muzafer Sherif, "Experiments in Group Conflict," *Scientific American* 195 (1956): 54–58; Edgar H. Schein, *Organizational Psychology*, 3d ed. (Englewood Cliffs, N.J.: Prentice-Hall, 1980).

5. M. Ascalur Rahin, "A Strategy for Managing Conflict in Complex Organizations," *Human Relations* 38 (1985): 81–89; Kenneth Thomas, "Conflict and Conflict Management," in M. D. Dunnette, ed., *Handbook of Industrial and Organizational Psychology* (Chicago: Rand McNally, 1976); Stuart M. Schmidt and Thomas A. Kochan, "Conflict: Toward Conceptual Clarity," *Administrative Science Quarterly* 13 (1972): 359–70.

6. L. David Brown, "Managing Conflict among Groups," in David A. Kolb, Irwin M. Rubin, and James M. McIntyre, eds., *Organizational Psychology: A Book of Readings* (Englewood Cliffs, N.J.: Prentice-Hall, 1979), 377–89; Robert W. Ruekert and Orville C. Walker, Jr., "Interactions between Marketing and R&D Departments in Implementing Different Business Strategies," *Strategic Management Journal* 8 (1987): 233–48.

7. Amy Barrett, "Indigestion at Taco Bell," *Business Week,* 14 December 1994, 66–67; Greg Burns, "Fast-Food Fight," *Business Week,* 2 June 1997, 34–36; and Nicole Harris, "Flying into a Rage," *Business Week,* 27 April 1998; David Whitford, "Arthur, Arthur," *Fortune,* 10 November 1997, 1690–178; and Elizabeth MacDonald and Joseph B. White, "How Consulting Issue is Threatening to Rend Andersen Worldwide," *The Wall Street Journal,* 4 February 1998, A1, A10.

8. Thomas A. Kochan, George P. Huber, and L. L. Cummings, "Determinants of Intraorganizational Conflict in Collective Bargaining in the Public Sector," *Administrative Science Quarterly* 20 (1975): 10–23.

9. Eric H. Neilsen, "Understanding and Managing Intergroup Conflict," in Jay W. Lorsch and Paul R. Lawrence, eds., *Managing Group and Intergroup Relations* (Homewood, Ill.: Irwin and Dorsey, 1972), 329–43; Richard E. Walton and John M. Dutton, "The Management of Interdepartmental Conflict: A Model and Review," *Administrative Science Quarterly* 14 (1969): 73–84.

10. Jay W. Lorsch, "Introduction to the Structural Design of Organizations," in Gene W. Dalton, Paul R. Lawrence, and Jay W. Lorsch, eds., *Organization Structure and Design* (Homewood, Ill.: Irwin and Dorsey, 1970), 5.

11. Morty Lefkoe, "Why So Many Mergers Fail," *Fortune,* 20 June 1987, 113–14; Afsaneh Nahavandi and Ali R. Malekzadeh, "Acculturation in Mergers and Acquisitions," *Academy of Management Review* (1988): 79–90.

12. James D. Thompson, *Organizations in Action* (New York: McGraw-Hill, 1967), 54–56.

13. Walton and Dutton, "Management of Interdepartmental Conflict."

14. Joseph McCann and Jay R. Galbraith, "Interdepartmental Relationships," in Paul C. Nystrom and William H. Starbuck, eds., *Handbook of Organizational*

Design, vol. 2 (New York: Oxford University Press, 1981), 60–84.

15. Roderick M. Cramer, "Intergroup Relations and Organizational Dilemmas: The Role of Categorization Processes," in L. L. Cummings and Barry M. Staw, eds., *Research in Organizational Behavior,* vol. 13 (New York: JAI Press, 1991), 191–228; Neilsen, "Understanding and Managing Intergroup Conflict"; Louis R. Pondy, "Organizational Conflict: Concepts and Models," *Administrative Science Quarterly* 12 (1968): 296–320.

16. Jeffrey Pfeffer, *Power in Organizations* (Marshfield, Mass.: Pitman, 1981).

17. John R. P. French, Jr., and Bertram Raven, "The Bases of Social Power," in *Group Dynamics,* D. Cartwright and A. F. Zander, eds. (Evanston, Ill.: Row Peterson, 1960), 607–23.

18. Ran Lachman, "Power from What? A Reexamination of Its Relationships with Structural Conditions," *Administrative Science Quarterly* 34 (1989): 231–51; Daniel J. Brass, "Being in the Right Place: A Structural Analysis of Individual Influence in an Organization," *Administrative Science Quarterly* 29 (1984): 518–39.

19. Robert A. Dahl, "The Concept of Power," *Behavioral Science* 2 (1957): 201–15.

20. W. Graham Astley and Paramijit S. Sachdeva, "Structural Sources of Intraorganizational Power: A Theoretical Synthesis," *Academy of Management Review* 9 (1984): 104–13; Abraham Kaplan, "Power in Perspective," in Robert L. Kahn and Elise Boulding, eds., *Power and Conflict in Organizations* (London: Tavistock, 1964), 11–32.

21. Gerald R. Salancik and Jeffrey Pfeffer, "The Bases and Use of Power in Organizational Decision-Making: The Case of the University," *Administrative Science Quarterly* 19 (1974): 453–73.

22. Richard M. Emerson, "Power-Dependence Relations," *American Sociological Review* 27 (1962): 31–41.

23. Rosabeth Moss Kanter, "Power Failure in Management Circuits," *Harvard Business Review* (July-August 1979): 65–75.

24. A. J. Grimes, "Authority, Power, Influence, and Social Control: A Theoretical Synthesis," *Academy of Management Review* 3 (1978): 724–35.

25. Russ Baker, "Edged Out," *Inc.,* August 1998, 69–77.

26. Astley and Sachdeva, "Structural Sources of Intraorganizational Power."

27. Jeffrey Pfeffer, *Managing with Power: Politics and Influence in Organizations* (Boston: Harvard Business School Press, 1992).

28. Robert L. Peabody, "Perceptions of Organizational Authority," *Administrative Science Quarterly* 6 (1962): 479.

29. Richard S. Blackburn, "Lower Participant Power: Toward a Conceptual Integration," *Academy of Management Review* 6 (1981): 127–31.

30. Kanter, "Power Failure in Management Circuits," 70.

31. Astley and Sachdeva, "Structural Sources of Intraorganizational Power"; Noel M. Tichy and Charles Fombrun, "Network Analysis in Organizational Settings," *Human Relations* 32 (1979): 923–65.

32. Eryn Brown, "9 Ways to Win on the Web," *Fortune,* 24 May 1999, 112–25.

33. Charles Perrow, "Departmental Power and Perspective in Industrial Firms," in Mayer N. Zald, ed., *Power in Organizations* (Nashville, Tenn.: Vanderbilt University Press, 1970), 59–89.

34. D. J. Hickson, C. R. Hinings, C. A. Lee, R. E. Schneck, and J. M. Pennings, "A Strategic Contingencies Theory of Intraorganizational Power," *Administrative Science Quarterly* 16 (1971): 216–29; Gerald R. Salancik and Jeffrey Pfeffer, "Who Gets Power—and How They Hold onto It: A Strategic-Contingency Model of Power," *Organizational Dynamics* (Winter 1977): 3–21.

35. Pfeffer, *Managing with Power;* Salancik and Pfeffer, "Who Gets Power"; C. R. Hinings, D. J. Hickson, J. M. Pennings, and R. E. Schneck, "Structural Conditions of Intraorganizational Power," *Administrative Science Quarterly* 19 (1974): 22–44.

36. Carol Stoak Saunders, "The Strategic Contingencies Theory of Power: Multiple Perspectives," *Journal of Management Studies* 27 (1990): 1–18; Warren Boeker, "The Development and Institutionalization of Sub-Unit Power in Organizations," *Administrative Science Quarterly* 34 (1989): 388–510; Irit Cohen and Ran Lachman, "The Generality of the Strategic Contingencies Approach to Sub-Unit Power," *Organizational Studies* 9 (1988): 371–91.

37. Emerson, "Power-Dependence Relations."

38. Michel Crozier, *The Bureaucratic Phenomenon* (Chicago: University of Chicago Press, 1964).

39. Salancik and Pfeffer, "Bases and Use of Power in Organizational Decision-Making," 470.

40. Hickson, et al., "Strategic Contingencies Theory."

41. Pettigrew, *Politics of Organizational Decision-Making.*

42. Hickson, et al., "Strategic Contingencies Theory."

43. Ibid.

44. G. Bruce Knecht, "Retail Chains Emerge as Advance Arbiters of Magazine Content," *The Wall Street Journal,* 22 October 1997, A1, A13.

45. Jeffrey Gantz and Victor V. Murray, "Experience of Workplace Politics," *Academy of Management Journal* 23 (1980): 237–51; Dan L. Madison, Robert W. Allen, Lyman W. Porter, Patricia A. Renwick, and Bronston T. Mayes, "Organizational Politics: An Exploration of Managers' Perception," *Human Relations* 33 (1980): 79–100.

46. Gerald R. Ferris and K. Michele Kacmar, "Perceptions of Organizational Politics," *Journal of Management* 18 (1992): 93–116; Parmod Kumar and Rehana Ghadially, "Organizational Politics and its Effects on Members of Organizations," *Human Relations* 42 (1989): 305–14; Donald J. Vredenburgh and John G. Maurer, "A Process Framework of Organizational Politics," *Human Relations* 37 (1984): 47–66; Gerald R. Ferris, Dwight D. Frink, Maria Carmen Galang, Jing Zhou, Michele Kacmar, and Jack L. Howard, "Perceptions of Organizational Politics: Prediction, Stress-Related Implications, and Outcomes," *Human Relations* 49, no. 2 (1996): 233–66.

47. Ferris, et al., "Perceptions of Organizational Politics: Prediction, Stress-Related Implications, and Outcomes"; John J. Voyer, "Coercive Organizational Politics and Organizational Outcomes: An Interpretive Study," *Organization Science* 5, no. 1 (February 1994): 72–85; James W. Dean, Jr., and Mark P. Sharfman, "Does Decision Process Matter? A Study of Strategic Decision-Making Effectiveness," *Academy of Management Journal* 39, no. 2 (1996): 368–96.

48. Jeffrey Pfeffer, *Managing With Power: Politics and Influence in Organizations* (Boston, Mass.: Harvard Business School Press, 1992).

49. Amos Drory and Tsilia Romm, "The Definition of Organizational Politics: A Review," *Human Relations* 43 (1990): 1133–54; Vredenburgh and Maurer, "A Process Framework of Organizational Politics."

50. Pfeffer, *Power in Organizations,* p. 70.

51. Madison, et al., "Organizational Politics"; Jay R. Galbraith, *Organizational Design* (Reading, Mass.: Addison-Wesley, 1977).

52. Gantz and Murray, "Experience of Workplace Politics"; Pfeffer, *Power in Organizations.*

53. Daniel J. Brass and Marlene E. Burkhardt, "Potential Power and Power Use: An Investigation of Structure and Behavior," *Academy of Management Journal* 38 (1993): 441–70.

54. Hickson, et al., "A Strategic Contingencies Theory."

55. Pfeffer, *Power in Organizations.*

56. Ibid.

57. V. Dallas Merrell, *Huddling: The Informal Way to Management Success* (New York: AMACON, 1979).

58. Vredenburgh and Maurer, "A Process Framework of Organizational Politics."

59. Ibid.

60. Pfeffer, *Power in Organizations.*

61. Ibid.

62. Ibid.

63. Kanter, "Power Failure in Management Circuits"; Pfeffer, *Power in Organizations.*

64. Robert R. Blake and Jane S. Mouton, "Overcoming Group Warfare," *Harvard Business Review* (November–December 1984): 98–108.

65. Blake and Mouton, "Overcoming Group Warfare"; Paul R. Lawrence and Jay W. Lorsch, "New Management Job: The Integrator," *Harvard Business Review* 45 (November–December 1967): 142–51.

66. Robert R. Blake, Herbert A. Shepard, and Jane S. Mouton, *Managing Intergroup Conflict in Industry* (Houston: Gulf Publishing, 1964); and Doug Stewart, "'Expand the Pie Before You Divvy It Up,'" *Smithsonian,* November 1997, 78-90.

67. Kenneth Labich, "Fasten Your Seat Belts," *Fortune,* 10 May 1999, 114–18.

68. Robert R. Blake and Jane S. Mouton, "Overcoming Group Warfare"; Schein, *Organizational Psychology*; Blake, Shepard, and Mouton, *Managing Intergroup Conflict in Industry*; Richard E. Walton, *Interpersonal Peacemaking: Confrontation and Third-Party Consultations* (Reading, Mass.: Addison-Wesley, 1969).

69. Mark S. Plovnick, Ronald E. Fry, and W. Warner Burke, *Organizational Development* (Boston: Little, Brown, 1982), 89–93; Schein, *Organizational Psychology,* 177–78, reprinted by permission of Prentice-Hall, Inc.

70. Neilsen, "Understanding and Managing Intergroup Conflict"; Joseph McCann and Jay R. Galbraith, "Interdepartmental Relations."

71. Neilsen, "Understanding and Managing Intergroup Conflict"; McCann and Galbraith, "Interdepartmental Relations"; Sherif et al., *Intergroup Conflict and Cooperation.*

72. Dean Tjosvold, Valerie Dann, and Choy Wong, "Managing Conflict between Departments to Serve Customers," *Human Relations* 45 (1992): 1035–54.

adaptability/entrepreneurial culture a culture characterized by strategic focus on the external environment through flexibility and change to meet customer needs.

administrative principles a closed systems management perspective that focuses on the total organization and grows from the insights of practitioners.

ambidextrous approach a characteristic of an organization that can behave both in an organic and a mechanistic way.

analyzability a dimension of technology in which work activities can be reduced to mechanical steps and participants can follow an objective, computational procedure to solve problems.

authority a force for achieving desired outcomes that is prescribed by the formal hierarchy and reporting relationships.

benchmarking process whereby companies find out how others do something better than they do and then try to imitate or improve on it.

boundary spanning roles activities that link and coordinate an organization with key elements in the external environment.

bounded rationality perspective how decisions are made when time is limited, a large number of internal and external factors affect a decision, and the problem is ill-defined.

buffering roles activities that absorb uncertainty from the environment.

bureaucracy an organizational framework marked by rules and procedures, specialization and division of labor, hierarchy of authority, technically qualified personnel, separate position and incumbent, and written communications and records.

bureaucratic control the use of rules, policies, hierarchy of authority, written documentation, standardization, and other bureaucratic mechanisms to standardize behavior and assess performance.

bureaucratic culture a culture that has an internal focus and a consistency orientation for a stable environment.

bureaucratic organization a perspective that emphasizes management on an impersonal, rational basis through such elements as clearly defined authority and responsibility, formal recordkeeping, and uniform application of standard rules.

Carnegie model organizational decision making involving many managers and a final choice based on a coalition among those managers.

centrality a trait of a department whose role is in the primary activity of an organization.

centralization refers to the level of hierarchy with authority to make decisions.

change process the way in which changes occur in an organization.

charismatic authority based in devotion to the exemplary character or heroism of an individual and the order defined by him or her.

clan control the use of social characteristics, such as corporate culture, shared values, commitments, traditions, and beliefs, to control behavior.

clan culture a culture that focuses primarily on the involvement and participation of the organization's members and on rapidly changing expectations from the external environment.

closed system a system that is autonomous, enclosed, and not dependent on its environment.

coalition an alliance among several managers who agree through bargaining about organizational goals and problem priorities.

collective bargaining the negotiation of an agreement between management and workers.

collectivity stage the life cycle phase in which an organization has strong leadership and begins to develop clear goals and direction.

competition rivalry between groups in the pursuit of a common prize.

computer-integrated manufacturing (CIM) computer systems that link together manufacturing components, such as robots, machines, product design, and engineering analysis.

confrontation a situation in which parties in conflict directly engage one another and try to work out their differences.

contextual dimensions traits that characterize the whole organization, including its size, technology, environment, and goals.

contingency a theory meaning one thing depends on other things; the organization's situation dictates the correct management approach.

continuous process production a completely mechanized manufacturing process in which there is no starting or stopping.

cooptation occurs when leaders from important sectors in the environment are made part of an organization.

coping with uncertainty a source of power for a department that reduces uncertainty for other departments by obtaining prior information, prevention, and absorption.

craft technology technology characterized by a fairly stable stream of activities but in which the conversion process is not analyzable or well-understood.

creative departments organizational departments that initiate change, such as research and development, engineering, design, and systems analysis.

culture the set of norms, values, beliefs, understandings, and ways of thinking that is shared by members of an organization and is taught to new members as correct.

culture changes changes in the values, attitudes, expectations, beliefs, abilities, and behavior of employees.

culture strength the degree of agreement among members of an organization about the importance of specific values.

decision learning a process of recognizing and admitting mistakes that allows managers and organizations to acquire the experience and knowledge to perform more effectively in the future.

decision premises constraining frames of reference and guidelines placed by top managers on decisions made at lower levels.

departmental grouping a structure in which employees share a common supervisor and resources, are jointly responsible for performance, and tend to identify and collaborate with each other.

differentiation the cognitive and emotional differences among managers in various functional departments of an organization and formal structure differences among these departments.

direct interlock a situation that occurs when a member of the board of directors of one company sits on the board of another.

divisional grouping a grouping in which people are organized according to what the organization produces.

divisional structure the structuring of the organization according to individual products, services, product groups, major projects, or profit centers; also called product structure or strategic business units.

domain an organization's chosen environmental field of activity.

domains of political activity areas in which politics plays a role. Three domains in organizations are structural change, management succession, and resource allocation.

dual-core approach an organizational change perspective that identifies the unique processes associated with administrative change compared to those associated with technical change.

effectiveness the degree to which an organization realizes its goals.

efficiency the amount of resources used to produce a unit of output.

elaboration stage the organizational life cycle phase in which the red tape crisis is resolved through the development of a new sense of teamwork and collaboration.

engineering technology technology in which there is substantial variety in the tasks performed, but the activities are usually handled on the basis of established formulas, procedures and techniques.

entrepreneurial stage the life cycle phase in which an organization is born and its emphasis is on creating a product and surviving in the marketplace.

escalating commitment persisting in a course of action when it is failing; occurs because managers block or distort negative information and because consistency and persistence are valued in contemporary society.

ethical dilemma one in which each alternative choice or behavior seems undesirable because of a potentially negative ethical consequence.

ethics the code of moral principles and values that governs the behavior of a person or group with respect to what is right or wrong.

ethics committee a group of executives appointed to oversee company ethics.

ethics ombudsperson a single manager who serves as the corporate conscience.

external adaptation the manner in which an organization meets goals and deals with outsiders.

focus strategy a strategy in which an organization concentrates on a specific regional market or buyer group.

formalization the degree to which an organization has rules, procedures, and written documentation.

formalization stage the phase in an organization's life cycle involving the installation and use of rules, procedures, and control systems.

functional grouping the placing together of employees who perform similar functions or work processes or who bring similar knowledge and skills to bear.

functional matrix a structure in which functional bosses have primary authority and product or project managers simply coordinate product activities.

functional structure the grouping of activities by common function.

garbage can model model that describes the pattern or flow of multiple decision within an organization.

general environment includes those sectors that may not directly affect the daily operations of a firm but will indirectly influence it.

goal approach an approach to organizational effectiveness that is concerned with output and whether the organization achieves its output goals.

Hawthorne Studies a series of experiments on worker productivity begun in 1924 at the Hawthorne plant of Western Electric Company in Illinois; attributed employees' increased output to managers' better treatment of them during the study.

heroes organizational members who serve as models or ideals for serving cultural norms and values.

high-velocity environments industries in which competitive and technological change is so extreme that market data is either unavailable or obsolete, strategic windows open and shut quickly, and the cost of a decision error is company failure.

horizontal linkage the amount of communication and coordination that occurs horizontally across organizational departments.

horizontal linkage model a model of the three components of organizational design needed to achieve new product innovation: departmental specialization, boundary spanning, and horizontal linkages.

idea champions organizational members who provide the time and energy to make things happen; sometimes called "advocates," "intrapreneurs," and "change agents."

incremental decision process model a model that describes the structured sequence of activities undertaken from the discovery of a problem to its solution.

indirect interlock a situation that occurs when a director of one company and a director of another are both directors of a third company.

integration the quality of collaboration between departments of an organization.

integrator a position or department created solely to coordinate several departments.

intensive technologies a variety of products or services provided in combination to a client.

interdependence the extent to which departments depend on each other for resources or materials to accomplish their tasks.

intergroup conflict behavior that occurs between organizational groups when participants identify with one group and perceive that other groups may block their group's goal achievement or expectations.

interlocking directorate a formal linkage that occurs when a member of the board of directors of one company sits on the board of another company.

internal integration a state in which organization members develop a collective identity and know how to work together effectively.

internal process approach an approach that looks at internal activities and assesses effectiveness by indicators of internal health and efficiency.

intuitive decision making the use of experience and judgment rather than sequential logic or explicit reasoning to solve a problem.

job design the assignment of goals and tasks to be accomplished by employees.

job enlargement the designing of jobs to expand the number of different tasks performed by an employee.

job enrichment the designing of jobs to increase responsibility, recognition, and opportunities for growth and achievement.

job rotation moving employees from job to job to give them a greater variety of tasks and alleviate boredom.

job simplification the reduction of the number and difficulty of tasks performed by a single person.

joint optimization the goal of the sociotechnical systems approach, which states that an organization will function best only if its social and technical systems are designed to fit the needs of one another.

joint venture a separate entity for sharing development and production costs and penetrating new markets that is created with two or more active firms as sponsors.

language slogans, sayings, metaphors, or other expressions that convey a special meaning to employees.

large group intervention an approach that brings together participants from all parts of the organization (and may include outside stakeholders as well) to discuss problems or opportunities and plan for change.

large-batch production a manufacturing process characterized by long production runs of standardized parts.

learning organization an organization in which everyone is engaged in identifying and solving problems, enabling the organization to continuously experiment, improve, and increase its capability.

legends stories of events based in history that may have been embellished with fictional details.

legitimacy the general perspective that an organization's actions are desirable, proper, and appropriate within the environment's system of norms, values, and beliefs.

level of analysis in systems theory, the subsystem on which the primary focus is placed; four levels of analysis normally characterize organizations.

liaison role the function of a person located in one department who is responsible for communicating and achieving coordination with another department.

life cycle a perspective on organizational growth and change that suggests organizations are born, grow older, and eventually die.

long-linked technology the combination within one organization of successive stages of production, with each stage using as its inputs the production of the preceding stage.

low-cost leadership a strategy that tries to increase market share by emphasizing low cost compared to competitors.

management champion a manager who acts as a supporter and sponsor of a technical champion to shield and promote an idea within the organization.

management control systems the formalized routines, reports, and procedures that use information to maintain or alter patterns in organizational activity.

management science approach organizational decision making that is the analog to the rational approach by individual managers.

managerial ethics principles that guide the decisions and behaviors of managers with regard to whether they are morally right or wrong.

market control a situation that occurs when price competition is used to evaluate the output and productivity of an organization.

mass customization the use of computer-integrated systems and flexible work processes to enable companies to mass produce a variety of products or services designed to exact customer specification.

matrix structure a strong form of horizontal linkage in which both product and functional structures (horizontal and vertical) are implemented simultaneously.

mechanistic an organization system marked by rules, procedures, a clear hierarchy of authority, and centralized decision making.

mediating technology the provision of products or services that mediate or link clients from the external environment and allow each department to work independently.

meso theory a new approach to organization studies that integrates both micro and macro levels of analysis.

mission the organization's reason for its existence.

mission culture a culture that places emphasis on a clear vision of the organization's purpose and on the achievement of specific goals.

multifocused grouping a structure in which an organization embraces structural grouping alternatives simultaneously.

myths stories that are consistent with the values and beliefs of the organization but are not supported by facts.

negotiation the bargaining process that often occurs during confrontation and enables the parties to systematically reach a solution.

network centrality top managers increase their power by locating themselves centrally in an organization and surrounding themselves with loyal subordinates.

new-venture fund a fund that provides financial resources to employees to develop new ideas, products, or businesses.

nonprogrammed decisions novel and poorly defined, these are used when no procedure exists for solving the problem.

nonroutine technology technology in which there is high task variety and the conversion process is not analyzable or well understood.

nonsubstitutability a trait of a department whose function cannot be performed by other readily available resources.

official goals the formally stated definition of business scope and outcomes the organization is trying to achieve; another term for mission.

open system a system that must interact with the environment to survive.

operative goals descriptions of the ends sought through the actual operating procedures of the organization; these explain what the organization is trying to accomplish.

organic an organization system marked by free-flowing, adaptive processes, an unclear hierarchy of authority, and decentralized decision making.

organization theory a macro approach to organizations that analyzes the whole organization as a unit.

organizational behavior a micro approach to organizations that focuses on the individuals within organizations as the relevant units for analysis.

organizational change the adoption of a new idea or behavior by an organization.

organizational decision making the organizational process of identifying and solving problems.

organizational development a behavioral science field devoted to improving performance through trust, open confrontation of problems, employee empowerment and participation, the design of meaningful work, cooperation between groups, and the full use of human potential.

organizational environment all elements that exist outside the boundary of the organization and have the potential to affect all or part of the organization.

organizational goal a desired state of affairs that the organization attempts to reach.

organizational innovation the adoption of an idea or behavior that is new to an organization's industry, market, or general environment.

organizational politics activities to acquire, develop, and use power and other resources to obtain one's preferred outcome when there is uncertainty or disagreement about choices.

organizations social entities that are goal-directed, deliberately structured activity systems linked to the external environment.

organized anarchy extremely organic organization characterized by highly uncertain conditions.

personnel ratios the proportions of administrative, clerical and professional support staff.

political model a definition of an organization as being made up of groups that have separate interests, goals, and values in which power and influence are needed to reach decisions.

political tactics for using power these include build coalitions, expand networks, control decision premises, enhance legitimacy and expertise, and make preferences explicit while keeping power implicit.

pooled interdependence the lowest form of interdependence among departments, in which work does not flow between units.

power the ability of one person or department in an organization to influence others to bring about desired outcomes.

power sources there are five sources of horizontal power in organizations: dependency, financial resources, centrality, nonsubstitutability, and the ability to cope with uncertainty.

problem identification the decision-making stage in which information about environmental and organizational conditions is monitored to determine if performance is satisfactory and to diagnose the cause of shortcomings.

problem solution the decision-making stage in which alternative courses of action are considered and one alternative is selected and implemented.

problemistic search occurs when managers look around in the immediate environment for a solution to resolve a problem quickly.

product and service changes changes in an organization's product or service outputs.

product matrix a variation of the matrix structure in which project or product managers have primary authority and functional managers simply assign technical personnel to projects and provide advisory expertise.

programmed decisions repetitive and well-defined procedures that exist for resolving problems.

quality circles groups of six to twelve volunteer workers who meet to analyze and solve problems.

rational approach a process of decision making that stresses the need for systematic analysis of a problem followed by choice and implementation in a logical sequence.

rational-legal authority based on employees' belief in the legality of rules and the right of those in authority to issue commands.

rational model a description of an organization characterized by a rational approach to decision making, extensive and reliable information systems, central power, a norm of optimization, uniform values across groups, little conflict, and an efficiency orientation.

reasons organizations grow growth occurs because it is an organizational goal; it is necessary to attract and keep quality managers; or it is necessary to maintain economic health.

reciprocal interdependence the highest level of interdependence, in which the output of one operation is the input of a second, and the output of the second operation is the input of the first (for example, a hospital).

reengineering a cross-functional initiative involving the radical redesign of business processes to bring about simultaneous changes in organization structure, culture, and information technology and produce dramatic performance improvements.

resource-based approach an organizational perspective that assesses effectiveness by observing how successfully the organization obtains, integrates, and manages valued resources.

resource dependence a situation in which organizations depend on the environment but strive to acquire control over resources to minimize their dependence.

rites and ceremonies the elaborate, planned activities that make up a special event and often are conducted for the benefit of an audience.

routine technology technology characterized by little task variety and the use of objective, computational procedures.

rule of law that which arises from a set of codified principles and regulations that describe how people are required to act, are generally accepted in society, and are enforceable in the courts.

satisficing the acceptance by organizations of a satisfactory rather than a maximum level of performance.

scientific management a classical approach that claims decisions about organization and job design should be based on precise, scientific procedures.

sectors subdivisions of the external environment that contain similar elements.

sequential interdependence a serial form of interdependence in which the output of one operation becomes the input to another operation.

service technology technology characterized by simultaneous production and consumption, customized output, customer participation, intangible output, and being labor intensive.

simple-complex dimension the number and dissimilarity of external elements relevant to an organization's operation.

small-batch production a manufacturing process, often custom work, that is not highly mechanized and relies heavily on the human operator.

social responsibility management's obligation to make choices and take action so that the organization contributes to the welfare and interest of society as well as itself.

sociotechnical systems approach an approach that combines the needs of people with the needs of technical efficiency.

sources of intergroup conflict factors that generate conflict, including goal incompatibility, differentiation, task interdependence, and limited resources.

stable-unstable dimension the state of an organization's environmental elements.

stakeholder any group within or outside an organization that has a stake in the organization's performance.

stakeholder approach also called the constituency approach, this perspective assesses the satisfaction of stakeholders as an indicator of the organization's performance.

stories narratives based on true events that are frequently shared among organizational employees and told to new employees to inform them about an organization.

strategic contingencies events and activities inside and outside an organization that are essential for attaining organizational goals.

strategy the current set of plans, decisions, and objectives that have been adopted to achieve the organization's goals.

strategy and structure changes changes in the administrative domain of an organization, including structure, policies, reward systems, labor relations, coordination devices, management information control systems, and accounting and budgeting.

structure the formal reporting relationships, groupings, and systems of an organization.

subcultures cultures that develop within an organization to reflect the common problems, goals, and experiences that members of a team, department, or other unit share.

subsystems divisions of an organization that perform specific functions for the organization's survival; organizational subsystems perform the essential functions of boundary spanning, production, maintenance, adaptation, and management.

switching structures an organization creates an organic structure when such a structure is needed for the initiation of new ideas.

symbol something that represents another thing.

symptoms of structural deficiency signs of the organizational structure being out of alignment, including delayed or poor-quality decision making, failure to respond innovatively to environmental changes, and too much conflict.

system a set of interacting elements that acquires inputs from the environment, transforms them, and discharges outputs to the external environment.

tactics for enhancing collaboration techniques such as integration devices, confrontation and negotiation, intergroup consultation, member rotation, and shared mission and superordinate goals that enable groups to overcome differences and work together.

tactics for increasing power these include entering areas of high uncertainty, creating dependencies, providing resources, and satisfying strategic contingencies.

task a narrowly defined piece of work assigned to a person.

task environment sectors with which the organization interacts directly and that have a direct effect on the organization's ability to achieve its goals.

task force a temporary committee composed of representatives from each department affected by a problem.

team building activities that promote the idea that people who work together can work together as a team.

teams permanent task forces often used in conjunction with a full-time integrator.

technical champion a person who generates or adopts and develops an idea for a technological innovation and is devoted to it, even to the extent of risking position or prestige; also called product champion.

technical complexity the extent of mechanization in the manufacturing process.

technology the tools, techniques, and actions used to transform organizational inputs into outputs.

technology changes changes in an organization's production process, including its knowledge and skills base, that enable distinctive competence.

total quality management an organizational approach in which workers, not managers, are handed the responsibility for achieving standards of quality.

traditional authority based in the belief in traditions and the legitimacy of the status of people exercising authority through those traditions.

uncertainty occurs when decision makers do not have sufficient information about environmental factors and have a difficult time predicting external changes.

variety in terms of tasks, the frequency of unexpected and novel events that occur in the conversion process.

venture teams a technique to foster creativity within organizations in which a small team is set up as its own company to pursue innovations.

vertical linkages communication and coordination activities connecting the top and bottom of an organization.

whistle-blowing employee disclosure of illegal, immoral, or illegitimate practices on the part of the organization.

ame Index

Company Name Index

$\mathscr{S}$ubject Index